Syncretism: The Politics of Economic
Restructuring and System Reform in Japan

SYNCRETISM

The Politics of

Economic Restructuring

and System Reform

in Japan

Edited by
Kenji E. Kushida, Kay Shimizu, and Jean C. Oi

 THE WALTER H. SHORENSTEIN
ASIA-PACIFIC RESEARCH CENTER

THE WALTER H. SHORENSTEIN ASIA-PACIFIC RESEARCH CENTER (Shorenstein APARC) is a unique Stanford University institution focused on the interdisciplinary study of contemporary Asia. Shorenstein APARC's mission is to produce and publish outstanding interdisciplinary, Asia-Pacific–focused research; to educate students, scholars, and corporate and governmental affiliates; to promote constructive interaction to influence U.S. policy toward the Asia-Pacific; and to guide Asian nations on key issues of societal transition, development, U.S.-Asia relations, and regional cooperation.

The Walter H. Shorenstein Asia-Pacific Research Center
Freeman Spogli Institute for International Studies
Stanford University
Encina Hall
Stanford, CA 94305-6055
tel. 650-723-9741
fax 650-723-6530
http://aparc.stanford.edu

Syncretism: The Politics of Economic Restructuring and System Reform in Japan may be ordered from:
The Brookings Institution
c/o DFS, P.O. Box 50370, Baltimore, MD, USA
tel. 1-800-537-5487 or 410-516-6956
fax 410-516-6998
http://www.brookings.edu/about/press

Library of Congress Cataloging-in-Publication Data
Syncretism : the politics of economic restructuring and system reform in Japan / edited by Kenji E. Kushida, Kay Shimizu, and Jean C. Oi.
    pages cm
ISBN 1-931368-23-6 (pbk.)
 1. Japan—Economic policy—1989–2. Corporate reorganizations—Japan. 3. Corporate governance—Japan. 4. Industrial policy—Japan. I. Kushida, Kenji E. II. Shimizu, Kay (Kaoru) III. Oi, Jean Chun.
    HC462.95.S96 2013
    338.952—dc23

                                                                 2013049187

First printing, 2013
ISBN 978-1-931368-23-0

Typeset by Classic Typography in 10.5/13 Sabon MT Pro

We dedicate this volume to Daniel I. Okimoto, for his years of mentorship and his dedication to understanding Japan and building bridges across the Pacific.

Contents

Tables and Figures

Tables

Figures

Abbreviations

BOJ	Bank of Japan
BRP	book-reserve plan
CB	cash-balance plan
CEFP	Council on Economic and Fiscal Policy
CME	coordinated market economy
CO	Cabinet Office
COLI	corporate-owned life insurance
CRO	contract research organization
DB	defined benefit
DC	defined contribution
DER	debt-equity ratio
DIK	Dai-Ichi Kangyo Bank
DIR	Daiwa Institute of Research
DPJ	Democratic Party of Japan
EFPIA	European Federation of Pharmaceutical Industries and Associations
EPF	employee pension fund
FDA	U.S. Food and Drug Administration
FDI	foreign direct investment
FIEL	Financial Instruments and Exchange Law
FILP	Fiscal Investment and Loan Program
FSA	Financial Services Agency

IBJ	Industrial Bank of Japan
ICH	International Conference on Harmonization
ICT	information and communications technology
IRCJ	Industrial Revitalization Corporation of Japan
ISP	Internet service provider
JCGR	Japan Corporate Governance Research Institute
JFC	Japan Finance Corporation
JFTC	Japan Fair Trade Commission
JGB	Japan Government Bond
JILPT	Japan Institute for Labour Policy and Training
JPI	Japan Post Insurance
JPMA	Japan Pharmaceutical Manufacturers Association
JSDA	Japan Securities Dealers Association
JSP	Japan Socialist Party
KDDI	Kokusai Denshin Denwa (telecommunications carrier)
LDP	Liberal Democratic Party
LME	liberal market economy
LTCB	Long-Term Credit Bank
METI	Ministry of Economy, Trade, and Industry
MHLW	Ministry of Health, Labor, and Welfare
MHW	Ministry of Health and Welfare
MIC	Ministry of Internal Affairs and Communications
MITI	Ministry of International Trade and Industry
MMD	multi-member district
MNC	multinational corporation
MOF	Ministry of Finance
MOSS	"market-oriented sector-selective"
MP	member of parliament
MPT	Ministry of Posts and Telecommunications
MR	medical representative
NCB	Nippon Credit Bank
NHI	National Health Insurance
NLI	Nihon Life Institute
NNKK	Nikkeiren Nōryōkushugi Kanri Kenkyūkai (business organization study group)

NPL	non-performing loan
NTT	Nippon Telegraph and Telephone Corporation
OECD	Organisation for Economic Co-operation and Development
PARC	Policy Affairs Research Council
PhRMA	Pharmaceutical Research and Manufacturers of America
PR	proportional representation
SMD	single-member district
SME	small and medium enterprise
SPVA	single premium variable annuity
TDB	Teikoku Databank
TK	Tōyō Keizai (publisher)
TQPP	tax-qualified pension plan
TSE	Tokyo Stock Exchange
UNCTAD	United Nations Conference on Trade and Development
VoC	Varieties of Capitalism
WTO	World Trade Organization

Glossary

amakudari "descent from heaven": post-retirement position, usually for ex-bureaucrats

antei kabunushi stable shareholder

Chūshō Kigyō Kihon Hō Basic Law Governing Small and Medium Enterprises

Chūshō Kigyō Kinyū Kōko Japan Finance Corporation for Small and Medium Enterprise

Daini Rinchō Second Administrative Reform Committee

himawari social services component of the old postal system

jigyōsho establishments

jūsen housing finance company

jūgyōin employees

kaisha company

kampo life insurance services

keiretsu horizontal inter-market business group

Keizai Doyukai Japanese Association of Corporate Executives

kigyō enterprise

kōenkai candidate support group

Kokumin Seikatsu Kinyū Kōko People's Finance Corporation

Kokusai Kyōryoku Ginkō Japan Finance for International Cooperation

Kōei Kigyō Kinyū Kōko   Japan Finance Corporation for Municipal Enterprises

mochiai kabunushi   mutual shareholders

MOF-tan   dense interpersonal relationships between banks and MOF officials and bank employees (Ministry of Finance "handlers")

nenreikyū   age pay

Nihon Shintō   Japan New Party

Nippon Ishin-no-Kai   Japan Restoration Party

Nippon Yūsei Kōsha   Japan Post

Noringyogyō Kinyū Kōko   Agriculture, Forestry and Fisheries Finance Corporation

purosesu jūshigata seika shugi   process-oriented performance-based salary system

seisekikyū   performance pay

senmon iinkai   special expert committee

sentaku to shūchū   "choose and focus" reorganization

Shinseitō   Japan Renewal Party

shita-uke   dedicated suppliers

Shōkō Kumiai Chuō Kinko   Shoko Chukin Bank

shokunō shikaku seido   skill-grading system

shokunōkyū   ability/skill pay

shōtengai   shopping district

shuntō   yearly wage negotiation cycle

yakuwarikyū   role/job pay

yūcho   postal savings account

Yūsei Jigyōchō   Postal Services Agency

zaikai   business world

Zenkoku Seikatsu Eisei Dōgyō Kumiai Rengō (Seiei)   Japan Association of Life Sanitation Industries

zoku   "tribes," referring to politicians specializing in particular areas

Contributors

HARALD CONRAD is the Sasakawa Lecturer in Japan's Economy and Management at the University of Sheffield's School of East Asian Studies. He holds a PhD in economics from Cologne University, Germany. From 2000 to 2008 he worked in Japan as research fellow and deputy director of the German Institute for Japanese Studies and associate professor at Ritsumeikan Asia Pacific University. Conrad's research focuses on Japanese social policy, human resource management, economic issues related to demographic change, and intercultural business negotiation. His latest journal articles have appeared in the *Social Science Japan Journal, International Journal of Human Resource Management,* and *Journal of Social Policy.* A forthcoming book chapter is in the *Oxford Handbook of Employment Relations: Comparative Employment Systems.* Since April 2011 Conrad has been coeditor of *Japan Forum.*

KENJI E. KUSHIDA is the Takahashi Research Associate in Japanese Studies at the Walter H. Shorenstein Asia-Pacific Research Center at Stanford University. He holds a PhD in political science from the University of California, Berkeley. Kushida's research focuses on comparative political economy, particularly in the areas of information technology and comparative capitalist systems. His streams of research include commoditization in information technology sectors around the world, cloud computing, Japan–Korea comparisons in the broadband and wireless industries, Japan's "Galapagos" IT sector, the Fukushima nuclear disaster, systemic change in Japan's financial sector, the effects of multinational corporations in Japan, and Silicon Valley–Japan relationships. His publications include *Japan under the DPJ: The Politics of Transition and Governance* (coedited with Phillip Y. Lipscy) and articles in journals including *Socio-Economic Review, Social Science Japan Journal, Communications & Strategies, Japanese Political Economy, Journal of Industry, Competition and Trade, Asian Survey,* and the *Journal of Information Technology and Politics.*

GREGORY W. NOBLE is professor of politics and administration in the Institute of Social Science at the University of Tokyo, where his research focuses on comparative political economy in East Asia. After receiving his PhD from Harvard University's Department of Government, he taught at the University of California and the Australian National University before moving to Tokyo. His publications include *Collective Action in East Asia: How Ruling Parties Shape Industrial Policy; The Asian Financial Crisis and the Structure of Global Finance* (coedited with John Ravenhill); "Power Politics: Elections and Electricity Regulation in Taiwan" (with Stephan Haggard) in *Presidents, Parliaments, and Policy;* and "The Chinese Auto Industry as Challenge, Opportunity and Partner" in *The Third Globalization,* as well as articles in journals including *International Relations of the Asia-Pacific, Journal of East Asian Studies,* and *Business and Politics.*

JEAN C. OI is the William Haas Professor in Chinese Politics in the Department of Political Science and a senior fellow at the Freeman Spogli Institute for International Studies at Stanford University. She directs the Stanford China Program at the Walter H. Shorenstein Asia-Pacific Research Center and is the Lee Shau Kee Director of the newly established Stanford Center at Peking University. Her work focuses on comparative politics, with special expertise on Chinese political economy. Her books include *Adapt, Fragment, Transform: Corporate Restructuring and System Reform in South Korea* (2012), coedited with Byung-Kook Kim and Eun Mee Kim; *Going Private in China: The Politics of Corporate Restructuring and System Reform* (2011); *Growing Pains: Tensions and Opportunity in China's Transformation* (2010), coedited with Scott Rozelle and Xueguang Zhou; *Rural China Takes Off: Institutional Foundations of Economic Reform* (1999); *Property Rights and Economic Reform in China* (1999), coedited with Andrew Walder; and *State and Peasant in Contemporary China: The Political Economy of Village Government* (1989). Currently, Oi continues her research on rural finance and local governance in China and has started a new project on the challenges of governance in China's rapid urbanization.

ULRIKE SCHAEDE is professor of Japanese business at the University of California, School of International Relations and Pacific Studies (IR/PS). She studies Japan's corporate strategy, business organization, management, financial markets, and government-business relations. Her book *Choose and Focus: Japanese Business Strategies for the 21st Century* (Cornell, 2008) explains the strategic inflection point of the early 2000s, when Japan's business architecture began to change. Her current research concerns the management practices of "New Japan" companies that have assumed global supply chain leadership in materials and components. She also works on corporate restructuring, changing human resources practices, regulation, and entrepreneurship in Japan. She holds an MA from Bonn University, and a PhD from the Philipps-Universtät in Marburg, Germany. Schaede is trilingual and has spent more than eight years of research and study in Japan.

KAY SHIMIZU is assistant professor of political science at Columbia University. Her work focuses on comparative politics, with a focus on the fiscal and financial politics of Japan and China. Her works include *Political Change in Japan: Electoral Behavior, Party Realignment, and the Koizumi Reforms* (2009), coedited with Steven R. Reed and Kenneth Mori McElwain, along with publications in *Socio-Economic Review* and *Journal of East Asian Studies*. Currently, Shimizu is completing a book manuscript on Japan's post-bubble political economy, entitled *Private Money as Public Funds: The Politics of Japan's Fiscal Austerity*, and has started a new project on changing notions of citizenship in urbanizing China.

Preface

This volume originated in a conference held in the summer of 2006 at Stanford University's Walter H. Shorenstein Asia-Pacific Research Center (Shorenstein APARC). Organized by Jean C. Oi, Byung-Kook Kim, and Jennifer Amyx, it was part of a broad project covering China, the Republic of Korea, and Japan. The goal was to understand the politics of corporate restructuring and economic reform in the three countries. As is often the case with comparisons between these three very different countries, the dilemma was how to maximize comparability, while recognizing that the institutions required to facilitate economic and corporate restructuring would differ in each country. The idea of one large volume quickly grew into an ambitious strategy to orchestrate a volume for each country.

A central theoretical question linking the three countries was: to what degree was system change driven by firms or the state? The conference followed the lead of the Varieties of Capitalism framework articulated by Peter Hall and David Soskice. Their framework not only placed the activities of firms as central to the diverse organization of capitalist systems around the world, but also posited that firms were the primary drivers of systemic change. This was a proposition worth examining in Northeast Asia, where states and governments played critical roles in economic development.

The China volume, *Going Private in China: The Politics of Corporate Restructuring and System Reform*, and Korea volume, *Adapt, Fragment, Transform: The Politics of Corporate Restructuring and System Reform in South Korea*, were both published by Shorenstein APARC in 2011 and 2012, respectively.

The theoretical finding from these volumes, put simply, was that firms had relatively little autonomy to drive change in the way that the Varieties of

Capitalism conception contended. In China, state-owned enterprises were clearly unable to influence their surrounding environment in areas such as labor and pension schemes. In Korea as well, politics rather than firm behavior was the primary driver of system change. The Japanese case, as analyzed in the chapters of this volume, also demonstrates system change occurring as a result of politics driving regulatory reforms, leading to economic and industrial restructuring.

Along the road to publication, authors in this volume gained many insights from the period of remarkable change and continuity for Japan between 2006, when the first batch of papers from the conference was presented, and 2012, when the final set of chapters was completed.

Politically, in 2006, the ruling Liberal Democratic Party (LDP) had an almost unprecedented number of seats in the National Diet, after Prime Minister Koizumi had orchestrated a landslide victory for the LDP in the 2005 election. Yet, just three years later, the LDP lost power in a historical electoral defeat to the Democratic Party of Japan (DPJ), ending its almost continuous reign since 1955. Yet, the DPJ only lasted for three years before the LDP came back as powerful as ever, gaining majorities in both the Lower House and Upper House.

In 2006, the Japanese economy seemed to be on a trajectory of sustained growth, buoyed by regulatory reforms and corporate restructuring. However, the 2007–8 global financial crisis hit Japan hard—not in the financial sector, but in exports, as demand plunged around the world. Then, even as the economy was recovering quickly, the 2011 Great East Japan earthquake and tsunami hit, devastating regional economies and disrupting supply chains. While the longevity of the recent resurgence of Japan's economy under Prime Minister Abe's "Abenomics" has yet to be seen, the Japanese economy has undoubtedly undergone numerous major changes over the past two decades.

There is much uncertainty about the challenges Japan faces, ranging from demographic change of a rapidly aging society, new waves of globalization in production networks, uncertainty surrounding the future of its energy sources after the Fukushima nuclear disaster, to the government's large fiscal debt. However, what is certain is that Japan's trajectory of change will be shaped by aspects of Japan's political economy covered in the chapters that follow.

There are many people we would like to thank for enabling this volume. Paper presenters and discussants at the original conference helped formulate the original research questions and stimulated discussion that shaped the trajectory of this volume. In particular, input from Alicia Ogawa, Daniel

Okimoto, Yves Tiberghien, Steven Vogel, and Anthony Zaloom were invaluable in setting the direction of the volume. We extend particular thanks to Jennifer Amyx, who spearheaded organizing the conference and provided feedback to early versions of papers. We thank George Krompacky for his patience and tireless efforts shepherding this project to its completion. We would like to express our gratitude to Gi-Wook Shin and the Shorenstein APARC staff. A very special note of thanks goes to the Japan Fund at the Freeman Spogli Institute, which provided the final source of funding to get this volume published.

Kenji Kushida, Kay Shimizu, and Jean Oi

Stanford, USA and Beijing, China

Syncretism: The Politics of Economic
Restructuring and System Reform in Japan

1 Introduction: Syncretism in Japan's Political Economy Since the 1990s

NEW, TRADITIONAL, AND HYBRID FORMS COEXISTING

Kenji E. Kushida and Kay Shimizu

Japan had a remarkable twentieth century. It began as a rapid industrializer and, despite its wartime devastation, grew economically to become second only to the United States. Yet during the last decade of the century, Japan faltered, spectacularly. In the 1990s, Japan's economy had the slowest growth among the major advanced industrial nations. Observers both inside and outside of Japan pointed to an ever-expanding list of structural, political, and economic problems facing the country. Extensive scholarship has been devoted to understanding the lack of change in Japan despite (or because of) its lackluster economic performance following the 1990 burst of the asset-price bubble.[1]

Japan's first decade of the twenty-first century was both disappointing and bewildering, producing wildly contrasting evaluations. The domestic and international press, as well as the Japanese public at large, have come to call this period the "second lost decade," characterized by policy paralysis and overall lackluster economic growth. Japanese often reflect on the decades since 1990 with pessimism.

1 For example, see Jennifer A. Amyx, *Japan's Financial Crisis: Institutional Rigidity and Reluctant Change* (Princeton: Princeton University Press, 2004); Richard Katz, *Japan, the System that Soured: The Rise and Fall of the Japanese Economic Miracle* (New York: M.E. Sharpe, 1998); Edward J. Lincoln, *Arthritic Japan: The Slow Pace of Economic Reform* (Washington, DC: Brookings Institution Press, 2001); Bai Gao, *Japan's Economic Dilemma: The Institutional Origins of Prosperity and Stagnation* (New York: Cambridge University Press, 2001); William W. Grimes, *Unmaking the Japanese Miracle: Macroeconomic Politics, 1985–2000* (Ithaca, NY: Cornell University Press, 2001); Adam S. Posen, *Restoring Japan's Economic Growth* (Washington, DC: Institute for International Economics, 1998).

However, for those who study Japan more closely, the same decades reveal nothing short of a broad transformation in many of the core tenets of Japan's postwar political economy.

In the economy, the financial system, which was once dominated by main-bank–centered financing, increasingly has come to accommodate a capital market-based system. Employers depend much more heavily on non-regular workers, overwriting the once predominant image of lifetime employment in large firms.[2] Foreign multinational corporations have made significant inroads into traditionally closed sectors such as banking and insurance. Corporate governance practices have changed with the adoption of holding companies and international accounting standards. Regulatory changes in a wide range of sectors have reshaped industry dynamics, including retail, finance, pharmaceuticals, telecommunications, and distribution.[3] Large firms have become increasingly more selective and specialized in their product and service offerings, with a new focus on profitability and returns on investment.[4] And new firms, such as Softbank, Rakuten, and Uniqlo, have grown into major global corporations, reshaping their respective industries to become symbols of the "New Japan" and are characterized by visionary and daring entrepreneurs, disruptive market strategies, a global outlook, and a new dynamism.

Politically, major changes have been under way. In 1993, the Liberal Democratic Party (LDP) lost power for the first time since 1955, but less than a year later it quickly regained power by entering into a series of coalition governments. A shift in electoral rules restructured the logic of electoral competition, and a wave of scholarship was devoted to understanding the broad effects of this institutional change.[5] A decade later, in 2005, the LDP won a landslide victory due to mold-breaking Prime Minister Koizumi Junichirō, who was not a product of standard LDP factional politics. He captured widespread popular support by promising to destroy the "old LDP" by reforming it. But the LDP's revival was short-lived as Koizumi's

2 See Shimizu, chapter 6, in this volume.

3 Kenji E. Kushida, "Inside the Castle Gates: How Foreign Companies Navigate Japan's Policymaking Processes," Ph.D. diss., University of California, Berkeley, 2010.

4 Ulrike Schaede, *Choose and Focus: Japanese Business Strategies for the 21st Century* (Ithaca, NY: Cornell University Press, 2008).

5 For example, see Frances McCall Rosenbluth and Michael F. Thies, *Japan Transformed: Political Change and Economic Restructuring* (Princeton: Princeton University Press, 2010); Ellis S. Krauss and Robert Pekkanen, *The Rise and Fall of Japan's LDP: Political Party Organizations as Historical Institutions* (Ithaca, NY: Cornell University Press, 2011); Ikuo Kabashima and Gill Steel, *Changing Politics in Japan* (Ithaca, NY: Cornell University Press, 2010).

successors succumbed to intra-party jostling and backtracked on many of the Koizumi-era reforms. In 2009, Japan experienced its first direct electoral change in power during the postwar period, with the Democratic Party of Japan (DPJ) ousting the LDP from power.[6]

In policymaking, new regulations and practices changed the relationship between politicians and bureaucrats, reducing bureaucratic discretion. At the end of the millennium, elite ministries that were rocked by scandals in the 1990s were reorganized. Most notably, the powerful Ministry of Finance (MOF) was broken apart.[7] The political leadership increasingly asserted greater authority over bureaucrats with a strengthened Cabinet Office and more political appointments to top ministerial positions.

The role of informal coordination between politicians, bureaucrats, and economic actors—the so-called "iron triangle"—was also weakened, driven by regulatory changes and normative shifts following the burst of the bubble in 1990. In a variety of domestic-oriented sectors, new business strategies swept away traditional business models that had emphasized government relations. In finance, for example, a regulatory overhaul led to new competitive dynamics, rendering the "MOF handlers" (*MOF-tan*), employees devoted to cultivating relations with MOF officials, obsolete.[8]

Although Japan's political economy has transformed decisively and irreversibly, it has also exhibited a remarkable amount of structural resilience.[9] In the economy, few major firms went bankrupt or were sold off. Longstanding interfirm relationships, such as those between the main banks and the *keiretsu* corporate groups, did not disappear; instead, they bifurcated, with the main banks strengthening control over weaker firms and the *keiretsu* groups changing their functions. Nor has long-term employment in large firms fully disappeared. It has only declined in numbers as firms have increased their reliance on temporary workers in order to cut costs.

On a more basic level, Japan's national debt, though climbing to over 200 percent of GDP by 2010, was purchased almost entirely by domestic entities and kept within Japan. With Japanese banks, insurers, public pension funds,

---

6 For an overview of Japan under the DPJ, see Kenji E. Kushida and Phillip Y. Lipscy, eds., *Japan Under the DPJ: The Politics of Transition and Governance* (Stanford: Walter H. Shorenstein Asia-Pacific Research Center, Stanford University, 2013).

7 For details, see Tetsuro Toya, *The Political Economy of the Japanese Financial Big Bang: Institutional Change in Finance and Public Policymaking* (New York: Oxford University Press, 2006). For a list of prominent bureaucratic scandals in the 1990s, see Jennifer Ann Amyx and Peter Drysdale, eds., *Japanese Governance: Beyond Japan Inc.* (London: RoutledgeCurzon, 2003).

8 Amyx, *Japan's Financial Crisis*.

9 See Kushida and Shimizu, chapter 3, in this volume.

and households accounting for about 80 percent of Japanese Government Bond (JGB) purchases, a sudden run on the Japanese national debt is hard to conceive, particularly when the banks are aided by government-orchestrated mergers, and regional banks are required to buy low-risk assets. This underlying fiscal and financial stability contrasts with the sovereign debt problem in crisis-stricken Europe, for instance, in Greece and Spain where the national debt is largely held by foreign entities.[10]

Politically, even the charismatic Koizumi failed to usher in an entirely new era of reform and policy-oriented politics. His successors reverted to traditional LDP-style, non-populist politics by readmitting the LDP members that Koizumi had expelled. They even promulgated platforms aimed at "undoing the damage caused by the Koizumi reforms," which, as we will see later, were ultimately rejected by voters. Nor did the DPJ's historical win usher in decisively new politics because it too appealed to rural voters through direct financial assistance, and it became embroiled in intra-party infighting that hindered policymaking. In many areas, despite initial promises, DPJ policies did not differ much from those of the LDP.[11] On the contrary, the Great East Japan Earthquake disaster of March 2011 seemed to magnify the DPJ's lack of leadership experience, accelerating voter disillusionment and dissatisfaction with the DPJ; the LDP came back with a landslide victory in the December 2012 Lower House elections—albeit with a similar number of votes as when they lost.[12]

The Puzzle: Restructuring and Reform in Japan

The core questions that we seek to answer are about the dynamics of change and continuity: What drove the changes and shaped their trajectories? What was the pattern of change? Why do we see dramatic transformations as well as deep-seated continuities and resistance to change?

This volume originated as a conference held in 2006 at Stanford University. In hindsight, it was a propitious time to begin an analysis of how Japan was transforming. This was during the tail end of the major economic and political reforms, but it was followed by a period of significant reversals

10 For details on the technical difficulties of selling off large quantities of JGBs and Japan's capital-flight experience, see Masahiro Yamaguchi, *Naze Nihonkeizai wa sekai saikyo to iwareru no ka* [Why the Japanese economy is considered the world's strongest] (Tokyo: Toho Shuppan, 2012).

11 Kushida and Lipscy, eds., *Japan Under the DPJ*.

12 For more on the 2012 Lower House elections, see Robert Pekkanen, Steven R. Reed, and Ethan Scheiner, eds., *Japan Decides 2012: The Japanese General Election* (New York: Palgrave, 2013).

of fortune for the economy, for reform, and for the LDP. As the contributors revised, updated, and added new chapters, it became manifestly clear that many of the forces driving the Japanese political economy beyond 2010 cannot be understood without a clear picture of the late 1990s and early to mid-2000s. We firmly believe that any analysis of how, moving forward, the country will change must be rooted in an understanding of the transformation that has occurred since the 1990s.

Japan's Syncretic Model of Change

We contend that the transformation of Japan's political economy since the early 1990s is best characterized as syncretism, that is, new ideas, organizations, and practices combining and coexisting with previous ideas, organizations, and practices.[13] We observe traditional and new elements of the Japanese "model" coexisting with one another, such as long-term employment and increasing reliance on a whole new market of temporary workers. We also observe hybrid forms of organization and strategies, such as multiple employment systems within single firms—a track with higher upfront pay and lower job security and another track with seniority wages and higher job security. This combination of new, old, and hybrid elements best captures both the dramatic transformations and long-established characteristics that we are witnessing today.

In politics as well, new phenomena, such as greater electoral volatility and an emerging system of alternations of power among the parties, coexist with traditional forms of local electoral campaigning focused on more narrowly targeted support to rural and agricultural areas. Politicians with new strategies, such as Koizumi, were succeeded by traditional LDP interest-group leaders such as Asō Tarō. Even the DPJ quickly adopted many of the LDP's traditional tactics of appealing to the countryside. Yet the new focus on the media and on popular appeal did not disappear, as Osaka mayor Hashimoto Tōru rode a wave of populism to form a national-scale party, the Nippon Ishin-no-Kai (Japan Restoration Party), making a splash in national politics. With deregulation of campaign laws in 2013 enabling the advent of Internet-based campaigning, additional changes lurk on the horizon.

13 Syncretism, often used in the context of cultural or religious combinations, refers to the process of melding multiple forms of beliefs or practices. In Kenji E. Kushida, "Inside the Castle Gates: How Foreign Firms Navigate Japan's Policymaking Processes," Ph.D. diss., University of California, Berkeley, 2010, Kushida applies it to the context of Japan's transforming political economy. See also Kenji E. Kushida and Kay Shimizu,"Syncretism: The Politics of Japan's Financial Reforms," *Socio-Economic Review* 11, no. 2 (2013): 337–69.

Contributions to the Volume

The chapters in this volume provide important pieces to answer the puzzle of continuity and change in Japan since the early 1990s. Kushida and Shimizu, in chapter 2, first provide an overview presenting key data regarding Japan's political economy during the past twenty years.

In chapter 3, Kushida and Shimizu examine Japan's financial system, both the conventional financial sectors, such as banking, securities, and insurance, as well as the massive postal savings system. They argue that Japan's pattern of change is syncretic, whereby new ideas and practices are coexisting with pre-existing organizations and norms. Regulatory reforms allowed new entries, new possibilities for reorganization, and new strategies. Yet, although some financial institutions aggressively pursued new opportunities, others retained traditional organizations and strategies, and still others became hybrids. This has resulted in a syncretic system.

The authors go beyond the characterization of these transformations as syncretic to contend that a specific set of political dynamics shaped Japan's process of change, a process that they refer to as *syncretization*. This distinctive pattern of regulatory reform consisted of a strong political leadership pushing through reforms in the face of traditionally powerful interest groups. Such a pattern of reform left room for the long-standing and powerful interest groups to slow down or even reverse the reforms when the political impetus for reform waned.

In chapter 4, Ulrike Schaede stresses the extent to which the core tenets of the Japanese economy were transformed. She argues that Japan underwent a strategic inflection point between 1998 and 2006, when a reconstitution of the legal setting for business irreversibly transformed industrial dynamics and corporate strategies. She contends that in the new competitive environment, the traditional roles of the main banks, *keiretsu* business groups, and cross-shareholdings grew obsolete, and their continued existence was the result of inertia. Moreover, because they were a drag on the corporate strategies needed to compete, they provided examples of what not to do, actually driving change by pushing competitiveness-oriented firms away from these arrangements. This chapter reveals some of the dynamics of syncretism, as some firms moved toward new strategies and organizations while others, although outcompeted, failed to disappear overnight. This resulted in multiple coexisting norms and practices or hybrid forms.

Gregory Noble, in chapter 5, analyzes Koizumi's reform coalition: how it operated and the constraints it faced. He argues that Koizumi's reform coalition consisted of three complementary elements: political leadership from Koizumi himself, support from big business, and academic analysis by economists who provided the intellectual foundation for Koizumi's neoliberal reforms. Koizumi held together this coalition with pragmatism and persistence, despite broad opposition from a variety of forces, some even within the LDP. Koizumi's reforms were, however, also constrained by the main constituents that supported him, namely big business and the middle class, who were not fully dedicated to neoliberal competition and preferred to see society and government absorb some of the risk. Noble's chapter sheds light on how Japan underwent bold reforms in certain areas in the early to mid-2000s, and how opposition to these reforms later led to retrenchment once the political impetus for reform eroded.

Kay Shimizu, in chapter 6, examines small and medium enterprises (SMEs), which to date have received little attention in the political economy literature but deserve a much closer look, especially in Japan, where they employ nearly 70 percent of the labor force. Shimizu finds that SMEs have been bifurcating along two dimensions: by firm performance and by employment structure. On the one hand, zombie firms continue to be propped up by numerous government policies that align the interests of the lending banks, local politicians, and bureaucrats with SME borrowers. Such protective policies have also allowed the regional banks to remain above water by extending a helping hand to many of their weaker SME customers. On the other hand, Japan is also home to a vibrant group of SMEs that are competitive in the global marketplace and have become providers of niche products and parts for a wide range of businesses and their global supply chains. In order for both types of firms to remain financially viable, however, employers must rely more heavily on non-regular workers, creating a clear divide in earning power between regular and non-regular workers. Thus firm survival and low unemployment have come at a cost to Japan's non-regular workers, many of whom are young and underemployed.

In chapter 7, Harald Conrad examines the reforms in Japan's compensation system since the 1990s. He finds that even though performance factors have been gaining in importance, seniority-based wages continue to play an important role for blue-collar workers as well as for white-collar employees up to a certain managerial level. Wage systems and occupational pension systems remain highly complex, with a growing diversity of wage and benefit systems. Although overall coverage of retirement benefits has declined, the mix has changed significantly since the reforms in 2001–2, with defined contribution plans increasingly being replaced by defined-benefit pension plans. Conrad contends that even though certain aspects of human resource practices are increasingly market-based, they are hardly converging with the Anglo-American model. These findings support the volume's notion of syncretic outcomes in Japan's political economy; companies introducing new performance factors to their wage systems often continue to use a wide range of traditional welfare benefits, whereas others create hybrid systems that combine the existing and traditional systems.

Kenji Kushida, in concluding chapter 8, analyzes foreign multinational corporations in Japan, particularly in the financial, automobile, pharmaceuticals, and telecommunications sectors that absorbed massive foreign direct investment inflows after the mid-1990s. He finds that regulatory shifts, driven by political logic, reshaped the competitive environment facing the foreign firms. Not only were formal and informal entry barriers removed, but the rules governing industry dynamics shifted to the advantage of the business models of foreign firms over those of the domestic incumbents. The distinctive characteristics of Japan's political economy, such as the main banks, long-term labor, and *keiretsu* corporate groups, which had hitherto made it difficult for foreign firms to compete in Japan, actually were transformed functionally to aid foreign firms in making inroads into Japanese markets. Foreign firms often exploited gaps in the new regulatory structure, and took advantage of their ability to offer alternative employment structures and the slow adjustment of incumbent Japanese firms. They did not replace major Japanese firms, but they introduced new norms and practices that coexisted and melded syncretically with the older, pre-existing norms and practices.

Together, the chapters in this volume portray Japan's syncretic changes since the 1990s, in which new, traditional, and hybrid elements have coexisted during its transformation.

References

Amyx, Jennifer A. *Japan's Financial Crisis: Institutional Rigidity and Reluctant Change*. Princeton: Princeton University Press, 2004.

Amyx, Jennifer Ann, and Peter Drysdale, eds. *Japanese Governance: Beyond Japan Inc*. London: RoutledgeCurzon, 2003.

Gao, Bai. *Japan's Economic Dilemma: The Institutional Origins of Prosperity and Stagnation*. New York: Cambridge University Press, 2001.

Grimes, William W. *Unmaking the Japanese Miracle: Macroeconomic Politics, 1985–2000*. Ithaca, NY: Cornell University Press, 2001.

Kabashima, Ikuo, and Gill Steel. *Changing Politics in Japan*. Ithaca, NY: Cornell University Press, 2010.

Katz, Richard. *Japan, the System That Soured: The Rise and Fall of the Japanese Economic Miracle*. New York: M.E. Sharpe, 1998.

Krauss, Ellis S., and Robert Pekkanen. *The Rise and Fall of Japan's LDP: Political Party Organizations as Historical Institutions*. Ithaca, NY: Cornell University Press, 2011.

Kushida, Kenji E. "Inside the Castle Gates: How Foreign Companies Navigate Japan's Policymaking Processes." Ph.D. diss., University of California, Berkeley, 2010.

Kushida, Kenji E., and Phillip Y. Lipscy, eds. *Japan under the DPJ: The Politics of Transition and Governance*. Stanford: Walter H. Shorenstein Asia-Pacific Research Center, Stanford University, 2013.

Kushida, Kenji E., and Kay Shimizu. "Syncretism: The Politics of Japan's Financial Reforms." *Socio-Economic Review* 11, no. 2 (2013): 337–69.

Lincoln, Edward J. *Arthritic Japan: The Slow Pace of Economic Reform*. Washington, DC: Brookings Institution Press, 2001.

Pekkanen, Robert, Steven R. Reed, and Ethan Scheiner, eds. *Japan Decides 2012: The Japanese General Election*. New York: Palgrave, 2013.

Posen, Adam S. *Restoring Japan's Economic Growth*. Washington, DC: Institute for International Economics, 1998.

Rosenbluth, Frances McCall, and Michael F. Thies. *Japan Transformed: Political Change and Economic Restructuring*. Princeton: Princeton University Press, 2010.

Schaede, Ulrike. *Choose and Focus: Japanese Business Strategies for the 21st Century*. Ithaca, NY: Cornell University Press, 2008.

Toya, Tetsuro. *The Political Economy of the Japanese Financial Big Bang: Institutional Change in Finance and Public Policymaking*. New York: Oxford University Press, 2006.

Yamaguchi, Masahiro. *Naze Nihonkeizai wa sekai saikyo to iwareru no ka* [Why the Japanese economy is considered the world's strongest]. Tokyo: Toho Shuppan, 2012.

2 Overview: Japan's Political and Economic Transformations Since the 1990s

Kenji E. Kushida and Kay Shimizu

This chapter provides an overview of Japan's political economy since the 1990s as a backdrop for the rest of the volume. The information focuses on the question of what has changed and what has remained the same in core aspects of Japan's political economy. This chapter's distinctive contribution, the figures that plot each prime minister's administration as the horizontal axis for various indicators, provide a visual timeline useful for mapping the political dynamics onto the economic trends.

We begin by examining the political shifts during the last two decades, including the makeup of the National Diet seats and the approval ratings of the Prime Minister's Cabinet, before turning to the economic indicators— economic growth patterns, employment, national accounts, non-performing loans, public works spending, and various measures of internationalization.

National Diet Seats: The Transition from the Liberal Democratic Party (LDP) to the Democratic Party of Japan (DPJ)

Japan's party politics have experienced a combination of both major change and continuity. One of the most dramatic shifts was the rapid rise of the DPJ during the 2000s as a viable opposition party to the LDP, culminating in the DPJ taking power in the 2009 Lower House elections. However, one could argue that the resilience of Japan's traditional party politics reared its head when the DPJ was voted out of power in a landslide in December 2012, with the LDP again assuming power; in retrospect, the LDP's almost continuous rule from 1955 to 2009 had not ended, but was punctuated by just three years out of power.

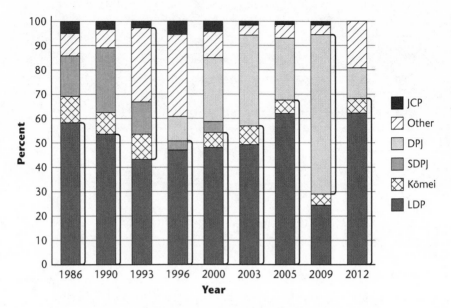

FIGURE 2.1 Party strength in Japan's House of Representatives
(Lower House), 1986–2012

Source: National Diet.

Note: Brackets indicate majority party or coalition after election.

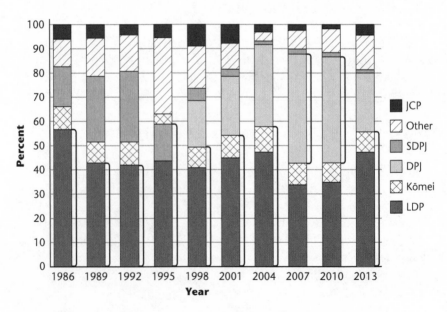

FIGURE 2.2 Party strength in Japan's House of Councillors (Upper House), 1986–2013

Source: National Diet.

Note: Brackets indicate majority party or coalition after election.

Figures 2.1 and 2.2, which show the percentages of seats held by each party (multiple parties or coalitions controlling the house are indicated by brackets), provide a visual representation of the new levels of electoral volatility—a significant change from previous stability. The figures clearly capture the remarkable boost that the LDP received under Koizumi Junichirō in the 2005 Lower House elections, the DPJ's rapid rise, and its dramatic fall.[1]

Recent scholarship has pointed to a shift in Japan's electoral logic stemming from the 1994 change in the Lower House electoral rules, which transformed Japan's multi-member district (MMD) system into a combination of a single-member district (SMD) and proportional representation (PR).[2] Scholars have argued that the new electoral system has increased electoral volatility by weakening incumbency advantages, contributing to more frequent power turnovers among the parties.[3]

Approval Ratings of the Prime Minister's Cabinet

A striking feature of Japanese politics in recent years is its succession of short-lived prime ministers. Although the LDP stayed in power almost continuously since 1955, in the twenty-odd years since 1990, Japan went through fifteen prime ministers (as of mid-2013). Since 2006, when Koizumi Junichirō stepped down, prime ministers have rotated on an almost annual basis.

Public opinion polls of the Prime Minister's Cabinet reveal the volatility in public opinion—a pattern of anticipation and disappointment with each new administration. At the most basic level, we see a pattern of approval ratings for each prime minister's administration falling below the disapproval ratings, followed by a new prime minister. This pattern offers some hints about the linkages between political leadership and reform. For example, the bursts of reform in Japan during the 1990s and 2000s, particularly under Prime Ministers Hashimoto Ryūtarō and Koizumi Junichirō,

---

1 For details on Japan's electoral politics up to the time of Koizumi, see, among others, the introductory chapter to Ellis S. Krauss and Robert Pekkanen, *The Rise and Fall of Japan's LDP: Political Party Organizations as Historical Institutions* (Ithaca, NY: Cornell University Press, 2011); Steven R. Reed, Kenneth Mori McElwain, and Kay Shimizu, eds., *Political Change in Japan: Electoral Behavior, Party Realignment, and the Koizumi Reforms* (Stanford: Walter H. Shorenstein Asia-Pacific Research Center, Stanford University, 2009).

2 For example, see Frances McCall Rosenbluth and Michael F. Thies, *Japan Transformed: Political Change and Economic Restructuring* (Princeton: Princeton University Press, 2010); Reed, McElwain, and Shimizu, eds., *Political Change in Japan*.

3 See the chapters by Ethan Scheiner and Kenneth MacElwain in Kenji E. Kushida and Phillip Y. Lipscy, eds., *Japan Under the DPJ: The Politics of Transition and Governance* (Stanford: Walter H. Shorenstein Asia-Pacific Research Center, Stanford University, 2013).

occurred in the context of high public approval ratings.[4] The three peaks of popularity occurred when the first non-LDP prime minister, Hosokawa Morihiro, came to power pledging reform, when Koizumi became prime minister promising to reform the fundamental politics of the LDP, and when the DPJ ascended to power, again on a platform of reform.

Figure 2.3 shows the approval and disapproval ratings of each Prime Minister's Cabinet from 1989 to 2000. After the bubble burst and a series of scandals plagued the elite bureaucracies and politicians, Prime Minister Miyazawa Kiichi's approval rating fell to the 10 percent level whereas his disapproval rating shot up to almost 80 percent. In the summer of 1993, when former LDP secretary general Ozawa Ichirō fled the long-ruling LDP and forged a coalition government of former opposition parties, the LDP lost its majority in the House of Representatives (Lower House). Hosokawa Morihiro of the Nihon Shintō (Japan New Party) led an eight-party coalition to become the first non-LDP prime minister since 1955.

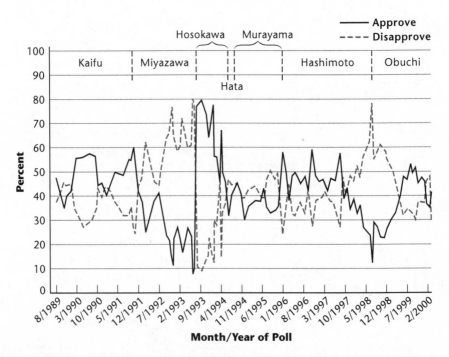

FIGURE 2.3 Prime Ministers' Cabinet approval ratings, 1989–2000
Source: TV Asahi.

4 See Kushida and Shimizu, chapter 3; Schaede, chapter 4; and Noble, chapter 5, all in this volume.

The general public had high hopes for the Hosokawa administration, giving it an initial rate of support of almost 80 percent. These ratings dropped, however, when bold reforms were blocked by disagreements within the eight-party ruling coalition. Allegations of misuse of public funds accelerated the end of Hosokawa's term as prime minister and he was replaced by Hata Tsutomu, head of the Shinseitō (Japan Renewal Party) that he formed with Ozawa. Hata enjoyed average approval and disapproval ratings, but even before the next election, the ruling coalition fell apart. Ozawa was largely blamed for driving the Japan Socialist Party (JSP)—the LDP's longtime rival and well-established primary opposition party—into an improbable alliance with its historical nemesis, the LDP. The LDP thus came back into the coalition, and JSP leader Murayama Tomiichi became prime minister. Murayama's approval ratings fell immediately upon taking office as he abandoned the JSP's historical policy positions that had differentiated it from the LDP, such as its opposition to Japan's alliance with the United States. His administration was also blamed for mishandling the Great Hanshin earthquake that struck the western city of Kobe and the surrounding areas in 1995.[5]

After this period of post-bubble political volatility, LDP leader Hashimoto Ryūtarō came to power in January 1996 with a reform platform. He passed numerous major reform bills, such as the financial "Big Bang," commercial code revisions, and a reorganization of the government bureaucracies that included splitting apart the powerful Ministry of Finance.[6] His high approval ratings, however, eroded rapidly and his disapproval ratings skyrocketed after he pushed through an ill-timed consumption tax hike. Enacted just as the 1997 Asian Financial Crisis hit, the tax hike was widely blamed for the economic recession that followed. The LDP's poor performance in the Upper House elections of 1998 forced Hashimoto to resign, and he was succeeded by Obuchi Keizō.

Obuchi's ratings took an unusual turn, as he started out being highly unpopular, but over time he experienced a dramatic upsurge in popularity. His quiet consensus-building style atnd his reforms were appreciated by the public as the economy began to recover.

Figure 2.4 shows the Prime Minister's Cabinet approval ratings from 2000 to 2009. The Mori Yoshirō administration that followed the Obuchi cabinet, in a dramatic reversal, was extremely unpopular—and it only worsened over time. Mori came to power through a series of backroom deals

5 For details on the government's mishandling of the Great Hanshin earthquake, see Richard J. Samuels, *3.11: Disaster and Change in Japan* (Ithaca, NY: Cornell University Press, 2013).

6 See the various chapters in this volume for the details and effects of these reforms.

after Obuchi's untimely passing in April 2000. The general public was skeptical of his leadership from the beginning, and his term as prime minister began with a high disapproval rating. As the global high-tech bubble burst in 2000, the GDP and stock market growth of the Obuchi years was reversed, further worsening Mori's approval ratings. Also, as a traditional LDP-style backroom deal-maker, Mori did not exude charisma or leadership in media appearances, and the press seized upon his many verbal gaffes. He earned the dubious distinction of setting records for the highest disapproval and lowest approval ratings in Japan's postwar era—his approval ratings declining to single digits.

Following Mori's extreme unpopularity, Koizumi Junichirō is widely regarded as having saved the LDP with unprecedented popularity by promising to undertake deep economic reforms and fundamentally reform the party itself—his slogan was "reform with no sanctuaries." Photogenic and with a staccato speech that made good sound bites for the media, Koizumi's initial approval ratings were unparalleled. The public thoroughly approved of Koizumi's promise to reform the old-style LDP politics, his maverick reputation, his hard-line stance against anyone who opposed his reforms, and his unprecedented media savvy. Although his approval ratings dropped

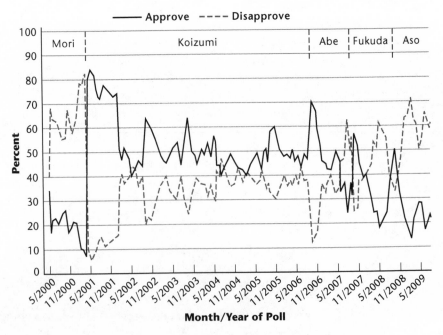

Figure 2.4 Prime Ministers' Cabinet approval ratings, 2000–2009
Source: TV Asahi.

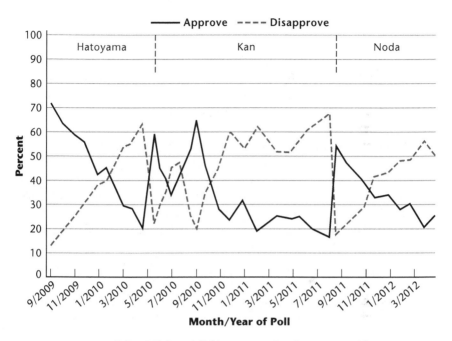

FIGURE 2.5 Prime Ministers' Cabinet approval ratings, 2009–mid-2012
Source: TV Asahi.

during the course of his tenure, they still hovered around 50 percent for most of his time in office.

Koizumi's successors, however, were a different story. Each started with high approval ratings only to see them drop precipitously as they progressively reverted to the traditional LDP politicking that Koizumi had rejected; Abe readmitted LDP members expelled by Koizumi, Fukuda appointed his cabinet according to traditional factional lines, and Asō campaigned to fix the "damage created by the Koizumi reforms." After the global financial crisis of 2007–8, which led to a precipitous drop in exports and a serious recession in Japan, Asō's popularity dropped sharply, although he never quite reached Mori's record lows. This was when the LDP was voted out of power in the DPJ landslide victory.

The DPJ's time in power was characterized by initial high expectations followed by deep public disappointment and disillusionment (see figure 2.5). The first DPJ prime minister, Hatoyama Yukio, came to power with high approval ratings, even approaching those of Hosokawa's first non-LDP government. However, these ratings quickly dropped as the DPJ seemed to have difficulty implementing policy and as Ozawa's campaign financing scandals gained media scrutiny. Ozawa had headed the DPJ until the financial scandals caused him to step down just before the Lower House elections.[7] When Hatoyama, close to Ozawa, became party leader and then prime minister after the DPJ victory, it became clear that the DPJ had become a two-headed monster.[8] Ozawa himself, who had long called for strengthening Cabinet leadership[9] and held much of the power within the party, was actually not in the Cabinet. This uncomfortable power structure, combined with a sense of policy paralysis and Ozawa's old-school politicking and behind-the-scenes leadership that undermined the DPJ's mantra of being anti-LDP, greatly weakened the DPJ's approval ratings. A financial contribution scandal involving Hatoyama—largely in the form of vast transfers of wealth from his mother, but also from several donors using the names of those who were found to be deceased—further drove down the approval ratings of his cabinet, and he was replaced by Kan Naoto.

Kan also enjoyed high initial approval ratings, especially as the economy recovered. However, after peaking in September 2010, his popularity began to slide as he became victim to intra-party struggles, resulting in a loss for the DPJ in the 2010 Upper House elections. After the March 11, 2011 Great East Japan Earthquake, the DPJ was criticized for the government's inadequate response to the crisis. In particular, with regard to the Fukushima nuclear accident, Kan's personal involvement in the recovery effort was attacked in the press, even further lowering his approval ratings.[10] Attacked from within his party as well as by the opposition LDP, which was rapidly gaining experience as an effective opposition party by undermining the credibility of the DPJ,[11] Kan resigned and was replaced by Noda Yoshihiko.

The approval ratings of Noda's Cabinet followed the familiar pattern of beginning high before sliding, as Noda pushed through an agreement for an unpopular consumption tax hike and seemed to rush to restart several nuclear power plants even before a new nuclear regulator was established.

7 Some observers have pointed to the odd timing and seemingly one-sided media coverage that focused on Ozawa's financial scandals involving a construction company that also implicated several LDP leaders. Martin Fackler, *"Hontou no koto" wo tsutae nai nihon no shinbun* [The Japanese newspapers do not report the "truth"] (Tokyo: Futaba Shinsho, 2012).

8 The authors wish to thank Steven Vogel for this characterization.

9 Ichirō Ozawa, *Nihon kaizō keikaku* [Japan transformation plan] (Tokyo: Kodansha, 1993).

10 For an analysis of the DPJ and Kan's involvement in the nuclear crisis, see Kenji E. Kushida, "The DPJ's Political Response to the Fukushima Nuclear Disaster," in *Japan Under the DPJ: The Politics of Transition and Governance*, ed. Kenji E. Kushida and Phillip Y. Lipscy (Stanford: Walter H. Shorenstein Asia-Pacific Research Center, Stanford University, 2013).

11 For an argument about how the LDP learned to become a more effective opposition party, see Masahisa Endo, Robert Pekkanen, and Steven R. Reed, "The LDP's Path Back to Power," in *Japan Decides 2012: The Japanese General Election*, ed. Robert Pekkanen, Steven R. Reed, and Ethan Scheiner (New York: Palgrave, 2013).

Weekly peaceful demonstrations, which began in early 2012, in front of the Prime Minister's Office against restarting the nuclear power plants grew to an estimated 10,000 to 20,000 participants by the end of June.

By the end of 2012, the DPJ had few active supporters and lost power to the LDP in the December 2012 Lower House elections. The LDP won, but with a similar number of votes as when it lost in 2009. Voters punished the DPJ, voting for third-party newcomers such as Osaka mayor Hashimoto Tōru and long-time Tokyo mayor Ishihara Shintarō's Nippon Ishin-no-Kai (Japan Restoration Party).[12]

Economic Growth Patterns: Not Simply "Two Lost Decades"

Japan's economy since the bubble burst in 1990, both within and outside Japan, tends to be described as "the lost decades," "stagnation," as well as by more colorful terms such as "moribund growth." This needs a corrective. Compared to the 1980s, growth rates in the 1990s and 2000s were far lower. Yet it was certainly not "two decades of recession" or "stagnation," since during the period there were actually only two pronounced recessions of limited duration. These recessions coincided with or immediately followed broader international crises: the 1997–98 Asian Financial Crisis and the global financial crisis of 2007–8 (see figure 2.6). A stream of more recent scholarship about Japan's transformation in the post-bubble years has moved beyond the last decades as "lost," but this point still needs to be emphasized, particularly in much of the press coverage.[13]

Figure 2.6 shows a pattern of recovery punctuated by abrupt drops into brief periods of recession. Note the first recovery was after the low point in 1993 that ended in 1997, and the second was from about 2002 to 2007. The listing of prime ministers along the horizontal axis provides context to Prime Minister Mori Yoshirō's extremely low public support (the sharp decline in economic growth) and Koizumi's high support (sustained growth). Japan's sharp recession after the 2007–8 global financial crisis—announced after the fact, as these economic indicators are—fueled the sharp drop in support for the Aso administration to the point that the LDP lost control of the government in a landslide election.

A look at the Nikkei Stock Index across time provides further context. Figure 2.7 shows the magnitude of the bubble, as the Nikkei peaked at about 40,000 yen, dropped precipitously, and then hovered between 15,000 and 20,000

12 For details on the 2012 Lower House elections and DPJ rule, see Kushida and Lipscy, "The Rise and Fall of the Democratic Party of Japan," in *Japan Decides 2012: The Japanese General Election*, ed. Robert Pekkanen, Steven R. Reed, and Ethan Scheiner (New York: Palgrave, 2013).

13 In particular, in chapter 4 in this volume, Schaede points to the deep, irreversible changes to Japan's economic structure during the 1990s and 2000s.

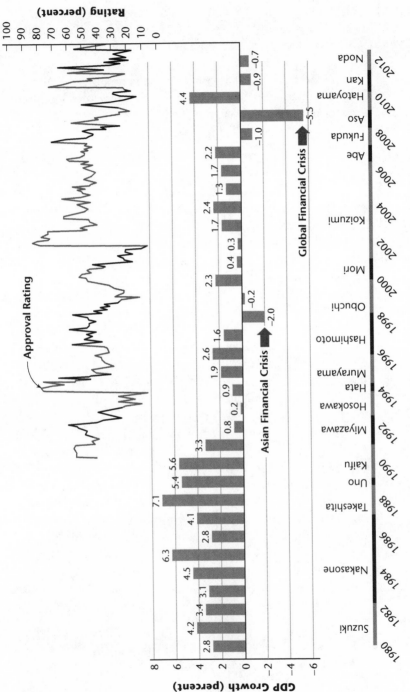

FIGURE 2.6 Japan's GDP growth, prime ministers, and Prime Ministers' Cabinet approval ratings, 1980–2012

Source: TV Asahi; Ministry of Internal Affairs and Communications, Statistics Bureau, http://www.stat.go.jp.

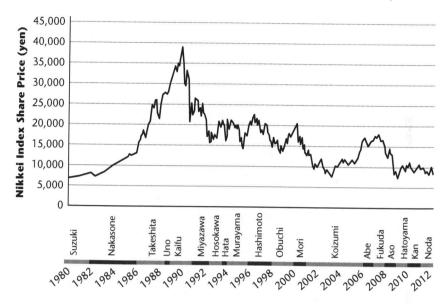

FIGURE 2.7 Japan's Nikkei Index share prices and prime ministers, 1980–2012
Source: Thomson-Reuters.

yen for much of the 1990s. The figures also show the continued decline during the Mori administration and the first years of the Koizumi administration as the index value dropped by almost one-half. Thereafter, it almost doubled, from just less than 8,000 yen to about 17,000 yen. This partly explains the optimistic mood that took hold among all sorts of investors during the Koizumi administration. Enthusiasts, including many households that regained confidence after being burned by the bursting of the bubble, reentered the stock markets, with some making substantial gains. Images of a "second lost decade" too often overlook the details of this time—after all, the stock market doubled during the period, and it was only the global financial crisis that sent it plunging again.

Employment: The Rise of Non-Regular Employees

Japan's changing employment structure has been one of the key transformations in Japan's political economy since 1990. The typical narrative is that unemployment rose and temporary or non-regular labor increasingly replaced Japan's vaunted lifetime employment. However, figure 2.8 reveals that the number of employed people in Japan actually increased throughout the 1990s and 2000s, although the growth rate was slow.[14] We also see that although the number of "regular" employees dropped, the rise of non-regular

14 It should be noted that the self-employed are not included in these data.

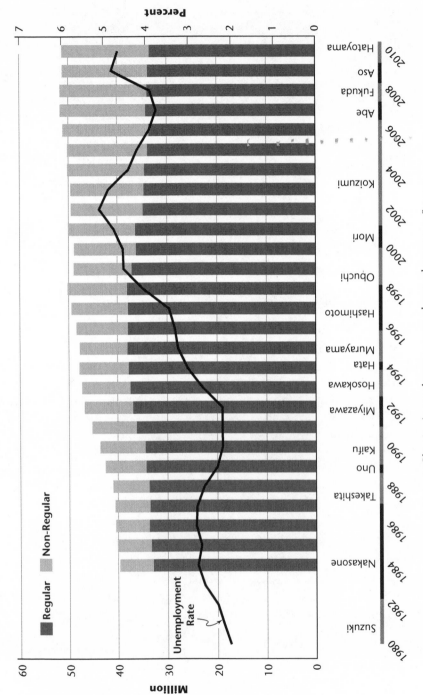

FIGURE 2.8 Changes in regular vs. non-regular employment, 1980–2010

Source: Ministry of Internal Affairs and Communications, Statistics Bureau.

employees (including temporary and part-time employees) certainly did not become a majority in the workforce.

The Koizumi years stand out as exceptional for the modest levels of employment growth and falling unemployment. Political campaigns waged by Koizumi's successors—Asō Tarō, in particular—tended to blame the Koizumi reforms for the rise in income inequality. However, the growth of non-regular employment began well before Koizumi came to power and unemployxment actually dropped during his tenure.

The shifting composition of the labor market is also illustrated by the rapid growth of a new industry that barely existed under the traditional postwar Japanese model: temporary labor, or "dispatch worker" agencies. Dispatch worker agencies serve the needs of large companies that need short-term employees, either white collar or blue collar, whom they can deploy flexibly. This industry doubled in size between 1992 and 2000, but then grew exponentially beginning in 2004, when the revisions to the Labor Law and the Worker Dispatch Law took effect, enabling a more flexible deployment of temporary workers (see figure 2.9).[15]

Expenditures, Savings, and Deflation: Buying More, Getting More, and Saving Less

The cognitive dissonance that struck most who visited Japan during the "lost decades" was that Japan had seemed to become wealthier, particularly in the urban areas. Despite media articles portraying Japan facing "anemic" growth or a "moribund" economy, one did not feel on the surface that there was a prolonged recession, particularly in the urban areas, where prominent downtown real estate was redeveloped into shiny high-rise buildings. Household consumption expenditures, adjusted for inflation, dropped after its peak of 1992 (see figure 2.10). However, the full impact of decreasing consumption levels was ameliorated by the falling nominal prices as Japan experienced bouts of deflation between 1998 and 2002, as seen in figure 2.11.

The other side of rising consumption, however, was a marked decrease in household savings rates; people were consuming more, but saving less, breaking the postwar image of Japan as a country of high savers. Figure 2.12 shows the drop in household savings as a percentage of household income.

15 For details, see Steven K Vogel, *Japan Remodeled: How Government and Industry are Reforming Japanese Capitalism* (Ithaca, NY: Cornell University Press, 2006): 81–82. For shifts in Japan's lifetime employment, see Ulrike Schaede, *Choose and Focus: Japanese Business Strategies for the 21st Century* (Ithaca, NY: Cornell University Press, 2008): 174–99. For a note on how a foreign firm pioneered the temporary worker agency industry in Japan, see Kenji E. Kushida, "Inside the Castle Gates: How Foreign Multinational Firms Navigate Japan's Policymaking Processes," Ph.D. diss., University of California, Berkeley, 2010: 75–76.

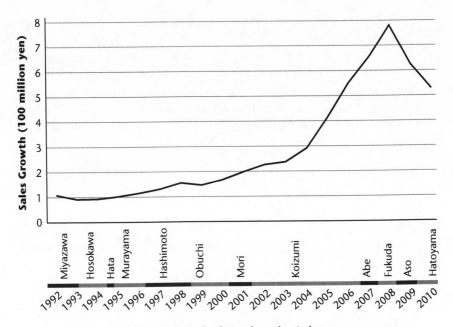

FIGURE 2.9 Sales growth in the dispatch worker industry, 1992–2010
Source: Ministry of Health, Labor, and Welfare.

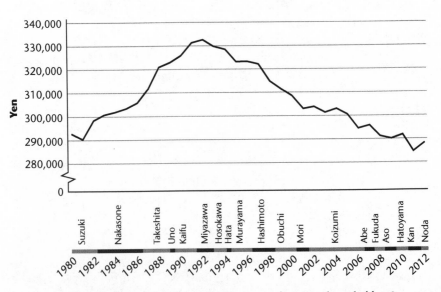

FIGURE 2.10 Japan's average monthly consumption expenditures per household, 1980–2012
Source: Ministry of Internal Affairs and Communications, Statistics Bureau.
Note: Adjusted to 2005 price levels using Consumer Price Index (CPI).

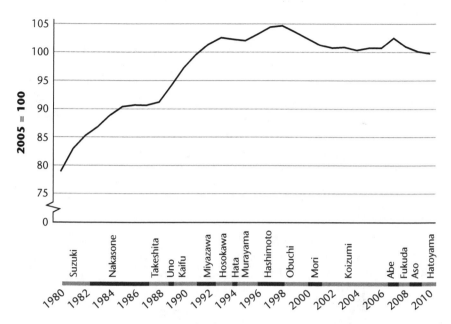

FIGURE 2.11 Japan's price levels: consumer price index, 1980–2010
Source: Ministry of Internal Affairs and Communications, Statistics Bureau.

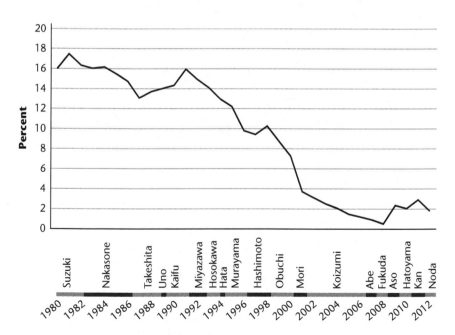

FIGURE 2.12 Japan's household savings rates, 1980–2012 (percentage of household income)
Source: OECD Economic Outlook, based on Ministry of Finance data.

Non-Performing Loans: A Crisis Diffused

A major looming crisis in Japan during the late 1990s was the sharp increase in non-performing loans (NPLs) held by the banking sector, particularly following the 1997 Asian Financial Crisis. Analyses often pointed to the rising NPLs as outgrowths of systemic flaws in Japan's political economy.[16] However, as Gregory Noble notes in chapter 5 in this volume, arguably the most notable achievement of the Koizumi administration was to decrease the burden of non-performing loans held by banks (along with overcoming Japan's deflationary spiral). Figure 2.13 clearly shows the decrease in NPL levels during the Koizumi administration.

Notably, the NPL decreases occurred primarily in city banks rather than regional banks. This supports Kushida and Shimizu's contention in chapter 3 in this volume about syncretic outcomes in Japan's financial sector, with the coexistence of new, traditional, and hybrid features. The regional banks remained in their traditional form, even retaining their NPL

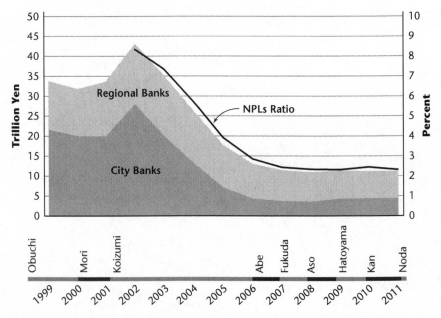

FIGURE 2.13 Non-performing loans in Japan's banking sector
and ratio of NPLs in total loan portfolios, 1999–2011
Source: Financial Services Agency.

16 For example, see Richard Katz, *Japan the System that Soured: The Rise and Fall of the Japanese Economic Miracle* (NY: M.E. Sharpe, 1998); Bai Gao, *Japan's Economic Dilemma: The Institutional Origins of Prosperity and Stagnation* (New York: Cambridge University Press, 2001).

burdens,[17] while city banks embraced hybrid structures as they merged and branched out into new activities such as securities and insurance.

Public Works Spending

Public works spending, a staple of the clientelistic politics characterizing the LDP's traditional "pork-barrel" exchange of local votes for infrastructure projects, declined after the late 1990s. Figure 2.14 shows the amount of public works spending in the government annual budget. Note that the sharpest decrease came under the first Koizumi budget, and this trend was continued by his successors until Aso. Aso increased public works spending as part of a stimulus package after the global financial crisis. Also note that the lowest expenditures were under the DPJ governments—although the latest budget is likely to reflect spending to rebuild the areas devastated by the earthquake and tsunami in the Tohoku region. As a sign of the resilience of local public works spending, however, the new LDP administration has pledged massive spending, including for public works, to stimulate the economy.

Japan's Continuing Internationalization: Investment Flows

Since the early 1990s, Japan's economy has become far more enmeshed in the global economy. Figure 4.4 in chapter 4 shows how the percentage of foreign ownership on Japan's Tokyo Stock Exchange grew from around 4 percent in 1990 to just over 25 percent in 2010. Foreign direct investment flows are shown in figure 2.15 below. The figure shows how inward foreign direct investments rose in the late 1990s before dipping in the mid-2000s, then rising in about 2008 before dipping again. Outward flows rose rapidly, spiking just before the global financial crisis hit Japan's economy in 2007–8.

Sources of Stability: Japan's Export Dependence, Foreign Assets, and National Debt Held by Domestic Entities

The previous sections provided a brief overview of several major substantial changes in Japan's political economy since the 1980s. Yet, as we point out through our framing of syncretism, many aspects of Japan's political economy remained surprisingly stable. This section reveals a few sources of that stability based on economic indicators that we believe have not received adequate attention.

First, the image that Japan's economy is still heavily dependent on exports is misleading. In fact, as a percentage of GDP, Japan's export dependence was only 15 percent in 2010, compared to over 50 percent in Korea and 27 percent in China (see figure 2.16).

17 For details, see Kay Shimizu, "Private Money as Public Funds," Ph.D. diss., Stanford University, 2009.

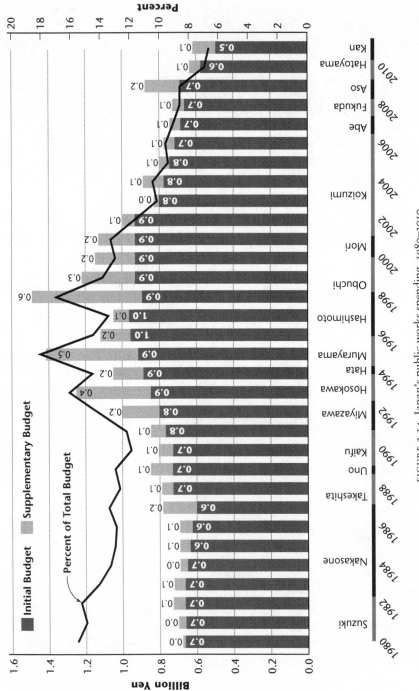

FIGURE 2.14 Japan's public works spending, 1980–2010
Source: Ministry of Finance.

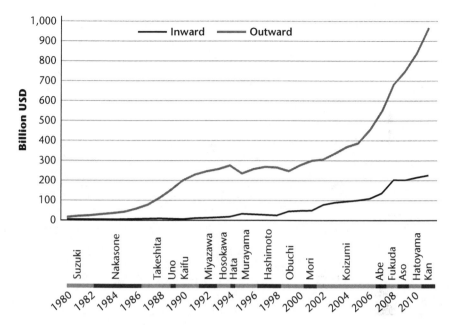

FIGURE 2.15 Japan's inward and outward foreign direct investment flows, 1980–2010
Source: UNCTAD.
Note: 2012 exchange rates.

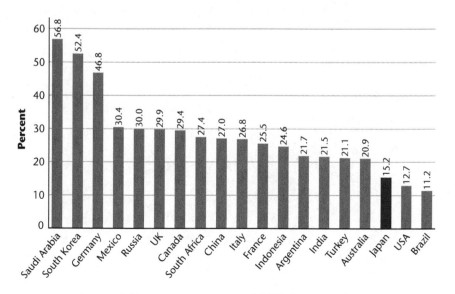

FIGURE 2.16 Exports as a percentage of GDP, G-20 countries, 2010
Source: United Nations Statistics Division, *National Accounts Main Aggregates Database*, 2010.

The effects of a stronger yen, which hit its first peak in 1996 and approached similar levels in 2012, are not necessarily disadvantageous to the economy to the degree that many (relatively uninformed) observers suggest.

Second, Japan's manufacturing portion of the economy consisted of only 19.4 percent of its economy in 2010, a decrease from 27 percent in 1980, 26 percent in 1990, and 21 percent in 2000. See figure 2.17 for a comparison among the G-20 countries. With few natural resources and shrinking agriculture, the majority of Japan's economy consists of services. This trend has increased as manufacturing operations have been increasingly taken abroad due to the pressures and opportunities created by a strong yen (see figure 2.18).

Combined with the low export dependence noted above, Japan's economy is strongly supported by internal demand.

Third, it should be pointed out that Japan is the world's largest creditor nation. Figure 2.19 shows the net international investment positions of the G8 countries, as well as China, Taiwan, and Switzerland.

Finally, as mentioned briefly at the beginning of this chapter, Japan's record-high national debt is unlikely to create an immediate crisis. JGBs (Japanese Government Bonds) are held overwhelmingly by domestic entities, as seen in figure 2.20. Moreover, most of the domestic JGB holders are highly unlikely to suddenly jettison their JGB holdings, since banks are essentially rescued by government-orchestrated mergers, and insurers and pension funds are mandated to hold a significant proportion of safe assets, which include JGBs. (See figure 2.21.) In any case, a massive sell-off would

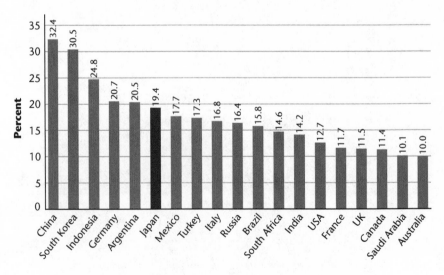

FIGURE 2.17 Manufacturing as a percentage of GDP,
G8 countries, and China and South Korea, 2010

Source: United Nations Statistics Division, *National Accounts Main Aggregates Database*, 2010.

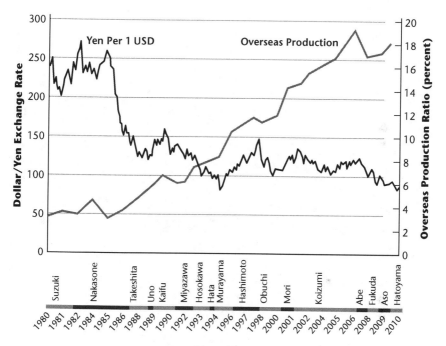

FIGURE 2.18 Yen–dollar exchange rate and overseas
manufacturing production, 1980–2010

Source: Ministry of Economy, Trade, and Industry, *Survey of Overseas Business Activities.*

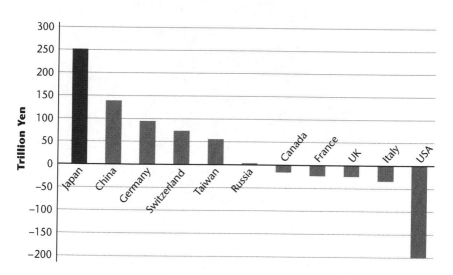

FIGURE 2.19 Net international investment positions, G8 countries,
and China, Taiwan, and Switzerland, 2011

Source: Ministry of Finance Net International Investment Positions 2012.

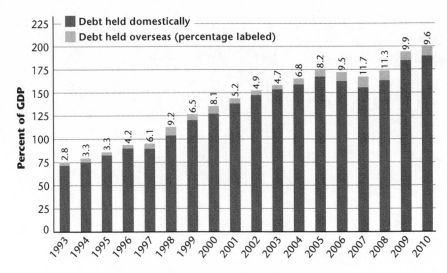

FIGURE 2.20 Japanese government debt as a percentage of GDP,
percentage held domestically vs. overseas, 1993–2010

Source: Adapted from Ministry of Finance, *Japanese Public Finance Fact Sheet 2011*, and Ministry of Finance, *Debt Management Report 2011*.

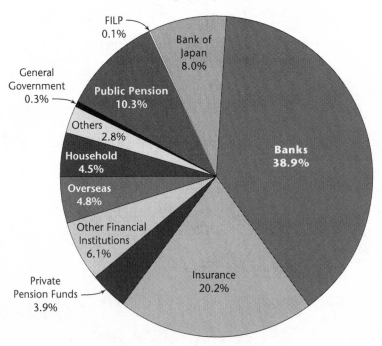

FIGURE 2.21 Japanese government bond holders, 2010 (shares)
Source: Ministry of Finance, *Debt Management Report 2011*.

raise interest rates, thereby creating vast new demand for JGB holdings.[18] Thus, the Japanese national debt situation is surprisingly stable for at least the short-to-medium term.[19]

Conclusion

In sum, Japan's political economy since 1990 has been characterized by significant transformations, but also important continuities. The argument put forth in the introduction to this volume, that Japan's pattern of change has been syncretic with the coexistence of new, traditional, and hybrid elements, is supported by many of the figures introduced in this overview. Although electoral volatility increased with the rise of the DPJ, the LDP retained its position as a viable political party, and has since reclaimed power. The promise of reform has been popular, but the public was deeply disappointed by the post-Koizumi LDP leadership, as well as by the DPJ leadership that promised but failed to deliver the reforms it had promised.

The economy, far from being "two decades of stagnation," actually followed a pattern of growth punctuated by sharp declines. The approval ratings of the Prime Minister's Cabinet were somewhat correlated to economic performance. Total employment actually increased since the 1980s, but much of the increase was due to rising non-regular employment, though it was far from displacing the levels of regular employment. Consumption rose during the 1990s and 2000s, explaining some of the cognitive dissonance of Japan's seemingly wealthier urban areas, particularly given the generally flat price levels with some deflationary periods that increased purchasing power. However, household savings did decrease during this period.

Japan's NPL crisis of the late 1990s was largely solved under the Koizumi administration as major city banks wrote off their bad loans. NPLs in regional banks, however, remained at relatively unchanged levels until the 2007–8 financial crisis. Public works spending decreased, and Japan became increasingly enmeshed in the global economy, with rising inward and outward foreign direct investment flows.

18 For an extended version of this argument, see Masahiro Yamaguchi, *Naze Nihonkeizai wa sekai saikyo to iwareru no ka* [Why the Japanese economy is considered the world's strongest] (Tokyo: Toho Shuppan, 2012).

19 In the medium to long term, however, prominent economists have argued that such stability is unlikely to continue. Takeo Hoshi and Takatoshi Itō write, "If and when the JGB rates rapidly rise, the Japanese financial institutions that hold a large amount of JGBs will sustain losses and the economy will suffer from fiscal austerity, financial instability, and inflation," in "Defying Gravity: How Long Will Japanese Bond Prices Remain High?" NBER Working Paper, No. 18287, August 2012, accessed June 11, 2013, http://www.nber.org/papers/w18287.

There are several aspects of Japan's economy that provide sources of stability. Contrary to many popular images of the Japanese economy, Japan is relatively less export-dependent than many other advanced industrial countries as well as its neighbors such as China and South Korea. It is also less manufacturing-dependent than many assume, and the strong yen from the late 1990s has accelerated offshore production considerably. Japan has one of the largest net positive investment positions, and its large national debt is held overwhelmingly by domestic lenders, many of which are large financial institutions that depend on the government for continued protection.

As Japan continues to evolve over the coming decades, many of the themes raised in this overview, and in this volume, on the extensive transformations coexisting with the traditional sources of core stability are likely to remain. We contend that syncretism will be the likely pattern of change for the foreseeable future.

References

Endō, Masahisa, Robert Pekkanen, and Steven R. Reed. "The LDP's Path Back to Power." In *Japan Decides 2012: The Japanese General Election*, edited by Robert Pekkanen, Steven R. Reed, and Ethan Scheiner. New York: Palgrave, 2013.

Fackler, Martin. *"Hontou no koto" wo tsutae nai Nihon no shinbun* [The Japanese newspapers do not report the "truth"]. Tokyo: Futaba Shinsho, 2012.

Gao, Bai. *Japan's Economic Dilemma: The Institutional Origins of Prosperity and Stagnation*. New York: Cambridge University Press, 2001.

Hoshi, Takeo, and Takatoshi Ito, "Defying Gravity: How Long Will Japanese Bond Prices Remain High?" NBER Working Paper, No. 18287, August 2012, accessed June 11, 2013, http://www.nber.org/papers/w18287.

Katz, Richard. *Japan, the System That Soured: The Rise and Fall of the Japanese Economic Miracle*. NY: M.E. Sharpe, 1998.

Krauss, Ellis S., and Robert Pekkanen. *The Rise and Fall of Japan's LDP: Political Party Organizations as Historical Institutions*. Ithaca, NY: Cornell University Press, 2011.

Kushida, Kenji E. "Inside the Castle Gates: How Foreign Companies Navigate Japan's Policymaking Processes." Ph.D. diss., University of California, Berkeley, 2010.

———. "The DPJ's Political Response to the Fukushima Nuclear Disaster." In *Japan under the DPJ: The Politics of Transition and Governance*, edited by Kenji E. Kushida and Phillip Y. Lipscy. Stanford: Walter H. Shorenstein Asia-Pacific Research Center, Stanford University, 2013.

Kushida, Kenji E., and Phillip Y. Lipscy, eds. *Japan under the DPJ: The Politics of Transition and Governance*. Stanford: Walter H. Shorenstein Asia-Pacific Research Center, Stanford University, 2013.

———. "The Rise and Fall of the Democratic Party of Japan." In *Japan under the DPJ: The Politics of Transition and Governance*, edited by Kenji E. Kushida and Phillip Y. Lipscy. Stanford: Walter H. Shorenstein Asia-Pacific Research Center, Stanford University, 2013.

Ozawa, Ichirō. *Nihon kaizō keikaku* [Japan transformation plan]. Tokyo: Kodansha, 1993.

Pekkanen, Robert, Steven R. Reed, and Ethan Scheiner, eds. *Japan Decides 2012: The Japanese General Election*. New York: Palgrave, 2013.

Reed, Steven R., Kenneth Mori McElwain, and Kay Shimizu, eds. *Political Change in Japan: Electoral Behavior, Party Realignment, and the Koizumi Reforms*. Stanford: Walter H. Shorenstein Asia-Pacific Research Center, Stanford University, 2009.

Rosenbluth, Frances McCall, and Michael F. Thies. *Japan Transformed: Political Change and Economic Restructuring*. Princeton: Princeton University Press, 2010.

Samuels, Richard J. *3.11: Disaster and Change in Japan*. Ithaca, NY: Cornell University Press, 2013.

Schaede, Ulrike. *Choose and Focus: Japanese Business Strategies for the 21st Century*. Ithaca, NY: Cornell University Press, 2008.

Shimizu, Kay. "Private Money as Public Funds," Ph.D. diss., Stanford University, 2009.

Vogel, Steven K. *Japan Remodeled: How Government and Industry Are Reforming Japanese Capitalism*. Ithaca, NY: Cornell University Press, 2006.

Yamaguchi, Masahiro. *Naze Nihonkeizai wa sekai saikyo to iwareru no ka* [Why the Japanese economy is considered the world's strongest]. Tokyo: Toho Shuppan, 2012.

3 The Politics of Syncretism in Japan's Political Economy

FINANCE AND POSTAL REFORMS

Kenji E. Kushida and Kay Shimizu

The theme of this volume is how Japan's political economy has evolved over the past few decades. This chapter analyzes Japan's financial system—the lynchpin of Japan's distinctive postwar economic structure.

First we situate this inquiry in the context of broader scholarship. The question of how diversely organized capitalist societies evolve in an age of ever-increasing internationalization has been a longstanding area of scholarly inquiry.[1] Mechanisms of institutional change in particular have been a recent focus, as political scientists and sociologists move beyond simple models of exogenous, shock-precipitated change to examine a variety of gradual transformations and patterns of change.[2] A core element of how each political economy is organized, and consequently a key driver of how each changes, has been the financial system, from which other aspects such as corporate governance and employment patterns stem.[3]

In almost all typologies of how diverse capitalist systems are organized, Japan is commonly situated at one extreme; Japan, along with Germany,

1 For an excellent overview of the "comparative capitalisms" literature, see Gregory Jackson and Richard Deeg, "From Comparing Capitalisms to the Politics of Institutional Change," *Review of International Political Economy* 15 (2008): 680–709.

2 For an overview, see Glenn Morgan et al., eds., *The Oxford Handbook of Comparative Institutional Analysis* (Oxford, New York: Oxford University Press, 2010), particularly the chapters by Thelen, Campbell, Streeck, and Jackson.

3 See, in particular, the seminal work of John Zysman, *Governments, Markets, and Growth: Financial Systems and the Politics of Industrial Change* (Ithaca, NY: Cornell University Press, 1983).

This chapter is a modified version of Kenji E. Kushida and Kay Shimizu, "Syncretism: the Politics of Japan's Financial Reforms," *Socio-Economic Review* 11 (2013): 337–69.

has long been considered the polar opposite of Anglo-American, market-centered models of capitalism, and has been described variously as a non-liberal[4] or coordinated market economy,[5] with a bank-centered financial system with heavy state intervention to shape the economy.[6]

An examination of extremes—Japan in this case—often reveals processes of change most clearly. Japan's financial system has greatly transformed over the past couple of decades, in part by incorporating many aspects of Anglo-American financial systems. However, convergence to an Anglo-American system does not seem likely any time soon. Instead, Japan has crafted a more diversified financial system that has retained some of the features of a non-liberal system, adopted some features of an Anglo-American system, and also created some new practices that are distinct from any of the pre-existing systems. This non-convergence, in a form we term *syncretism*, actually shielded Japan's financial system from the 2007 global financial crisis, which severely damaged financial sectors worldwide, by limiting Japan's exposure to global finance.[7] Therefore, understanding how Japan's financial system is now configured, and uncovering the mechanisms of how it transformed, provides useful insights into the fast-growing scholarship exploring processes of institutional change.

Syncretism: The Observed Outcome in Japan's Financial System

Japan's financial system was long bifurcated into a "developmental" or "strategic" side in the commercial and policy bank systems and a "clientelistic" or "pork-barrel" side involving the massive postal banking system. Each side fit into the scheme of Japan's postwar model of rapid economic growth, and each side had its own political logic. These two sides of Japan's financial system are rarely examined together in political economy scholarship because they long operated under very different political dynamics, playing contrasting roles in Japan's postwar economy.

On the one hand, the commercial and policy bank systems were central to Japan's strategic, or developmental, politics. This side of the financial

4 Kozo Yamamura and Wolfgang Streeck, *The End of Diversity? Prospects for German and Japanese Capitalism* (Ithaca, NY: Cornell University Press, 2003).

5 Peter A. Hall and David Soskice, "An Introduction to Varieties of Capitalism," in *Varieties of Capitalism: The Institutional Foundations of Comparative Advantage*, ed. Peter A. Hall and David Soskice (New York: Oxford University Press, 2001), 1–68.

6 Zysman, *Governments, Markets, and Growth*.

7 As noted in the introduction, syncretism is a word often used for cultural or religious combinations, referring to the process of melding multiple different forms of beliefs or practices. Kushida applied it to Japan's transforming political economy. Kenji E. Kushida, "Inside the Castle Gates: How Foreign Firms Navigate Japan's Policymaking Processes" (Doctoral Dissertation, University of California Berkeley, 2010).

system took deposits from households and firms, and used these funds to provide loans to industry. The Ministry of Finance (MOF) and the Bank of Japan deployed a variety of formal and informal measures to shape the country's investment profile, targeting strategic sectors such as heavy industries to promote long-term industrial growth.[8]

On the other hand, the postal banking system, which contained the largest financial institution in the world in terms of deposits, was long at the core of Japan's clientelistic politics. It took advantage of the nationwide network of post offices to gather deposits from households around the country, and invested largely in infrastructure projects. It acted as a "second budget," enabling politicians to allocate capital to electorally important sectors and to public works projects in their local districts in exchange for votes. The postal bank was therefore a critical factor in keeping the Liberal Democratic Party (LDP) in power for over fifty years.

This postwar Japanese financial system was closed to new entrants and carefully segmented into subcategories such as banking, insurance, and securities industries, each with strictly limited business models. Individual asset investment opportunities were essentially limited to domestic deposit-taking institutions and kept within the country.

Since the 1980s, Japan's financial system has undergone an extensive transformation, becoming far more open and diverse. By the late 2000s, bond and equity markets were highly developed, and a variety of new entrants, both domestic and foreign, brought a wide range of new business models. The banking system played a smaller role in the economy, foreign insurers and securities firms became major players, and the postal savings system became corporatized, en route to full privatization and competition in the same markets as private sector firms. The overall complexity of the financial system increased considerably, a trend shared worldwide. It has been pointed out that labeling these new, more heterogeneous forms of financial systems everywhere has become exceedingly difficult.[9]

8 The Ministry of Finance used its licensing authority over bank branches to informally shape investment decisions of commercial banks, and a set of policy banks, such as the Developmental Bank of Japan and the Long-Term Credit Bank, were mobilized to lend to target industries. The Bank of Japan, particularly during periods of tight monetary policy, used "window guidance" to guide the lending of major city banks. Takeo Hoshi, David Scharfstein, and Kenneth J. Singleton, "Japanese Corporate Investment and Bank of Japan Guidance of Commercial Bank Lending," in *Japanese Monetary Policy*, ed. Kenneth J. Singleton (Chicago: University of Chicago Press, 1993), 63–94.

9 Richard Deeg, "Institutional Change in Financial Systems," in *The Oxford Handbook of Comparative Institutional Analysis*, ed. Glenn Morgan et al. (New York, NY: Oxford University Press, 2010), 309–34.

We contend that Japan's new financial system is best characterized as syncretic, in which new, old, and hybrid forms of practices, norms, and modes of organization coexist. The old have not been simply replaced by the new, nor entirely morphed into hybrid forms. While the breadth of the new has expanded, and hybridization is occurring to a significant degree, large portions of very traditional organizations, norms, and practices remain within the industry. Syncretism, therefore, is a specific form of diversity. It is not simply hybridization, which is a mix of old and new elements, but instead retains old and new, as well as hybrid elements as distinct forms.[10]

The "new" are best represented by foreign investment banks, securities firms, insurers, and some new Japanese entrants. They introduced new business models (such as derivatives and annuities), practices (particularly regarding employment and interfirm relations) and norms (their perceived raison d'etre is to maximize profit, and especially for many foreign firms, to maximize short-term shareholder returns).

The "hybrid" forms, which meld traditional and new elements, are best represented by the three major financial groups, Mizuho, Mitsubishi UFJ, and Mitsui Sumitomo, centered around their respective mega-banks. The mega-banks were created by mergers between historical main banks, and the resulting financial groups, organized as holding companies, were allowed to expand into previously restricted areas such as securities, trust banking, and insurance. The financial groups embrace a combination of new and old business models (ranging from traditional deposits to foreign currency-denominated accounts and a variety of annuities and insurance products), multiple forms of employment practices (traditional seniority-based banks versus performance-oriented securities subsidiaries, for example), as well as new and old interfirm relations (acting as relational "main banks," but also entering into joint ventures and tie-ups with foreign financial institutions).

The "old" are exemplified by regional banks, which overwhelmingly retain traditional strategies (continued heavy reliance on retail banking), organizational structures (main bank relationships, seniority-based hierarchies), and norms (regionally based with close ties to local governments and an emphasis on relationship banking as a key source of client information).

10 Aoki and collaborators empirically show Japanese firms clustering around several corporate forms: the traditional J-firm model (with at least three subcategories), and multiple subtypes of two hybrid models. Our conception of syncretism is simpler, more easily capturing the dynamics of change. Masahiko Aoki, Gregory Jackson, and Hideaki Miyajima, eds., *Corporate Governance in Japan: Institutional Change and Organizational Diversity* (Oxford: Oxford University Press, 2007); Masahiko Aoki, *Corporations in Evolving Diversity: Cognition, Governance, and Institutions* (New York, NY: Oxford University Press, 2010).

The postal banking system has also become a combination of the new, old, and hybrid. The corporate form is new, with the corporatized Japan Post Holding Company fully owning the bank, insurance, and postal services as subsidiary companies. Top management was given to private sector businessmen, with a new concern for profitability, and employees—including postmasters—are no longer public servants. The postal companies also offer new products and services, such as mutual funds and credit cards, with tie-ups to foreign firms' insurance and annuity products. At the same time, Japan Post Bank is a hybrid in that the government currently still owns 100 percent of the shares of the parent holding company, with plans for the government to retain one-third of the shares. This hybrid ownership form, where the organization is that of a corporatized holding company but the controlling shares belong to the state, has led to calls of unfair competition from Japan Post's private sector and foreign competitors. However, the core business remains traditional: the Japan Post Bank takes retail deposits through its nationwide network, and it is a significant buyer of Japanese government bonds—about one-third of the 700-trillion-yen Japanese Government Bond (JGB) market.

In Japan's new financial system, the new, old, and hybrid coexist. Table 3.1 shows the roughly similar deposit amounts in each area. Note that the total amount of deposits in Japan's sixty-odd regional banks even slightly

TABLE 3.1

Japan's banking system—developmental and clientelistic sides, ranked by deposit size, 2005 and 2010 (trillion yen)

Date	City Banks	Regional Banks	Postal Savings
Deposits			
1995	209.0	217.7	–
2000	230.6	235.0	–
2005	255.7	245.9	200.0
2010	270.3	272.6	175.8
Assets			
1995	346.9	194.7	–
2000	373.0	200.5	–
2005	395.5	216.7	194.7
2010	419.4	240.1	264.9

Source: Bank of Japan.

Note: Postal savings adapted from Japan Post Bank Co. non-consolidated financial data.

TABLE 3.2

Comparison of Japan's financial groups and Japan Post Bank (trillion yen)

	2005			2010	
	Deposits	Total Assets		Deposits	Total Assets
Japan Post	200.0	247.7	Japan Post	175.8	194.7
Mitsui Sumitomo Financial Group	71.2	99.7	Mitsubishi UFJ Financial Group	123.9	204.1
Mitsubishi Tokyo Financial Group	70.4	110.0	Mitsui Sumitomo Financial Group	90.5	123.0
Resona Holdings	33.0	40.0	Resona Holdings	34.1	42.7

Source: Kaisha Shikiho, Summer 2005; company financial reports.

exceeded those of city banks (including mega-banks and some others) by 2010. And the Japan Post Bank, as a single financial institution, still dwarfs the mega-banks (see table 3.2).

Syncretization: The Pattern and Process of Change

The core question posed by this chapter is: How and why did this observed syncretism in Japan's financial sectors occur?

The diversification of financial sectors into new, traditional, and hybrid components is not entirely an expected outcome, given the most common expressions of the idea of institutional complementarity. In the influential scholarship on comparative capitalisms,[11] institutions are considered complementary, or having a good "fit" with one another, when the presence of one enhances the function of another, and so on, creating a matrix of interlocking institutions.[12] Piecemeal change should therefore be difficult, and it may be expected to lower overall performance.[13] It also raises the question of whether the observation of syncretism in Japan is simply transitory: Is it an interlude before the set of institutions converge to a new set of

11 See Jackson and Deeg, "Comparative Capitalisms."

12 For an overview of the varying conceptions of institutional complementarities, see Colin Crouch. "Complementarity," in *The Oxford Handbook of Comparative Institutional Analysis*, ed. Glenn Morgan et al. (New York, NY: Oxford University Press, 2010), 117–38.

13 Hall and Gingerich contend that changes in one institution without changes in the complementary institutions lead to inferior economic outcomes. Peter A. Hall and Daniel W. Gingerich, "Varieties of Capitalism and Institutional Complementarities in the Political Economy: An Empirical Analysis," *British Journal of Political Science* 39 (2009): 449–82.

complementarities (closer to an Anglo-American model, for example), or will they revert back to a more traditional Japanese model?

Our observation of syncretic outcomes also raises the issue of the process of change. A prominent thrust of scholarship is aimed at understanding gradual but transformative change that arises endogenously rather than from exogenous shocks. Pierson brings attention to time horizons in the causes and outcomes of change, and Streeck and Thelen articulate several patterns of gradual institutional change.[14] Mahoney and Thelen go on to stipulate the political conditions, in terms of veto possibilities and characteristics of the target institutions, for each pattern of change to occur.[15] The question for this study is therefore: Was syncretism in Japan's financial sectors a case of gradual, endogenous, transformative change, and if so, does it follow previously identified patterns?

The main contentions of this chapter are as follows. The pattern of change entailed a period of gradual adjustment, with incremental regulatory reforms driving marginal changes in industry dynamics, followed by a burst of regulatory reform that significantly reshaped the actors, business strategies, and patterns of interaction to create the observed syncretic outcome. Particularly in the case of Japan Post, the burst of reform was followed by partial retrenchment of those reforms over a longer period.

The *driver of change* was political—a particular pattern of interest-group politics we call *syncretization*. The prolonged gradual adjustment period was driven by traditional interest group politics dominated by the large, domestic financial institutions and mediated by the bureaucracy. At the junctures of rapid change, however, major political thrusts for reform were driven by the ruling party's acute electoral concerns over its survival in power. Traditional political bargains and historical industry-level policy processes were discarded by the political leadership, which called for reform as a platform for survival.

The key point is that *the actors pushing for reform were not the incumbent, traditionally powerful interest groups most affected by reform.* The impetus for reform came, instead, from strong political leadership spearheading reform as a critical electoral strategy for the party's survival. Since

---

14 Paul Pierson, "Big, Slow-Moving, and Invisible," in *Comparative Historical Analysis in the Social Sciences,* ed. James Mahoney and Dietrich Rueschemeyer. (New York, NY: Cambridge University Press, 2003); Wolfgang Streeck and Kathleen A. Thelen, *Beyond Continuity: Institutional Change in Advanced Political Economies* (Oxford: Oxford University Press, 2005).

15 James Mahoney and Kathleen A. Thelen, *Explaining Institutional Change: Ambiguity, Agency, and Power* (Cambridge: Cambridge University Press, 2010).

the incumbent major players in the financial system were not pushing for reforms, only some players immediately rushed to embrace the new possibilities the reforms enabled. Hence, old, new, and hybrid elements coexisted. Moreover, particularly for postal reforms, since the interests pushing reforms were not in line with those being reformed, once the political leadership lost its drive for reform, the process slowed, and even reversed in some cases.

Implications for Understanding Institutional Change

When theorizing about institutional change, Campbell reminds us to carefully specify the institutions we examine.[16] Regarding the conceptualization of institutions themselves, while various notions of institutions have developed over the past few decades, we settle with an increasingly widespread middle-of-the-road conception: (a) they include formal and informal "rules of the game," which can include external structures and cognitive frames, and (b) they include not only the rules of the game, but also how those rules are concretely played out.[17]

In the financial sector, the main rules of the game include the formal legal regulatory framework as ultimately determined by politicians, bureaucratic discretion to interpret and enforce the regulatory framework, and firm strategies about how to operate—both in markets and in political strategies—to influence policy. Norms play a significant role in determining what firms are maximizing (e.g., shareholder returns versus longevity as a corporate entity), and how they pursue strategies in the face of uncertainty (e.g., business models, and how and when to lobby the government for what), particularly when governance structures provide leeway for interpretive ambiguity (such as shareholders not actively demanding immediate maximum returns).

This chapter finds that the rules of the game in Japan's financial sectors shifted in the following manner. In the private sector financial system, formal regulatory frameworks shifted gradually since the late 1970s, guided by bureaucratic leadership in the context of global financial market liberalization. Then, in the mid-1990s, a major thrust of political leadership-driven reform significantly accelerated liberalization while restructuring bureaucratic financial oversight. The leadership's reform focus, in turn, was driven

16 John L. Campbell, *Institutional Change and Globalization* (Princeton, NJ: Princeton University Press, 2004).

17 Marie-Laure Djelic, "Institutional Perspectives—Working Towards Coherence or Irreconcilable Diversity?" in *The Oxford Handbook of Comparative Institutional Analysis*, ed. Glenn Morgan et al. (New York: Oxford University Press, 2010), 15–40.

by a normative political institutional change; for the first time since the LDP took power in 1955, it was electorally vulnerable: expectations shared by voters and the LDP of the LDP's continued rule no longer held, with electoral defeat a real possibility.

The new financial regulatory framework enabled new entrants, who brought new business models and norms into the sector, altering the dynamics of competition in many areas, shaping the new and hybrid areas. In the postal system, a far stronger, electorally motivated, politically led reform drive spearheaded legislation to corporatize and privatize the entire postal system. However, political backlash against efforts to disrupt long-practiced forms of redistributive politics gradually eroded the initial reform plans, ending in a revised Postal Privatization Law under the new political leadership in April 2012.

So where does this lead us with respect to theoretical discussions of institutional change and complementarity? First, this chapter empirically supports calls by more theoretical work to reintroduce the notion of power struggles in shaping change or sustaining existing arrangements, and to avoid overly functional analysis that infers the purpose of institutions from their current function.[18] In doing so, this study brings attention to the role of political struggles in shifting the mode and speeds of change—from a mode of gradual, incremental change following a longstanding set of interest-group politics, to another mode of rapid politician-spearheaded reform driven by electoral concerns, and then, to a degree, back to the initial mode of incremental change.

This chapter's findings most closely support the theory of institutions and institutional change put forth by theoretical economist Aoki's recent, highly sophisticated conceptual approach.[19] He offers an alternative approach to institutions and institutional complementarity, which rejects the notion that institutional complementarity necessarily constrains partial change, or that partial change causes extremely low performance.

Aoki provides a complex, game theory-centered, but far more holistic conception of institutions, complementarity, and change. He builds upon a concept of associational cognition to construct frameworks of the organizational architecture of firms, and how they fit within broader societal

18 Jackson and Deeg, "From Comparing Capitalisms to the Politics of Institutional Change"; Kathleen A. Thelen, "Beyond Comparative Statics: Historical Institutional Approaches to Stability and Change in the Political Economy of Labor," in *The Oxford Handbook of Comparative Institutional Analysis*, ed. Glenn Morgan et al. (New York: Oxford University Press, 2010), 41–62.

19 Aoki, *Corporations in Evolving Diversity*.

rules, which are themselves shared cognitive frames. In this conception, institutional complementarities occur as one of multiple possible strategic equilibria resulting from interactions by agents across domains. He shows how this implies that changes in quasi-parameters can shift the marginal payoffs among agents, which can then lead to conflicting strategic responses due to policy changes or the endogenous accumulation of physical or cognitive assets, which can cause conflicting strategic responses in complementary domains.[20] Applying this to the Japanese context, Aoki posits that "the emerging diversity in the corporate domain and the gradual demise of the bureaucracy-mediated state in the political exchange domain are mutually complementary and reinforcing of each other."[21] In other words, the shift towards a more diverse industry structure is actually complementary with Japan's postwar political economic system moving away from a policy model strongly mediated by the bureaucracy. We apply his framework more fully in the conclusion after elaborating on our findings.

The remainder of this chapter examines the transformation of the private sector financial system, followed by the postal system reforms. The conclusion ties the chapter into the rest of the book by suggesting how the pattern of syncretism, driven by the politics of syncretization, might apply beyond finance, and beyond Japan.

Reform of the "Developmental" Private Sector Financial System

In the private sector financial system, MOF carefully managed a gradual liberalization of Japan's postwar bank-centered, government-directed financial system since the late 1970s, as finance liberalized globally. Traditional patterns of interest-group politics consisted of bureaucracy-mediated compromises pushed by intense lobbying from large Japanese financial institutions.

In the mid-1990s, however, Prime Minister Hashimoto's Cabinet promulgated the financial "Big Bang" reforms, driven by electoral concerns since the LDP faced unprecedented vulnerability; shared expectations of LDP's continuing electoral victories no longer held, an institutional change in the realm of norms.[22] The reforms drastically dismantled much of the regulatory apparatus of Japan's postwar "developmental" financial system. The reforms accelerated liberalization by breaking down sectoral compartments, enabling new entrants, and providing a wide range of new options

---

20 Ibid., 136.

21 Ibid., 167.

22 Tetsuro Toya, *The Political Economy of the Japanese Financial Big Bang: Institutional Change in Finance and Public Policymaking* (New York: Oxford University Press, 2006).

for corporate organization and business strategies. MOF itself—the lead ministry directing the flow of investments in the "developmental" system—was broken apart and its vast discretionary authority was sharply curtailed. The breakup and weakening of MOF precipitated normative shifts surrounding firms' market and political strategies as a rules-based regulatory model took hold. New entrants also brought new norms, organizations, and business strategies, altering the very dynamics of competition—what firms competed over—in the sector.

These reforms did not follow historical patterns of bureaucracy-mediated compromises pushed by intense lobbying by large Japanese financial institutions. Nor were they the result of political pressures from the greatest beneficiaries of reform—foreign financial institutions. Instead, the financial Big Bang reforms were spearheaded by the political leadership despite intense opposition from the domestic financial industry. The reforms were broader in scale and deeper in scope than previous reforms, MOF lost its historical control of the reform agenda, and industry groups that were strongly opposed were successful only in slowing the pace rather than altering the content of the reforms.

Japan's Big Bang financial reforms also contrasted with those in the United States and UK during the 1980s, where major financial reforms were pushed by the firms most affected (domestic financial firms). Our contention is that because Japan's Big Bang reforms were not pushed through by the interest groups that were most affected (large incumbent Japanese financial institutions), Japanese incumbent firms did not rush to embrace new business models and organizations enabled by the reforms. The reforms themselves did not mandate a complete abandonment of previous practices, organizations, and business models. As a result, Japan's financial sectors did not converge to those of the United States or UK, leaving a different configuration of strategies and firms. Therefore the industry developed following a pattern of syncretism, with old practices coexisting with new practices and strategic adjustments by incumbent players against the backdrop of new rules.

An unexpected benefit of the lack of convergence by Japan's financial system to those of the United States and UK was that the financial system emerged largely unscathed from the 2007–8 global financial crisis. The primary cost was that the inefficient assets held by large and regional banks were not put to productive use. In the political realm, since the financial reforms were not the result of financial interest-group politics, such as was the case in the United States and UK in the 1980s, political pressures for further reforms after Japan's late 1990s financial Big Bang were not particularly strong—especially since the industry remained largely intact after the 2007–8 global financial crisis.

The Traditional "Japanese Model" of Financial
Sectors and Gradual Reform

Japan's traditional financial model, commonly labeled "bank-centered," relied on a high domestic household savings rate and tightly restricted household investment opportunities. Banks and the postal system were the primary repositories for capital, and MOF channeled investments into strategic sectors such as heavy industries and manufacturing. Without including the postal savings system, banks were the largest actors, followed by life insurance firms.[23]

The *traditional industry model* entailed MOF closely managing competition through a variety of formal and informal policy tools. First, MOF compartmentalized the sectors into different segments, including banking, securities, and insurance. It further subdivided each segment. The banking segment included large commercial banks ("city" banks), regional banks, long-term credit banks specializing in long-term industrial loans, policy banks, trust banks specializing in managing pensions and trust investments, and a single bank for foreign currency transactions. Insurance was divided into life, casualty, and, later, a "third sector" in which a small number of foreign insurers were allowed to operate. Securities were kept strictly separate from commercial banking through legislation modeled after the U.S. Glass-Steagall Act, a partition initially imposed by the Occupation authorities but thereafter retained by MOF.

Second, MOF restricted market entry by requiring licenses. It had discretionary authority over the granting of licenses to new entrants and, with the exception of a few foreign banks, until the late 1990s it licensed almost no new banks. With no new banks, MOF could utilize its existing relationships with banks, cultivated over time, to better manage the sector.

Third, MOF tightly managed firms' business models by limiting the products and services that each type of firm was allowed to offer. For example, the interest rates that banks were permitted to offer depositors were fixed, as were commission fee rates at securities brokerages.

In exchange for relinquishing control and complying with the government's investment objectives,[24] MOF provided financial institutions an im-

---

23 By the 1970s, an astonishing 90-plus percent of the population was estimated to have life insurance policies, much of it in the form of "group insurance" offered via employers. Mitsumasa Okamoto, *Gyōkai kenkyū shirīzu: Seiho sonpo* [Industry analysis series: life insurance, casualty insurance] (Tokyo: Nikkei Bunko, 2006).

24 As Vogel writes, "Unlike their counterparts in the United States, Japanese financial institutions rarely tested the rules without the blessing of the authorities. . . ." Steven K. Vogel, "The Bureaucratic Approach to the Financial Revolution: Japan's Ministry of Finance and Financial System Reform," *Governance* 7, no. 3 (1994): 225.

plicit guarantee against insolvency, usually through government-orchestrated mergers. This is commonly known as the "convoy system," named after a convoy of ships that travel at the speed of the slowest one.[25]

The result was a remarkable homogeneity in the products and services offered across firms within each sector. For example, for city banks, because their interest rates and products were limited, competition was based on the number of retail branches available to receive deposits. MOF licensed retail branches, leading to dense interpersonal relationships between banks and MOF officials via bank employees, known as *MOF-tan*, whose mission was to court, and wine and dine, MOF officials to obtain and exchange information.[26]

The *traditional policy model* entailed dense informal bargaining and co-ordination between industry actors, MOF, and LDP politicians, especially those specializing in financial affairs (known as financial *zoku,* or tribe politicians).[27] Gradual regulatory reforms to the financial sectors that began in the late 1970s followed this traditional pattern.

MOF gradually de-compartmentalized the sectors and incrementally deregulated business model restrictions such as brokerage fees, carefully maintaining a balance between each industry segment.[28] For example, in insurance, in the early 1970s, American insurer Aflac wanted to offer cancer insurance, a product that did not fit either the "life" or "casualty" insurance categories. After much deliberation, MOF created a third insurance industry segment, the "third sector," in which Aflac and another U.S. insurer could operate. This industry segment was limited to foreign firms, and major Japanese insurers were restricted from it. In trust banking, foreign firms

25 For more on the "convoy system" see Masahiko Aoki, *Information, Incentives, and Bargaining in the Japanese Economy* (New York: Cambridge University Press, 1988).

26 Jennifer A. Amyx, *Japan's Financial Crisis: Institutional Rigidity and Reluctant Change* (Princeton, NJ: Princeton University Press, 2004).

27 Notable conceptions include "bureaupluralism" (in Masahiko Aoki, *Information, Incentives, and Bargaining in the Japanese Economy* [New York: Cambridge University Press, 1988]); "compartmentalized pluralism" (in Seizaburō Satō and Tetsuhisa Matsuzaki, *Jimintō seiken* [The LDP in power], Shohan ed. [Tokyo: Chūō Kōronsha, 1986]); "bureaucratic-inclusive pluralism" (in Takashi Inoguchi, *Gendai Nihon seiji keizai no kōzu: Seifu to shijō* [The structure of contemporary Japan's political economy: Government and markets] [Tokyo: Tōyō Keizai Shinpōsha, 1983]); and "reciprocal consent" (in Richard J. Samuels, *The Business of the Japanese State: Energy Markets in Comparative and Historical Perspective* [Ithaca, NY: Cornell University Press, 1987]).

28 Vogel, in "The Bureaucratic Approach to the Financial Revolution" (219) writes, "While MoF officials have been forced to make concessions to industry groups and to adjust to unforeseen developments along the way, they have maintained overall control of the reform process."

partnered with Japanese securities firms to enter the sector in the 1980s, buoyed by foreign diplomatic pressures combined with MOF's interest in allowing reciprocal access for Japanese financial institutions to overseas markets.[29] In 1985 MOF allowed securities firms to trade in the secondary market for certificates of deposits and to lend to customers with government bonds as collateral. In return for allowing securities firms to enter new business areas, MOF allowed banks to offer government bond accounts and to participate in the new bond futures markets.[30] These settlements were reached primarily through dense negotiations between MOF and the relevant industry actors, with the occasional involvement of politicians.

The Financial Big Bang Reforms

The financial Big Bang reforms, initially announced in 1996, rapidly accelerated the financial sector's liberalization. The political leadership, desperate to stay in power, cast itself as driving reform by taking the reform process out of MOF's control. The plan, a 1,000-page omnibus bill, revised twenty-four financial and tax laws. Passed in March 1998, it took effect that December, and was implemented in multiple phases through 2001.

The reforms covered the areas within MOF's domain—banking, securities, insurance, accounting, and foreign exchange. They did *not* cover the other portions of Japan's financial system—the postal savings system, under the jurisdiction of the Ministry of Posts and Telecommunications (MPT), or pension funds, under the Ministry of Health and Welfare.

The reforms consisted of several parts. The first part focused on enhancing competition and reducing government control of the sector. Notable measures included the liberalization of international capital transactions; product liberalization, such as securities, investment trusts, derivatives, and loan securitization; de-compartmentalization between banking, trust banking, securities, and insurance; removing the ban that had been in effect since 1945 on financial holding companies; and liberalizing fixed brokerage commissions.

The second part dealt with market development and transparency: harmonizing accounting standards with international practices; applying stricter disclosure rules for banks and securities firms; and creating safety nets for securities and insurance policyholders.

29 Kenji E. Kushida, "Inside the Castle Gates: How Foreign Companies Navigate Japan's Policymaking Processes," Ph.D. diss., University of California, Berkeley, 2010.

30 Frances McCall Rosenbluth, *Financial Politics in Contemporary Japan* (Ithaca, NY: Cornell University Press, 1989), 155.

The third part involved major organizational reforms to financial regulation: MOF was broken up, and the new Financial Services Agency (FSA) took over supervision of the banking, securities, and insurance sectors—previously the areas of highest prestige within MOF. The Bank of Japan (BOJ) Law was fully revised, drastically increasing BOJ's independence from MOF. Finally, there was an overall shift in the style of financial administration in the direction of rules-based market management.[31]

The Politics Driving the Big Bang Reforms: Syncretization

The Big Bang financial reforms were spearheaded by political leadership within the LDP, as the party faced unprecedented electoral vulnerability. As the LDP sought broad public approval, the political leadership took a leading role in controlling the reform agenda. MOF was weakened by scandals, bringing its reputation and prestige to an all-time low. Financial industry interest groups, with the most to lose, were largely excluded from the process.[32] In short, *the actors most affected by the reforms did not have a significant voice in the reform process.*

This was in significant contrast to Great Britain's 1980s financial "Big Bang" reforms, after which the Japanese financial reforms are named. In the British case, British brokerages lobbied the government to deregulate financial markets so they could compete against U.S. firms. As the British financial market rapidly lost business to the deregulated U.S. markets dominated by American firms, British cartel members actually lobbied to be deregulated, recognizing that if the British financial market failed to be deregulated, it would become irrelevant in global competition.[33] Japan's financial markets were experiencing a similar "hollowing out" by the mid-1990s, but domestic financial firms were not lobbying the government to liberalize the market; Japan's financial Big Bang was not the result of corporate lobbying.

In fact the politics of Japan's Big Bang reforms differed considerably between the first phase, promulgation of the reform initiative in 1996, and the second phase, the detailed reform plan of 1997 and implementation.

In the first phase, corporate interest groups were almost entirely left out. The LDP at the time faced unprecedented vulnerability, having lost power in 1993 for the first time in the postwar period, and returning in 1994 with coalition partners the New Party Sakigake and the Japan Socialist Party (JSP), the LDP's longtime opposition. Facing wide criticism from the public

31 Toya, *Political Economy of the Japanese Financial Big Bang.*
32 Ibid.
33 Laurence, *Money Rules.*

fund injections to bail out the housing loan cooperatives (known as *jūsen*), a declining stock market price and prolonged economic slump, the LDP pinned their electoral hopes onto major economic reforms in the run-up to the Lower House elections called for in October 1996. The electoral system change enacted in 1994 shifted electoral strategy toward broad-based appeals rather than the traditional practice of locally targeted distributions,[34] further making this reformist agenda politically attractive.

Hashimoto's reform initiative, which was announced before the October election, bypassed standard LDP legislative processes. Instead of going through the LDP's Policy Affairs Research Council (PARC) populated by industry-sympathizing financial *zoku* politicians, reformers, notably Mizuno Kiyoshi and Shiozaki Yasuhisa, had drafted a plan more comprehensive than the Big Bang reforms themselves, as part of the Administration Reform Promotion Headquarters set up by Prime Minister Hashimoto. Despite opposition from the LDP's financial *zoku*, a meeting of LDP top officials in mid-September 1996 decided to pursue electorally popular reform measures (including the breakup of MOF) at the expense of their hitherto powerful financial industry constituents.[35] The LDP was also capitulating to the demands of its coalition partners, Sakigake and JSP, who wanted to avoid being blamed for taxpayer costs incurred by being coalition partners with the LDP in its reform efforts. They insisted that MOF, who had been preparing for a more modest reorganization of its financial supervisory functions, be split apart—and the LDP agreed.[36]

At the time, the financial industry was weakened by multiple crises and scandals, and MOF, which had worked to protect the industry, was consequently under serious attack. A wave of credit cooperative bankruptcies and regional bank failures in 1994 were followed in 1995 by a crisis in which the seven *jūsen* housing loan companies faced insolvency. Many had former MOF officials in their upper management and had received special regulatory treatment.[37] Their losses amounted to 6.4 trillion yen,

34 For an overview of these arguments, see Frances McCall Rosenbluth and Michael F. Thies, *Japan Transformed: Political Change and Economic Restructuring* (Princeton, NJ: Princeton University Press, 2010).

35 Toya, *Political Economy of the Japanese Financial Big Bang*, 165–66.

36 Nobuhiro Hiwatari, "The Reorganization of Japan's Financial Bureaucracy: The Politics of Bureaucratic Structure and Blame Avoidance," in *Crisis and Change in the Japanese Financial System*, ed. Takeo Hoshi and Hugh Patrick (Boston: Kluwer Academic Publishers, 2000), 109–36.

37 They were free to invest in real estate even after MOF's banking bureau issued administrative guidance to curb such lending from banks. Major banks therefore used these housing loan companies to bypass the regulation. Toya, *Political Economy of the Japanese Financial Big Bang*, 115.

and a public bailout of 685 billion yen was incredibly unpopular—a 1996 poll by the *Asahi Shimbun* reported 87 percent of the public opposed it.[38] Large financial institutions were unwilling to shoulder the bailout as MOF initially hoped, fueling MOF unpopularity and causing concern among the LDP's coalition partners as well.[39] Other scandals, such as Daiwa Bank's losses from illegal bond trading in New York, which resulted in the U.S. government publically criticizing MOF for not acting on prior knowledge, further weakened MOF. A "Japan premium" developed, in which international financial institutions charged interest premiums on all transactions with Japanese banks in the interbank call market due to the lack of trust in MOF's supervision and Japanese financial institutions' financial well-being. Between 1994 and 1996, wining and dining scandals with Japanese financial firms lavishly entertaining MOF officials made headlines, leading to the unprecedented dismissal of MOF's two most senior officials.[40] The life insurance sector was also declining, partly due to the post-bubble economic slump, with the number of life insurance subscribers peaking in 1994. Many were in a financially vulnerable position, stuck with investment portfolios that yielded less than their "guaranteed return rates" promised to subscribers, due to the restricted investment targets and the low interest rate adopted by the government attempting to stimulate the economy.[41] In short, domestic and international public opinion toward Japan's financial institutions and MOF hit all-time lows, just when the LDP was most sensitive to broader public opinion, and vulnerable to the demands of coalition partners.

In the second phase of the Big Bang reforms, Hashimoto, bolstered by an electoral victory for the LDP, immediately moved to enact his reform agenda. Finance was central to his broader "Six Major Reforms" and Hashimoto wanted to push through reforms from the cabinet level rather than through PARC committees with *zoku* politicians. The LDP was not interested in consulting the broader industry at this juncture.[42]

MOF promptly supplied its reform plan, already having lost the battle over its breakup. Interested in preserving what public favor it could, it bypassed the standard industry consultations to avoid accusations of being too close to

---

38 Toya, *Political Economy of the Japanese Financial Big Bang*, 161.

39 Hiwatari, "Reorganization of Japan's Financial Bureaucracy."

40 Toya, *Political Economy of the Japanese Financial Big Bang*.

41 Ryōtaro Mitsuno, *Yokuwakaru hoken gyōkai: Gyōkai no saishin jōshiki* [The insurance industry explained: Up-to-date industry information] (Tokyo: Nihon Jitsugyō Shuppansha, 2006).

42 Toya, *Political Economy of the Japanese Financial Big Bang*.

industry. MOF therefore worked to enlist the support of the mass media, trading companies, and manufacturing firms. A top official is quoted as saying:

> Had we consulted the industries, they would have opposed us. We knew that public opinion would be on our side. . . . It was obvious that deregulated businesses would be in trouble. Thus we could not consult those industries that would have faced trouble due to deregulation.[43]

The financial industry was further weakened in 1997 with a series of racketeering scandals involving paying off organized crime to avoid disrupting shareholders' meetings,[44] reducing the industry's clout in narrowing the breadth and slowing down the reforms. Thus, large financial firms with the most to lose from the reforms succeeded only in slowing down the implementation of cross-entry into different segments by somewhat credibly pointing to the possibility of a wave of bankruptcies. Securities firms lobbied for a "soft landing," with complete brokerage commission liberalization in 1998, and entry of bank subsidiaries into the securities business delayed until 1999. The insurance industry, aided by incumbent foreign insurers who mobilized U.S. diplomatic pressure, successfully lobbied to delay bank entry into insurance until 2001, and even then, limited bank participation initially.[45] The insurance industry association was preoccupied with the problem of how to rescue and resuscitate a string of mid-sized life insurers that had failed, and was not in a strong bargaining position.[46]

Significantly, those with the most to gain—foreign financial institutions—were not strongly lobbying for the Big Bang reforms. Foreign diplomatic pressure mobilized by financial firms peaked in the mid- to late-1980s over the issue of market entry. Once inside, however, they did not organize into strong political associations, since their positions did not necessarily align on several key issues; some with longstanding ties to the Japanese government preferred to remain independent, while others were leery of political involvement.[47] Moreover, foreign firm industry associations within Japan, separated from major Japanese industry associations until after the

43 Eisuke Sakakibara and Soichiro Tahara, *Kinyū—keizai Nihon saisei* [Finance and economy: the resurrection of Japan] (Tokyo: Fusosha, 1999), 135–36. Quoted in Toya, *Political Economy of the Japanese Financial Big Bang,* 171.

44 In 1997 the public prosecutor's office investigated Nomura Securities, Daiichi Kangyo Bank and others, leading to arrests and MOF sanctions.

45 Toya, *Political Economy of the Japanese Financial Big Bang.*

46 Kushida, "Inside the Castle Gates."

47 Louis W. Pauly, *Regulatory Politics in Japan: The Case of Foreign Banking* (Ithaca, NY: China-Japan Program, Cornell University, 1987).

Big Bang, were seldom organized to exert political pressure. For example, the Foreign Banking Association established in 1984 revolved around European banks, represented only about 40 percent of foreign banks, and was primarily an information exchange association rather than a lobbying organization.

For many foreign firms, significant investments in Japan's existing industry arrangements was a deterrent from promoting liberalization or new entry. For example, joining the Tokyo Stock Exchange, opened to foreign members in 1986, cost up to a billion yen (including indirect costs). The twenty-two foreign firms that had joined by 1988 were, unsurprisingly, silent on the issue of liberalizing commission fees that would have nullified the benefits of their exclusive membership.[48] This was understandable, since, historically, liberalization of privileged foreign market segments, such as dollar-denominated "impact loans," had rapidly dried up in the face of competition from new entrants, both foreign and domestic.[49]

In short, the policy process for the financial Big Bang reforms departed considerably from the ongoing gradual reform process orchestrated by MOF. Driven by electoral considerations, in the context of Japan's political logic, and with prevailing circumstances weakening traditionally powerful interest groups, the political leadership drove a strong reform agenda.[50] This change in the pattern of interest-group politics led to syncretism in market outcomes.

Market Outcomes of the Financial Big Bang: Syncretism

The financial Big Bang reforms transformed the logic of competition in Japan's financial industry to a syncretic form. Foreign firms and new entrants took advantage of new opportunities to offer services and products, becoming highly profitable. Incumbent Japanese firms were disadvantaged, since their organizations and strategies were optimized for previous regulatory conditions of limited products and services. While free to enter new business areas, their existing workforces lacked the necessary expertise and radical workforce reductions were legally difficult and normatively prohibitive. After years of adjustment, many incumbents adopted hybrid structures, with holding companies, multiple employment structures, and diverse market strategies.

48 Laurence, *Money Rules*, 131.
49 Pauly, *Regulatory Politics in Japan*.
50 It should be clarified that Thelen and Streeck, and Mahoney and Thelen's conceptions of institutional change are limited to gradual transformative change, and do not include the type of rapid and sweeping changes constituting the Big Bang reforms.

Regional banks, with neither the resources nor the will to transform thoroughly, overwhelmingly adhered to traditional structures and strategies.[51]

The New: New Actors, New Strategies, New Products and Services.   The new areas of finance that the Big Bang reforms introduced entailed truly dramatic changes. Foreign firms, previously confined to relatively niche segments, became major players in almost all areas of Japanese finance. In the securities industry they were highly profitable, pioneering Wall Street–type employment with high salaries and bonuses, little job security, and fluid labor mobility among firms for mid-career professionals.[52] In insurance, they held prominent market shares, with several appearing in the top fifteen since 2000. In March 2011 American Family and Metlife Alico ranked numbers six and seven. And in banking, some spectacular turnarounds occurred with foreign investment funds. Shinsei Bank and Aozora Bank, the seventh and eighth largest banks in Japan (though far smaller than the four megabanks and the postal bank) that were both failed long-term credit banks were resuscitated by U.S. investment funds from Ripplewood and Cerberus, respectively.[53]

New Japanese entrants into banking, insurance, and securities were highly successful. By 2012, Seven Bank, a retail bank with ATMs in the ubiquitous 7–Eleven stores, owned by the retailing giant 7–Eleven Holdings, became a prominent player. In insurance, Sony Life and Sony Sonpo Casualty Insurance ranked eighth and tenth, respectively, in terms of policy-sales income. In securities, electronic trading company Rakuten Securities, a subsidiary of Japanese online commercial giant Rakuten, ranked among the top twenty (at number nineteen) in terms of operating income.[54]

As the major drivers of change, a more detailed examination of foreign firms is called for. In securities, the abolition of fixed commission rates led to a rapid undermining of Japanese securities firms' prevalent business model focused on achieving high trading volumes rather than offering diverse and profitable products and services. As soon as the Big Bang deregulations came into effect, foreign brokerages rapidly expanded their presence and excelled in introducing new products, such as convertible bonds, in which

51 Kay Shimizu, "Private Money as Public Funds: The Politics of Economic Downturn" (Doctoral Dissertation, Stanford University, 2009).

52 For an empirical study of foreign stock brokerages, see Glenn Morgan and Izumi Kubo, "Beyond Path Dependency? Constructing New Models for Institutional Change: The Case of Capital Markets in Japan," *Socio-Economic Review* 3 (2005): 55–82.

53 TDB, *TDB Report: Gyōkai dōkō 2012* [TDB report: Industry developments 2012], (Tokyo: Teikoku Databank, 2012).

54 Ibid.

they topped the list of trades and issuances. Their program trading algorithms were widely deemed to be superior, with greater flexibility and speed. Their advanced computer systems were capable of conducting large basket trades (trades involving a portfolio of multiple shares and bonds), leading even Japanese brokerages to place orders with the foreign firms.[55] Foreign research analysts also offered data and evaluations to institutional investors, services not traditionally provided by Japanese brokerages.[56]

The performance gap between domestic and foreign firms was stark. In 1996, operating profits of the Japanese members of the Japan Securities Dealers Association (JSDA) dropped 40 percent from the previous year, whereas those of foreign securities firms grew an incredible twenty-one-fold.[57] In 2000, the total operating income for the 238 domestic securities firms dropped 23 percent, reflecting a 45 percent drop in commission revenue, whereas that of the fifty foreign firms rose 33 percent, with revenue increasing by 44 percent.[58]

After 1998, Japan's financial Big Bang reforms enabled foreign trust banks to offer dollar-denominated overseas investment trusts. Combined with Japan's low interest rates and the banking crisis, this led to an inflow of Japanese savings; between 1998 and 1999, despite the overall shrinkage of Japanese corporate pension funds entrusted to major Japanese trust banks, the nine foreign trust banks recorded a combined 30 percent increase in corporate pension fund assets.[59] In the first half of fiscal year 1998, total assets held by foreign trusts increased by approximately 40 percent.[60] A particularly successful dollar-denominated investment trust developed by LTCB Warburg took in 50 billion yen in its first week.[61] By late 2004, a survey showed that

55 Basket trades were often used in the late 1990s to quietly unwind cross-shareholding. If it became clear that a major shareholder was unwinding, speculation could drive down share prices, reducing the value of the shares that the firm was attempting to unwind.

56 Interview with an investment banker who wishes to remain anonymous, Tokyo.

57 TDB, *TDB Report: Gyōkai dōkō 1998-I* [TDB report: Industry developments 1998-I] (Tokyo: Teikoku Databank, 1998): 370.

58 TDB, *TDB Report: Gyōkai dōkō 2002-I* [TDB report: Industry Developments 2002-I] (Tokyo: Teikoku Databank, 2002): 22. In 1999, small and medium firms, an estimated 80 percent of which were mostly reliant on commission revenue, began going out of business. TDB, *TDB Report: Gyōkai dōkō 1999-II* [TDB report: Industry developments 1999-II] (Tokyo: Teikoku Databank, 1999): 18.

59 Makoto Satō, "Realignments Sweep Trust-bank Sector: Government Push to Speed Disposal of Bad Loans Adds to Impetus for Change," *The Nikkei Weekly*, January 25, 1999.

60 TDB, *TDB Report: Gyōkai dōkō 1999-II*, 370.

61 Ibid.

foreign institutions held 26.5 percent of all shares managed by investment trusts, investment advisers, and pension funds, totaling 147 trillion yen, an increase of 80 percent since 1997.[62]

In a departure from the convoy system, in 1997 MOF allowed Yamaichi Securities, one of Japan's "big four" brokerages, to collapse. The remnants were purchased by Merrill Lynch, which purchased 33 retail branches and hired about 2,000 of the approximately 7,500 Yamaichi employees.[63]

The Hybrid. A range of interesting hybrid organizational forms became apparent as new firms, business models, and organizations appeared after the Big Bang reforms. Most prominently, multiple employment systems emerged within single firms.

A prime example is Shinsei Bank, the former Long Term Credit Bank that became insolvent in 1998 and was subsequently rescued and reformed by U.S. investment fund Ripplewood. Practices at the new bank, which began operations in June 2000, departed sharply from previous and prevailing banking practices. Most interestingly, the bank implemented a two-tiered compensation scheme. "Permanent staff" enjoyed higher job security but lower pay, whereas "market staff," mostly mid-career hires and foreigners, received higher pay in return for lower job security.[64] Firms such as Mizuho Securities and PWC Japan also implemented two-tiered employment schemes that allowed employees to choose whether to take longer-term employment at lower upfront pay or to take higher upfront pay with less employment security.

Since many of the major Japanese financial institutions were burdened with large numbers of employees but were unable to quickly convert them (either by replacing them or re-educating them) into workers who were familiar with the new products, the solution was to offer new products by partnering with foreign firms. In a sense, they created financial "supply chains" by selling products created by foreign firms through their own sales networks. Japanese banks, trust banks, insurers, and even securities firms thus sought partnerships with foreign firms in the mid-2000s. For example, Sumitomo Bank and Daiichi Kangyo Bank entered into tie-ups with Templeton and JP Morgan, respectively. Sumitomo Trust Bank partnered

---

62 Calculations by Cerulli Associates based on data from the Investment Trusts Association, the JSDA, the Japan Securities Investment Advisers Association, and other sources.

63 In 2002, however, Merrill, unable to make the enterprise profitable, closed all but two branches, losing an estimated US$900 million over the period of four years.

64 Vogel, *Japan Remodeled*, 182–83. For more, see Kushida, "Inside the Castle Gates."

with Chase Manhattan. Japan's largest life insurer, Japan Life, entered into a partnership with Deutsche Bank, Yasuda Life with PaineWebber, and Yasuda Fire and Marine with Cigna International. New joint ventures were created as well, including Prudential-Mitsui Trust Investments, Nomura BlackRock Asset Management, Meiji Dresdner Asset Management, and others.[65]

The Traditional. In contrast to the vast changes within Japan's mega-banks and the entry of new players, the regional banks by and large have retained their traditional forms.

Japan's sixty-four regional banks, located nationwide, originated as part of a postwar government effort to finance and rebuild the regional econo-mies. Regional banks make the majority of their profits from retail banking, catering to small and medium enterprises (SMEs) in their local economies. The SMEs that are their customers are politically salient largely due to their numbers; over 99 percent of the firms in Japan are SMEs, employing nearly 70 percent of the labor market.[66]

The preferential financing available for SMEs also protects regional banks via publicly funded credit guarantees. In lowering the risks associated with loans given to SMEs, credit guarantees allow regional banks to distrib-ute loans to SMEs that are financially weak. These credit guarantees also provide *amakudari*, or post-retirement positions, for local officials. As long as credit guarantees exist, many zombie SMEs will survive, and regional banks will also survive. That there is no market for middle-risk loans is a sign of the inefficiencies in this sector that can only be explained by govern-ment intervention.[67]

The second reason for the continued survival of regional banks in their traditional form is the strength of their relationship banking strategies. The practice of "relationship banking," whereby regional banks nurture close relationships with their SME customers over a long period of time, gives regional banks detailed, long-term information about their SME customers. Interviews with regional bank officers reveal that bankers see their SME cus-tomers at least once a week for banking purposes, but they often have even more frequent contact in various community settings. Bankers may visit their SME customers on site at their business locations not only to cultivate

65 Kushida, "Inside the Castle Gates."

66 The political salience of SMEs is investigated further by Shimizu in chapter 6 of this volume.

67 Ulrike Schaede, "The 'Middle Risk Gap' and Financial System Reform: Small Firm Financing in Japan," Discussion Paper No. 2004-E-11, accessed April 24, 2013, http://www.imes.boj.or.jp/english/publication/edps/2004/04-E-11.pdf.

good relations in hopes of increasing business, but also to get a better sense of their performance. More generally, regional banks have long-term relationships with their SME customers, averaging well over ten years.[68] Smaller SMEs tend to have shorter relationships with their banks, but this is more often due to the short lifespan of the very small SMEs. Overall, the length of the relationship is long enough for regional banks to evaluate the business history and future profitability of their SME customers.

The third reason for the survival of the regional banks in their traditional form is that each prefecture in Japan has at least one regional bank that serves as the designated financial institution of the local government. These designated financial institutions handle the financial transactions of local public institutions, including the prefectural and municipal governments. Their roles include handling fiscal cash management, managing payroll accounts of public officials, and financing local governments. Increasingly, these transactions have become a financial burden for regional banks, as until recently local governments paid no transaction fees for such services. At the same time, regional banks obtain precious information about the health of their regional economies through these transactions and services. Of particular value is their role as the administrator of local tax collection. Local citizens, and especially local businesses, must pay their taxes through the designated financial institution of their local government. Although regional banks play merely an administrative role, these tax remittances provide valuable information about the performance of individual local businesses, giving regional banks an advantage in the SME loan market.

Reform of "Clientelistic" Postal Savings Finance

Reform of the clientelistic side of Japan's financial system occurred through postal privatization. The postal system fueled clientelistic politics in two significant ways: it provided the funds necessary for distribution to specific sectors and geographic areas deemed most effective in influencing votes, and it provided a nationwide network of post offices and postmasters for organizing votes and influencing policymaking.

Japan's postal savings system is thought to be the world's largest holder of personal savings; at its peak in 1999 it held 224 trillion yen (approximately US$2 trillion at 1999 exchange rates) of household assets in its savings accounts (*yūcho*) and an additional 126 trillion yen (US$1.2 trillion)

---

68 See Small and Medium Enterprise Agency, ed., *2003 White Paper on Small and Medium Enterprises in Japan* (Tokyo: Ministry of the Economy, Trade, and Industry, 2003), fig. 2-3-10, for a graph on the average length of relationships that SMEs have with their main banks. Ten years is considered very short.

of household assets in its life insurance services (*kampo*). Together, its assets accounted for nearly one-third of Japan's household assets. With these funds, the postal savings system and the postal insurance system served as key contributors to the Fiscal Investment and Loan Program (FILP).[69] During the postwar years, FILP was the source of government investments in industrial development, small and medium enterprise support, public works, and other government-funded projects, thereby providing politicians with the ability to influence votes with public funds.[70] Japan's reformers saw postal privatization as a necessary part of Japan's overall financial reform and liberalization since postal savings and insurance, via the FILP, placed nearly one-third of household savings under government control.[71]

FILP played a key role in the postwar rebuilding of Japan by financing the construction of national highways and airports, providing funds for housing construction, and subsidizing social welfare facilities and other public works projects. However, as infrastructure saturated nearly all corners of Japan, the supply of funds began to exceed demand, creating abundant room for inefficient and more clientelistic spending. Doi and Hoshi estimate that in 2001, of the 350 trillion yen in outstanding loans from FILP, 75 percent went to recipients that were already insolvent, costing taxpayers 75 trillion yen, or 15 percent of GDP at the time.[72] Imai, using prefectural-level data on Japan's government loans from 1975 to 1992, shows that prefectures represented by more influential LDP members received more governmental loans from the FILP program, and more FILP loans went to prefectures where the ruling LDP candidates were more vulnerable electorally, a variation that was not observed in loans from private banks.[73] To address these problems, in

---

69 For more on the FILP, see Gene Park, *Spending Without Taxation: FILP and the Politics of Public Finance in Japan* (Stanford: Stanford University Press, 2011).

70 Jennifer Amyx, Harukata Takenaka, and A. Maria Toyoda, "The Politics of Postal Savings in Japan," *Asian Perspective* 29, no. 1 (2005): 23–48; Yasushi Iwamoto, "The Fiscal Investment and Loan Program in Transition," *Journal of the Japanese and International Economies* 16, no. 4 (2002): 583–604.

71 In 1997, deposits in private banks and the postal savings system totaled 474,629 billion yen and 237,782 billion yen, respectively. By the start of the privatization process in 2007, the amounts had shifted to 545,043 billion yen and 180,843 billion yen, respectively. Naoyuki Yoshino, "Yubin chokin no shorai to zaisei toyushi" [The future of postal savings and the fiscal investment and loan program], *Toshi mondai* 99, no. 11 (November 2008): 57–58.

72 Takero Doi and Takeo Hoshi, "Paying for the FILP," in *Structural Impediments to Growth in Japan*, ed. Magnus Blomström (Chicago: University of Chicago Press, 2003), 37–70.

73 Masami Imai, "Political Determinants of Government Loans in Japan," *Journal of Law and Economics* 52, no. 1 (2009): 41–70.

May 2000 a reform bill originally designed by Prime Minister Hashimoto's Administrative Reform Council ended compulsory deposits of postal savings and pension reserves into FILP. Under the new law, postal savings and insurance, as well as pension funds, were independently managed via the financial markets, though they continued to invest in FILP bonds and FILP agency bonds issued by public corporations, nominally on the basis of portfolio considerations. FILP, in turn, began to raise funds on an as-needed basis by floating FILP bonds on the market. These reforms severed the direct flow of funds between postal savings and politicians via FILP. Lending under FILP dropped by 63 percent between 1996 and 2006, from 40.5 trillion yen to 15.0 trillion yen. Today, roughly one-third of FILP funding still comes from postal savings and insurance.

With the influence of FILP greatly reduced, one way that politicians have retained control over the allocation of postal savings and insurance funds is through loans to local governments. Because local governments have very limited tax income and almost no power to impose their own taxes, postal savings and insurance funds continue to provide them with financing via local government bonds and FILP. The amounts and terms of the loans are not determined through negotiations with individual local governments to reflect the economic health of each locality, but rather by the Diet through the budgetary process. FILP disbursements to local governments in 2006, for example, included 170 billion yen from the postal savings fund and 310 billion yen from the postal insurance fund. Thus politicians have retained some political control over the allocation of postal savings and insurance funds.

In addition to providing politicians with the funds necessary for public investments, a nationwide network of post offices and postmasters provides organizational support for politicians. With over 24,000 post offices, nearly every small town and village in Japan has one. Among them, the more politically prominent are the 18,000 "special" post offices headed by commissioned postmasters. Unlike the postmasters in ordinary post offices, these commissioned postmasters are handpicked by postal bureaucrats from among a small group of candidates—often the sons or relatives of retiring postmasters—and in many cases are pre-approved by local LDP Diet members.[74] These postmasters in turn serve as vote-collecting machines and also provide logistical and financial support through organizations, such as the kōenkai (candidate support groups).

74 Patricia L. Maclachlan, *The People's Post Office: The History and Politics of the Japanese Postal System, 1871–2010* (Cambridge, MA: Asia Center, Harvard University, 2011).

Nurtured and fortified by former prime minister Tanaka Kakuei, the postal lobby had its heyday in the 1970s and 1980s. At its peak, it is said to have controlled roughly one million votes, primarily for LDP candidates in the rural areas.[75] Under the old electoral system, the influence of the postal lobby and the postmasters was electorally significant, but even then, their real influence was limited to the Upper House elections where they could carry one or two candidates at the national level. In the Lower House elections, the postal lobby had limited influence, and even less so after the 1994 changes in the electoral rules that required a larger proportion of voters to win a seat. Nonetheless, the postal lobby has long been seen as a key vote-gathering machine, not only by rural LDP politicians but also now by members of the Democratic Party of Japan (DPJ) as well as by the People's New Party.

Prior to the privatization efforts, the postal system offered postal and package delivery services, banking services, and life insurance, all under the name of the Postal Services Agency (Yūsei Jigyōshō). It had over 400,000 employees and ran 24,700 post offices throughout the country. The Postal Services Agency was the country's largest employer, employing one-third of all government employees. As a financial institution, its greatest advantages were derived from its nationwide network and its government ownership. Postal savings was a low-risk, convenient option for Japanese households, especially those households with lower incomes or living in remote areas with few alternative investment options. From the perspective of financial competitors, however, the Postal Services Agency had unfair advantages, creating an uneven playing field and hindering competition.

Politically Driven Reform

Postal privatization, like the private sector financial reforms discussed earlier, was a politically driven reform effort most closely associated with one individual, former prime minister Koizumi, who successfully passed the postal privatization bills in October 2005. Koizumi was a long-time proponent of postal privatization beginning in the 1980s when postal privatization was first discussed. His convictions were rooted in his origins in the Mori faction of the LDP and in the party's financial *zoku*, closely affiliated with MOF and the commercial banks. Koizumi regarded postal privatization as representative of a much broader program of market liberalization and structural reform. His views were supported by some bureaucrats, but especially by private banks and firms in the financial sector that saw government protection of postal savings and insurance as unfair competition.

75 Ibid.

Not surprisingly, opposition to postal privatization was fierce. Rooted in 130 years of postal history (postal savings was established in 1875 and postal insurance in 1916), the postal lobby headed by the postmasters was both the target of this reform and its most vociferous opponent. The postal lobby found support among politicians from both the LDP and the opposition parties who benefited from their political support. It also found some public support among those who viewed the old postal system as a symbol of Japan's bygone era of economic prosperity coexisting with social harmony. These citizens equated postal privatization with the evil forces of market liberalization and competition, an economic vision that saw little value in the social benefits and community services provided by postal workers.

Yet in the end, Koizumi's determination and political acumen prevailed. Despite resistance from not only the postmasters and their supporters in the general public, but also from within his own party, Koizumi successfully passed postal privatization by utilizing the institutions directly under his control. In particular, he used the Council on Economic and Fiscal Policy (CEFP), a policy group established by Prime Minister Hashimoto as part of his reorganizational plan for the national government. The CEFP is a deliberative body located within the Cabinet Office and is largely independent of interest-group politics. Koizumi astutely tapped the CEFP, then led by Heizō Takenaka, his minister for economic and fiscal policy, to design the postal privatization process. When opponents in the LDP backed by the postmasters tried to halt the policymaking process in the CEFP, and in the party more broadly, Koizumi moved the policymaking to a small group of allies in the Postal Privatization Preparation Office[76] also within the Cabinet Office, effectively shielding the process from its opponents. Koizumi also took an electoral gamble, linking the credibility of his opponents to passage of the postal privatization bills. By tying postal privatization to his overall stance on reform, Koizumi won a landslide victory in the so-called postal elections of September 2005, paving the way for the successful passage of the postal privatization bills the following month.

Over the longer run, however, Koizumi's overall strategy in passing the privatization bills had important implications in terms of their implementation and the ability of the opposition to limit their actual effects. Even though Koizumi did manage to pass the bills, his strategy was to weaken the opposition by refusing to endorse opposing politicians in the LDP rather than to strengthen the proponents of postal privatization by extolling its

---

76 The Postal Privatization Promotion Office, initiated by Takenaka, was set up in April 2004. Heizō Takenaka, *Kōzō kaikaku no shinjitsu* [The truth behind Japan's structural reforms] (Tokyo: Nihon Keizai Shinbunsha, 2006), 158.

benefits and winning greater popular support. This strategy ensured the success of the reforms only as long as a strong political maverick, such as Koizumi, remained in power. A closer look at the electoral outcomes of September 2005 suggests that Koizumi and his allies won critical votes from voters who rejected the opposition parties that were unable to provide a compelling alternative to postal privatization. The LDP share of the popular vote increased only marginally from the previous election, whereas of the sixteen anti–postal privatization candidates, thirteen were successful. Thus the bill passed but only narrowly. This meant that the opposition to postal privatization remained quite strong, leaving the reform vulnerable to future political compromises. The vulnerability of changing the rules (e.g., passing the postal privatization bills) despite resistance from the very actors they targeted (postmasters and consumers) is that the new rules can later be circumvented, or even reversed, as appears to be the trend thus far.

Postal Privatization and its Outcomes

An examination of the bills themselves as well as their implementation process helps explain the mixed outcomes of the postal reforms. The privatization bills left plenty of room for manipulation and circumvention by opponents of the reform, setting the stage for syncretic outcomes, with the old postal system combining and coexisting with the new businesses that were ushered in by the privatization process. Koizumi began the reform in 2003 by turning the old Postal Services Agency (Yūsei Jigyōchō) into a government-owned corporation, Japan Post (Nippon Yūsei Kōsha), as an intermediary step to outright privatization. Politically, this was an astute strategy, since the postmasters had thwarted his efforts to privatize the postal savings and insurance systems when he served as minister of health and welfare under Prime Minister Hashimoto. By the time Koizumi became prime minister in 2001, the political clout of the postmasters had sufficiently weakened and the more reformist politicians within the LDP had gained power, allowing the transformation of the state-run postal services into the independent government agency, Japan Post.

Although corporatization was an intermediary step, it initiated a number of reforms that provided incentives for Japan Post to think and act more like a corporation than a government agency. The top positions of its three divisions, Postal Services, Postal Savings, and Postal Life Insurance, were held by businessmen, mostly former corporate executives rather than the traditional retiring bureaucrats. Profitability became a priority, placing operational pressures on mail services and the network of post offices. Such pressures prompted the innovation of new products, such as mutual funds, and entry into new services, such as credit cards. These changes early on allowed Japan Post to taste the benefits of privatization while maintaining a de facto 100 percent government guarantee through government ownership, a situation that continues today.

The October 2005 Postal Privatization Bill paved the way for the privatization of Japan Post in October 2007. The bill split Japan Post into four separate companies: a bank, an insurance company, a postal service company, and a company to handle the post offices as the retail storefronts of the former three. These four companies came under the control of Japan Post Holdings Co., Ltd. (Nippon Yūsei Kabushikigaisha), which under the 2005 bill would begin to sell its shares in two financial corporations (Japan Post Bank and Japan Post Insurance) beginning in fall 2011 and ending in fall 2017 (see figure 3.1).

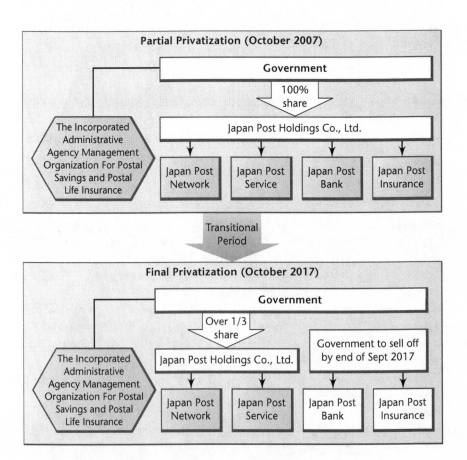

FIGURE 3.1 The 2005 Postal Privatization Bill

Source: Author, based on "Summary of the Revised Postal Privatization Bill," Jiji.com, April 27, 2012, http://www.jiji.com/jc/graphics?p=ve_pol_yusei20120427j-01-w460.

Entry into New Businesses

Setting the path to privatization gave the companies under Japan Post Holdings the green light to venture deeper into new lines of businesses while remaining under the protective umbrella of government ownership. Japan Post Bank now offers postal credit cards with access to the vast postal ATM network as well as some overseas ATMs. Additional services include annuity policies, mortgage and consumer loan intermediary services, and the sale of funds that invest in Japanese and foreign stocks, bonds, real estate investment trusts, and other assets. Alliances with foreign corporations have also opened up new business opportunities. By June 2008, Japan Post Bank and Japan Post Network were selling ING Life Japan's single premium variable annuity (SPVA) products and Japan Post Insurance was selling ING's corporate-owned life insurance (COLI) products. This partnership greatly extended ING's distribution network of banks and securities houses for SPVA products and independent agents for COLI products. In addition to ING Life Japan, a unit of Netherlands-based ING, Japan Post Bank and Japan Post Network also started selling variable annuity insurance products for Sumitomo Life Insurance, Mitsui Sumitomo MetLife Insurance, and Alico Japan, greatly expanding their sales outlets.

Japan Post Insurance (JPI) also ventured into new territory in late 2007 when it began offering products to corporate customers in partnership with life insurers. The eight companies working with JPI include ING Life Japan, Axa Life Insurance, American Life Insurance, Sumitomo Life Insurance, Tokio Marine & Nichido Life Insurance, Nippon Life Insurance, Mitsui Sumitomo Kirameki Life Insurance, and Meiji Yasuda Life Insurance. They are targeting smaller businesses that can utilize these policies as tax-break measures by recording premium payments as losses. JPI continues to push for further expansion of its business. In 2009 it filed an application with the Financial Services Agency and the Ministry of Internal Affairs and Communications (MIC) for approval of a new stand-alone insurance product that would compete directly with the private sector and foreign companies.[77] In 2010 a cabinet proposal was introduced that would raise caps on the amount of insurance coverage and reduce limits on the scope of JPI product offerings. The growing protests against such expansions—from the private sector and from foreign companies that were upset about the statutory, regulatory, and other governmental privileges afforded to JPI—attest to the considerable expansion of JPI.

77 American Council of Life Insurers, *Japan's Expression of Interest in the Trans-Pacific Partnership Negotiations* (Washington, DC, 2012).

Retrenching to a Hybrid Form

However, as the economy continued to suffer from deflation and the aftermath of the 2008 global financial recession, the public began to side with those opposed to full privatization. Riding this momentum, in November 2009 then DPJ prime minister Yukio Hatoyama froze the sale of shares in Japan Post's financial units, a significant retreat from Koizumi's pro-market reforms. In so doing, Hatoyama tried to appeal to those who saw Koizumi's reforms as excessively market-friendly, a line he had touted during his party's landslide victory earlier that year. At 330 trillion yen (US$3.6 trillion in 2009) in assets (with 240 trillion yen in Japan Post Bank), although Japan Post Holdings by then accounted for only one-fifth of Japan's total financial assets down from its peak of one-third, a significant portion still funded Japanese government bonds.

The current status of postal privatization is a combination of the old, the new, and the hybrid. For Japan Post Bank, the basic business model of taking retail deposits through its nationwide network remains intact. The social services component of the old postal system, such as *himawari*, or daily visits especially to the elderly, have been retained to the extent possible, although a special government fund earmarked for this purpose appears to have evaporated. Shares of the postal savings and postal insurance companies have yet to leave the hands of the state. Although it is no longer required that these funds be invested in the FILP, the practice continues, with Japan Post holding about one-third of the 700 trillion yen government bond market. And even though the postal lobby and postmasters have continued to lose their political influence, their jobs have been largely retained and additional jobs have been created in postal-related facilities, such as recreation centers and lodging. Ironically, as a result of the passage of the privatization bill, postmasters are no longer public servants and thus they are free to actively participate in political activities. But postmasters are by no means as electorally influential as they once were, even though they evidently retained enough political influence to win over the DPJ and its supporters during its time in power.[78]

In April 2012 a revision to the Postal Privatization Bill passed as a result of an agreement between the New Komeito and the LDP (see figure 3.2). The revision removed the December 2009 Freeze Law that had halted the sale of government-owned shares, thereby greatly dampening the incentives for privatization.[79] However, support for reform in the revision ended here. The

78 A leader of the postmasters group was quoted as saying that his group could guarantee at least 500,000 votes. ("Zentoku 'Kondo wa ribenji da' minshu, chihō-hyō ni shōjun," *Asahi Shinbun Globe*, June 8, 2009, http://globe.asahi.com/feature/090608/04_3.html)

79 Naoki Tanaka, "Report on the Postal Privatization Commission's Opinion Pertaining to the Comprehensive Review of Postal Privatization Progress," March 2012.

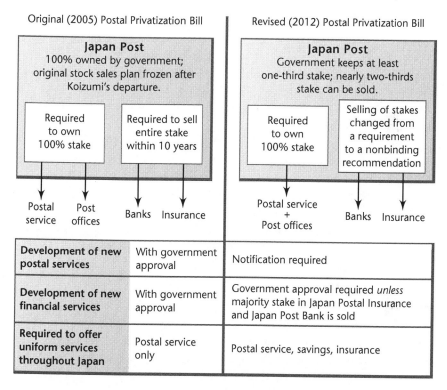

FIGURE 3.2. The April 2012 revision to the Postal Privatization Bill
Source: Nikkei Shimbun, May 13, 2012, morning edition.

revision also removed the requirement for the sale of government stakes in the two Japan Post financial institutions (bank and insurance) by September 2017, replacing it with a much weaker recommendation. Even though Japan Post Holdings President Jiro Saito has said that Japan Post aims to go public "at the earliest possible time," he has also said that "the shares could end up being handed over to trust banks or acquired by Japan Post Holdings group firms."[80] This, interestingly, contrasts with the position of Minister Kawabata (DPJ) of the MIC, a position stated in the Diet deliberations, that Japan Post shares should be sold publicly.

The revision to the Postal Privatization Bill also stipulated that in October 2012 Japan Post Service Company (mail delivery) and Japan Post Network Company (window services) would be merged. Proponents of reform saw serious pitfalls in this merger, as it raised the risk of a systemic

80 "Japan Post Eager to Enter SME Loan Markets: Interview with the President," *Nikkei Newspaper* (morning edition), May 9, 2012.

shock to Japan's financial system. The Commission Report by Naoki Tanaka (March 2012) states that combining the delivery and network companies with a holding company would raise serious doubts about isolating two of the world's largest financial institutions from the holding company's business risks. Rising levels of risk aside, however, this merger would also create a hybrid between a government-owned holding company and a privately held corporation. In regulatory terms, cross-subsidization among subsidiaries of Japan Post Holding Company is only permitted due to Japan Post's status as a government-owned business; in contrast, private holding companies must allow their subsidiaries to go bankrupt.

At the same time, however, the revision paves the way for greater expansion of Japan Post into new business areas. The revisions do not permit unfettered expansion into areas already dominated by the private sector, but the legislation does open the door to new businesses and it lowers the barriers to entry.

Conclusion

This chapter has examined reforms to Japan's financial system—the system at the core of its distinct model of capitalism. We have characterized the observed outcome of its transformation as syncretism, the coexistence and combination of traditional, new, and hybrid organizational structures and strategies. Analyzing both the traditional financial sectors of banking, securities, and insurance, as well as the financial firms within the massive postal system—the "developmental" and "clientelistic" sides of the economy—we contend that the particular pattern of interest-group politics that drove the reform led not only to syncretic industry outcomes, but also to distinct dynamics of reform. Major thrusts of reform occurred when the political leadership overwhelmed traditionally powerful vested interests; however, when the leadership advocating reform waned, the vested interests substantially slowed down further reform. We call this pattern of reform "syncretization."

This type of reform has several implications. We expect Japan's financial system to exhibit syncretism for at least the short to medium term. Therefore, although some areas of the system are rapidly converging with U.S.– and UK–style norms, organizations, and strategies, such as in securities and investment banking, others retain their traditional structures and strategies, such as the regional banks. The growth of hybrid practices and strategies also assures that convergence is unlikely any time soon. Even though inefficiencies remain, to a large degree the current state of affairs insulates Japan's financial system from international shocks, such as the 2007–8 financial crisis that damaged Japan's export sector but left most of the financial system largely intact.

The potential integration of Japan's postal savings and insurance systems into the mainstream financial system represents the entry of major new market-based players. Yet, given the shifting political trajectory with vested interests advocating a slowdown returning to political prominence, integration has been substantially decelerated. Japan Post Bank and Japan Post Insurance are still wholly held by Japan Post, itself held 100 percent by the Japanese government. In short, the reversals in the privatization process have created government-owned firms that directly compete with private firms, both domestic and international. This is another aspect of Japan's financial system that remains distinct from that in the United States or the UK. But even though Japan may be blazing its own path, these firms have the potential to create new headaches for the government as it attempts to steer Japan toward greater participation in both bilateral and regional trade agreements. In the recent negotiations for the Trans Pacific Partnership, for example, Japan met with U.S. opposition to plans for state-owned Japan Post Insurance to enter the cancer insurance market. Syncretism may be the distinct outcome of politically led reforms, but the lack of conformity may also lead to isolation and accusations of unfair play.

References

American Council of Life Insurers. *Japan's Expression of Interest in the Trans-Pacific Partnership Negotiations.* Washington, DC, 2012.

Amyx, Jennifer A. *Japan's Financial Crisis: Institutional Rigidity and Reluctant Change.* Princeton, NJ: Princeton University Press, 2004.

Amyx, Jennifer, Harukata Takenaka, and A. Maria Toyoda. "The Politics of Postal Savings in Japan." *Asian Perspective* 29, no. 1 (2005): 23–48.

Aoki, Masahiko. *Information, Incentives, and Bargaining in the Japanese Economy.* New York: Cambridge University Press, 1988.

Aoki, Masahiko, Gregory Jackson, and Hideaki Miyajima, eds. *Corporate Governance in Japan: Institutional Change and Organizational Diversity.* Oxford: Oxford University Press, 2007.

Campbell, John L. *Institutional Change and Globalization.* Princeton, NJ: Princeton University Press, 2004.

Crouch, Colin. "Complementarity." In *The Oxford Handbook of Comparative Institutional Analysis,* edited by Glenn Morgan, John Campbell, Colin Crouch, Ove Kaj Pedersen, and Richard Whitley, 117–39. New York: Oxford University Press, 2010.

Deeg, Richard. "Institutional Change in Financial Systems." In *The Oxford Handbook of Comparative Institutional Analysis,* edited by Glenn Morgan, John Campbell, Colin Crouch, Ove Kaj Pedersen, and Richard Whitley, 309–34. New York: Oxford University Press, 2010.

Djelic, Marie-Laure. "Institutional Perspectives—Working Towards Coherence or Irreconcilable Diversity?" In *The Oxford Handbook of Comparative Institutional Analysis,* edited by Glenn Morgan, John Campbell, Colin Crouch, Ove Kaj Pedersen, and Richard Whitley, 15–40. New York: Oxford University Press, 2010.

Doi, Takero, and Takeo Hoshi. "Paying for the FILP." In *Structural Impediments to Growth in Japan,* edited by Magnus Blomström, 37–70. Chicago: University of Chicago Press, 2003.

Dore, Ronald. *Stock Market Capitalism: Welfare Capitalism: Japan and Germany versus the Anglo-Saxons.* New York: Oxford University Press, 2000.

Hall, Peter, and Daniel W. Gingerich. "Varieties of Capitalism and Institutional Complementarities in the Political Economy: An Empirical Analysis." *British Journal of Political Science* 39 (2009): 449–82.

Hall, Peter, and David Soskice. "An Introduction to Varieties of Capitalism." In *Varieties of Capitalism: The Institutional Foundations of Comparative Advantage,* edited by Peter A. Hall and David Soskice, 1–68. New York: Oxford University Press, 2001.

Hiwatari, Nobuhiro. "The Reorganization of Japan's Financial Bureaucracy: The Politics of Bureaucratic Structure and Blame Avoidance." In *Crisis and Change in the Japanese Financial System,* edited by Takeo Hoshi and Hugh Patrick, 109–136. Boston: Kluwer Academic Publishers, 2000.

Hoshi, Takeo, David Scharfstein, and J. Kenneth Singleton. "Japanese Corporate Investment and Bank of Japan Guidance of Commercial Bank Lending." In *Japanese Monetary Policy,* edited by Kenneth J. Singleton, 63–94. Chicago: University of Chicago Press, 1993.

Imai, Masami. "Political Determinants of Government Loans in Japan." *Journal of Law and Economics* 52, no. 1 (2009): 41–70.

Inoguchi, Takashi. *Gendai Nihon seiji keizai no kōzu: seifu to shijō* [The structure of contemporary Japan's political economy: Government and markets]. Tokyo: Tōyō Keizai Shinpōsha, 1983.

Iwamoto, Yasushi. "The Fiscal Investment and Loan Program in Transition." *Journal of the Japanese and International Economies* 16, no. 4 (2002): 583–604.

Jackson, Gregory, and Richard Deeg. "From Comparing Capitalisms to the Politics of Institutional Change." *Review of International Political Economy* 15 (2008): 680–709.

Kabashima, Ikuo, and Gill Steel. *Changing Politics in Japan.* Ithaca, NY: Cornell University Press, 2010.

Kushida, Kenji E. "Inside the Castle Gates: How Foreign Companies Navigate Japan's Policymaking Processes." Ph.D. diss., University of California, Berkeley, 2010.

Kushida, Kenji E., and Kay Shimizu. "Syncretism: The Politics of Japan's Financial Reforms." *Socio-Economic Review* 11 (2013): 337–69.

Laurence, Henry. *Money Rules: The New Politics of Finance in Britain and Japan*. Ithaca, NY: Cornell University Press, 2001.

Maclachlan, Patricia L. *The People's Post Office: The History and Politics of the Japanese Postal System, 1871–2010*. Cambridge, MA: Asia Center, Harvard University, 2011.

Mahoney, James, and Kathleen A. Thelen. *Explaining Institutional Change: Ambiguity, Agency, and Power*. Cambridge: Cambridge University Press, 2010.

Milhaupt, Curtis J. "In the Shadow of Delaware? The Rise of Hostile Takeovers in Japan." *Columbia Law Review* 105, no. 7 (2005): 2171–216.

Mitsuno, Ryōtaro. *Yokuwakaru hoken gyōkai: Gyōkai no saishin jōshiki* [The insurance industry explained: Up-to-date industry information]. Tokyo: Nihon Jitsugyou Shuppansha, 2006.

Morgan, Glenn, John L. Campbell, Colin Crouch, Ove Kaj Pedersen, and Richard Whitley. *The Oxford Handbook of Comparative Institutional Analysis*. Oxford: Oxford University Press, 2010.

Morgan, Glenn. and Izumi Kubo. "Beyond Path Dependency? Constructing New Models for Institutional Change: The Case of Capital Markets in Japan." *Socio-Economic Review* 3 (2005): 55–82.

Ohmae, Kenichi. *End of the Nation State: The Rise of Regional Economies*. New York: Free Press, 1995.

Okamoto, Mitsumasa. *Gyōkai kenkyū shirīzu: Seiho sonpo* [Industry analysis series: Life insurance, casualty insurance]. Tokyo: Nikkei Bunko, 2006.

Park, Gene. *Spending without Taxation: FILP and the Politics of Public Finance in Japan*. Stanford: Stanford University Press, 2011.

Pauly, Louis W. *Regulatory Politics in Japan: The Case of Foreign Banking*. Ithaca, NY: China-Japan Program, Cornell University, 1987.

Rosenbluth, Frances McCall. *Financial Politics in Contemporary Japan*. Ithaca, NY: Cornell University Press, 1989.

Rosenbluth, Frances McCall, and Michael F. Thies. *Japan Transformed: Political Change and Economic Restructuring*. Princeton, NJ: Princeton University Press, 2010.

Sakakibara, Eisuke, and Soichiro Tahara. *Kinyū—keizai Nihon saisei* [Finance and economy: The resurrection of Japan]. Tokyo: Fusosha, 1999.

Samuels, Richard J. *The Business of the Japanese State: Energy Markets in Comparative and Historical Perspective*. Ithaca, NY: Cornell University Press, 1987.

Sato, Makoto. "Realignments Sweep Trust-Bank Sector: Government Push to Speed Disposal of Bad Loans Adds to Impetus for Change." *The Nikkei Weekly*, January 25, 1999.

Satō, Seizaburō, and Tetsuhisa Matsuzaki. *Jimintō seiken* [The LDP in power]. Shohan ed. Tokyo: Chūō Kōronsha, 1986.

Schaede, Ulrike. *Choose and Focus: Japanese Business Strategies for the 21st Century*. Ithaca, NY: Cornell University Press, 2008.

———. "The 'Middle Risk Gap' and Financial System Reform: Small Firm Financing in Japan." Discussion Paper No. 2004-E-11, http://www.imes .boj.or.jp/english/publication/edps/2004/04-E-11.pdf.

Shimizu, Kay. "Private Money as Public Funds: The Politics of Economic Downturn" Ph.D. diss. Stanford University, 2009.

Small and Medium Enterprise Agency, ed. *2003 White Paper on Small and Medium Enterprises in Japan*. Tokyo: Ministry of the Economy, Trade, and Industry,

Streeck, Wolfgang, and Kathleen Thelen, eds. *Beyond Continuity: Institutional Change in Advanced Political Economies*. New York: Oxford University Press, 2006.

Tahara, Soīchirō, and Eisuke Sakakibara. *Nihon saisei: Kin yū keizai jiyū kyōsō bannō wa macchigai da* [Finance and economy: The resurrection of Japan]. Tokyo: Fusosha, 1999.

Takenaka, Heizō. *Kōzō kaikaku no shinjitsu* [The truth behind Japan's structural reforms]. Tokyo: Nihon Keizai Shinbunsha, 2006.

Tanaka, Naoki. "Report on the Postal Privatization Commission's Opinion Pertaining to the Comprehensive Review of Postal Privatization Progress." March 2012.

TDB. *TDB Report: Gyōkai dōkō 1998-I* [TDB report: Industry developments 1998-I]. Tokyo: Teikoku Databank, 1998.

———. *TDB Report: Gyōkai dōkō 1999-I* [TDB report: Industry developments 1999-I]. Tokyo: Teikoku Databank, 1999.

———. *TDB Report: Gyōkai dōkō 1999-II* [TDB report: Industry developments 1999-II]. Tokyo: Teikoku Databank, 1999.

———. *TDB Report: Gyōkai dōkō 2002-I* [TDB report: Industry developments 2002-I]. Tokyo: Teikoku Databank, 2002.

———. *TDB Report: Gyōkai dōkō 2012* [TDB report: Industry developments 2012]. Tokyo: Teikoku Databank, 2012.

Toya, Tetsuro. *The Political Economy of the Japanese Financial Big Bang: Institutional Change in Finance and Public Policymaking*. New York: Oxford University Press, 2006.

Vogel, Steven K. "The Bureaucratic Approach to the Financial Revolution: Japan's Ministry of Finance and Financial System Reform." *Governance* 7, no. 3 (1994): 219–43.

———. *Japan Remodeled: How Government and Industry Are Reforming Japanese Capitalism*. Ithaca, NY: Cornell University Press, 2006.

Yamamura, Kozo, and Wolfgang Streeck. *The End of Diversity? Prospects for German and Japanese Capitalism.* Ithaca, NY: Cornell University Press, 2003.

Yoshino, Naoyuki. "Yūbin chokin no shōrai to zaisei tōyūshi" [The future of postal savings and the fiscal investment and loan program]. *Tōshi mondai* 99, no. 11 (November 2008): 57–58.

Zysman, John. *Governments, Markets, and Growth: Financial Systems and the Politics of Industrial Change.* Ithaca, NY: Cornell University Press, 1983.

4 System Change and Corporate Reorganization in Japan

THE STRATEGIC LOGIC OF BUSINESS GROUPS
AND MAIN BANKS, REVISITED

Ulrike Schaede

The 1990s are often referred to as Japan's "lost decade," marking ten years of limited economic growth after the collapse of the bubble economy of the 1980s. However, the decade also marked the launch of a fundamental transformation of Japan's industrial architecture from the previous postwar "developmental state" system. In about 1998 the country reached a tipping point when the banking crisis, the arrival of globalization to domestic markets, and the loss of Japan's previous competitive advantage in the mass manufacturing of consumer end products invited a legal change through a revision of virtually all laws pertaining to commerce. Under the leadership of Prime Ministers Ryūtarō Hashimoto and Junichirō Koizumi, who coined the label "leave it to the market," the earlier socialization of business risks was challenged and regulatory processes were oriented toward transparency and accountability. As a result, the context in which Japanese firms can now compete was completely altered. Indeed, the period from 1998 to 2006 crystallized into a strategic inflection point, i.e., a reversal in terms of what it takes to win within the Japanese setting.

In response to the lingering crisis, many Japanese companies embarked on a major journey of restructuring. This occurred in two forms: reactive and proactive. In cases where companies only reacted, they engaged in corporate restructuring narrowly defined. These were troubled firms that had no choice but to undergo layoffs, plant closures, and even bankruptcy

---

A detailed version of the argument proposed in this chapter can be found in Ulrike Schaede, *Choose and Focus: Japan's Business Strategies for the 21st Century* (Ithaca, NY: Cornell University Press, 2008).

procedures. Theirs is a story of stopping the bleeding and cleaning house. The second form was a wave of positive, forward-looking strategic repositioning by proactive firms that realized that the old system did not allow them to be as competitively sharp as they could be and should be in the new global competitive landscape. These reformers became the trailblazers of Japan's "choose and focus" (*sentaku to shūchū*) reorganization and their actions have since reoriented Japan's industrial architecture—including business groups, financing channels, and corporate governance—toward profitability and efficiency. These proactive companies operate in diverse industries such as materials and components (e.g., JSR, Nittō Denkō, and Ibiden), pharmaceuticals (Takeda and Astellas), chemicals (Toray, Teijin, and Fujifilm Holdings), and even steel (JFE Holdings). Because their products are not end products, and because many of these firms are not household names, their transformation has been largely underappreciated. Yet the consequences of their repositioning for Japan's entire business system have been far-reaching. This chapter is their story, as it analyzes the changes in Japan's political economy, the actions of these proactive companies, and the changes they brought to the old system of business groups and main banks.

System Change: The Strategic Inflection Point

In business strategy, an inflection point refers to a moment in time when the competitive environment changes such that the balance of forces shifts away from the existing paradigm.[1] Such an inflection affects industry dynamics and reorients corporate strategy, as it necessitates a transition from previous ways of doing business to new ones. For example, the arrival of Internet commerce brought a strategic inflection for the book industry, where the winning retail proposition shifted from store location, shelf presentation, and ambience, to immediacy in shipping, selection, and price. In Japan, as this chapter will argue, the far-reaching commercial reforms since 1998 have been so elemental that they resulted in a deep-seated restructuring of Japanese business organization.

For an inflection point to be truly strategic, it has to be irreversible. What has made system change in Japan irreversible is that it was not based on one single event or law, but rather on a confluence of factors that all pushed

1 Robert A. Burgelman and Andrew S. Grove, "Strategic Dissonance," *California Management Review* 38, no. 2: 8–28. In mathematics, an inflection point is reached when the first derivative (the slope of the trajectory) becomes zero, and the second trajectory (the rate of change) reverses its sign. See Ulrike Schaede, *Choose and Focus: Japan's Business Strategies for the 21st Century* (Ithaca, NY: Cornell University Press, 2008), chap. 2, for a more detailed account of the following summary.

Japan's industrial architecture in a new direction. During the 1990s, Japan irrevocably lost its previous cost advantages in mass-producing high quality, commoditized household goods for export, first to South Korea, followed by Taiwan, and later increasingly to China. Just as sales were lost to these competitors, the banking crisis of 1998 brought Japan perilously close to a financial meltdown. The crisis moment was exploited by entrepreneurial prime ministers Ryūtarō Hashimoto in the late 1990s and Junichirō Koizumi in the early 2000s, who both spearheaded a series of reforms that were unprecedented in terms of their reach and impact.[2] Even though the complete response to this strategic inflection point may take as long as one generation, 1998 can be regarded as the watershed year when Japan moved away from its previous postwar architecture. And even as laggard firms still slowed down the change process, by the mid-2000s two main pillars of "Old Japan" had been dismantled: the *keiretsu* (business groups) and the main bank system. For both, their strategic underpinnings had changed because the old construction had become irrelevant for successful Japanese companies. Where these groups and their protective mechanisms continued, members found themselves surrounded mostly by Old Japan firms. What we used to know about these two pillars in postwar Japan no longer applies.

The most visible event in the "tipping point" was the banking crisis. By 1997 the huge losses incurred by banks as a result of financial and real estate speculation during the bubble years (1987–91) could no longer be downplayed. With the bankruptcy of several large financial institutions in November 1997, and the Asian financial crisis of 1997–98, most large banks faced great difficulties to maintain the 8 percent capital adequacy ratio as required by the Basel Accord for banks operating internationally. If any large bank dropped below this ratio, it most likely would have folded, potentially causing a bank run. To avert this precarious scenario, the government injected a total of ¥9.3 trillion (roughly US$90 billion) into the country's leading banks. At the time, this was considered an enormous bailout, and it was accompanied by fierce political debate and stringent new rules on how to

2 Shifts in politics and vested interests were critically important during this process, but are better discussed in research on political change in Japan. See T.J. Pempel, *Regime Shift: Comparative Dynamics of the Japanese Political Economy* (Ithaca, NY: Cornell University Press, 1998), for a prescient analysis of the precursors to this "regime shift"; Steven K. Vogel, *Japan Remodeled: How Government and Industry are Reforming Japanese Capitalism* (Ithaca, NY: Cornell University Press, 2006), for the interplay of government and business during this reform process; and Jennifer A. Amyx, *Japan's Financial Crisis: Institutional Rigidity and Reluctant Change* (Princeton: Princeton University Press, 2004), on the role of the Ministry of Finance and the political background of the financial crisis in the 1990s.

improve bank business. Finding themselves in the spotlight, banks began to reorganize and clean up their non-performing loans. This was made possible by new laws that facilitated direct loan write-offs whereby the banks could sell off the assets of failing customers immediately, rather than organizing long-term informal debt workouts. This allowed the banks to clean up failing clients, with some hope to recoup at least a modicum of value from the failed loans. To allow the banks themselves to restructure, a 1998 legal revision allowed financial holding companies, and the previous thirteen leading banks merged into four large financial groups (MUFG, Mizuho, Sumitomo-Mitsui, and Resona). Also in 1998, two long-term credit banks came under government receivership and were subsequently sold to U.S. equity funds and became the Shinsei and Aozora Banks. In addition, the Financial Services Agency (FSA) was established as a supervisory agency independent from the Ministry of Finance. Finally, the Financial Reform Program of 2002, promoted by Prime Minister Junichirō Koizumi, established a rigid timetable for expunging non-performing loans, and the largest banks accomplished this by about 2006.

Meanwhile, manufacturing firms confronted the harsh reality that they had lost their erstwhile competitive advantage in exporting consumer end products. With the emergence of companies in South Korea and Taiwan as leaders in low-cost assembly, and the threat of China joining the ring, strategic Japanese companies had to identify ways to reposition themselves in higher margin segments where the new entrants could not (yet) compete in terms of technology and innovation. This meant they had to withdraw from commodity end-product assembly and move upstream in the value chain. For example, textile companies Toray and Teijin began to phase out standard textile production to become world leaders in carbon fiber, which is difficult to produce in large quantities at a consistent quality. The two leading steel companies (Nippon Steel and JFE) reduced their commodity steel segment and directed strategic efforts to becoming world leaders in advanced steel products. Panasonic began a long process of exiting most of its consumer product businesses, and instead built capacities in new "ideas for life" products (intelligent household applications) as well as advanced components, such as automobile lithium-ion batteries and solar energy. Moreover, new competitors emerged in the components and materials sectors. As of 2012, Japanese companies combined held roughly 70 percent of the world market share in fine chemicals for electronics. For example, Fujifilm Holdings is now one of a group of leaders in certain films that improve the quality of LCD panels. A large number of hitherto unknown Japanese companies have appeared on the global stage with similar strengths, such as JSR, a synthetic rubber company that has become a leader in photoresists (chemicals for semiconductor production) and materials needed for high-quality LCD panels.

The success of this repositioning is indicated by Japan's growing trade surplus with South Korea and Taiwan throughout the 2000s. Although electronics were increasingly assembled in China, China sourced parts for assembly in South Korea and Taiwan, which in turn purchased high-level input materials for these parts from Japan. However, in managerial terms—including labor relations and a reorientation of corporate culture toward efficiency—the transition from Old Japan to "New Japan" was a long-term process expected to last perhaps a generation.[3]

Legal Reforms

The strategic inflection was initiated by a change in Japan's rigid laws and rules for corporate reorganization. The far-reaching legal reforms of 1998–2007 can be grouped into four large categories. The first set of changes addressed regulation, transparency, and oversight. This began with Prime Minister Hashimoto's 1998 "Big Bang" financial reforms that covered all financial areas. Most critically, the reform program introduced more transparency into corporate accounting by (1) shifting from book-value reporting to market-value reporting beginning in 2000 (and including for cross-shareholdings beginning in 2001), and (2) mandating consolidated accounting, meaning that it was required that the financial situation of all subsidiaries be reported. The former measure radically changed the trade-off calculation for corporate stock ownership (as discussed below), whereas the latter ended long-standing practices of cross-subsidizing businesses and concealing losses in small subsidiaries. As a result of this new transparency, corporate financial statements became more meaningful for investors. It also made large numbers of subsidiaries, which previously had remained unreported if they incurred losses, much less useful for large companies. The new accounting rules were paired with a new approach to financial regulation, as the previous reliance on informal administrative guidance by the Ministry of Finance and behind-closed-doors workouts were replaced with by-the-book inspections and meaningful sanctions of violators by the new FSA.

A second important change was the introduction of new corporate turnaround and bankruptcy legislation. Throughout the postwar period, large

3 Ulrike Schaede, "From Developmental State to the 'New Japan': The Strategic Inflection Point in Japanese Business," *Asia Pacific Business Review* 18, no. 2 (2012): 167–85.

firms that fell into trouble typically were forced into an informal workout, usually guided by the main bank. Rarely was a company closed down, for the bank typically aimed to recoup the debt in the long run, as opposed to incurring a large one-time loss. The government had long supported this approach to restructuring, as it pursued a "too big to fail" policy to maintain employment. Companies in trouble had little choice but to rely on their bank because bankruptcy laws dating back to 1927 and 1951 were too cumbersome for alternative types of reorganization. During the postwar period banks had become quasi-monopolists in corporate restructuring, in an almost automated process: a firm falls into distress, the bank sends in an executive to structure a financial turnaround, the firm recovers and over time pays back the bank. Perhaps the biggest long-term problem with this approach was that the main bank typically focused on improving the financial situation (in which it specialized), but rarely did it care to create a new viable business model for the failing firm (about which it knew little). In the 1990s it became clear that decades of finance-oriented turnarounds void of business strategy reform had created an army of "zombies," that is, dead companies existing ominously in a depressed economy.[4] The average profitability data for stock-exchange–listed Japanese companies halved, from an unweighted average return on equity of about 10 percent in the early 1980s to 5 percent in the late 2000s; likewise, during the three decades operating margins halved from about 8 percent to 4 percent.[5] These are dismal numbers in international comparison: Japan had too many companies with suboptimal performance. Many of these companies knew this quite well, of course, but they were limited in their options on how to restructure.

In 2000, the new Civil Rehabilitation Law opened new legal processes for corporate restructuring, akin to a Chapter 11 process, and the 2003 revision of the Corporate Reorganization Law introduced new processes for efficiently structured turnarounds. The courts in Tokyo and Osaka established special divisions to handle such procedures. Further, the 2001 guidelines for "out-of-court workouts" clarified the structure of bank-led turnarounds. Finally, the 2004 revision of the Liquidation Law established clear-cut rules for a shutdown of debtors and the distribution of remaining assets. The new system afforded companies in distress a choice of alternative ways to reorganize. It also gave banks the option of refusing to bail out a client in trouble,

4 Takeo Hoshi, "Economics of the Living Dead," *Japanese Economic Review* 57, no. 1 (2006): 30–49.

5 Author's calculations based on Nikkei Needs data.

as the distribution of assets could now be left to the courts.[6] Overall, these changes brought about a series of shutdowns and reorganizations, greatly helping to clean up in the aftermath of the excesses of the bubble period.

A third set of reforms aimed to invite competitive repositioning by proactive restructuring, i.e., by companies that technically were not in distress. During the period of rapid growth, Japanese companies had grown by expanding into ever-more business areas. The Old Japan had rewarded size, as measured in sales, as it allowed the "best" (meaning large) firms access to industrial policies, talent (having first pick of each year's university graduates), and even higher stock price evaluations. Beginning in the 1990s, globalization brought extensive competition, including on the Japanese markets, and the old behemoths, some of which had hundreds of subsidiaries, were insufficiently nimble to compete.

Beginning in 1997, to allow these behemoths to reposition and regroup by exiting non-core or unprofitable businesses, the Commercial Code was revised annually. In 2006, this culminated in the new Corporation Law, which replaced the century-old Commercial Code. At the end of this process, Japanese companies had many options for reorganization through mergers and acquisitions, spin-offs, labor transfers, and exiting from entire business segments, i.e., the rules were reconfigured to facilitate the transfer and exchange of ownership stakes in business units and subsidiaries. This paved the way for a true market for corporate assets and led to a surge in mergers and acquisitions as companies focused on their main-business segments while exiting their peripheral activities.

Other laws, too, were revised, ranging from finance to antitrust and intellectual property protection to labor.[7] Taken together, in terms of corporate strategy this meant greatly increased flexibility for managers in terms of how to compete, with whom to merge, and which business units to spin off. Before 1998, companies that wanted to change were greatly hindered by archaic rules favoring stability, while those that attempted to "muddle through" could use the system rigidities (e.g., in the labor market) as an excuse. With these legal changes, proactive strategic players can aggressively reposition while laggards find it increasingly difficult to do nothing.

The 2006 Corporation Law is explicit about the new managerial flexibility, but it also prescribes new processes of oversight by shifting significant

6 Takeo Hoshi, Satoshi Koibuchi, and Ulrike Schaede, "Corporate Restructuring in Japan during the Lost Decade," in *Japan's Bubble, Deflation, and Long-Term Stagnation*, eds. Koichi Hamada, Anil K. Kashyap, and David E. Weinstein (Cambridge: MIT Press, 2011), 343–73.

7 Schaede, *Choose and Focus*.

monitoring powers to shareholders. A new 2007 Financial Instruments and Exchange Law (FIEL) brought J-SOX, a version of the U.S. Sarbanes-Oxley Law, which, among other things, stipulates fiduciary responsibility for board members, a larger proportion of whom must be external to the company (see below). This aimed to make the board of directors an entity with accountability, by empowering progressive companies to replace the rubber-stamp decision-making of boards and pro-forma annual shareholders' meetings of the past with more open and meaningful processes.[8]

Proactive Restructuring: Choose and Focus

To compete against new global competitors, Japan's competitive companies have proactively reorganized, in a shift that has come to be described in Japan as "choose and focus" (*sentaku to shūchū*). This term refers to strategies of corporate unbundling (through reorganization and spin-offs) and concentration on the core business (through organic growth or by acquiring or merging with competitors). A process was set in motion away from the previous dominant strategy of high diversification and conglomerate building toward attempts to focus on clearly defined core competencies with a more careful and guarded consolidation around the core. Many of Japan's former goliaths began to slim down in order to become more focused and more driven. Spinning off non-core operations helped to improve profitability as companies exited low-margin, commoditized product segments.[9] Refocusing has allowed targeted investments in R&D to increase differentiation through innovation.

An analysis of the Nikkei 500 firms for the 2000–6 period reveals that 75 percent of Japan's largest firms reported to have undergone proactive restructuring.[10] Even though one might expect firms to reorganize regularly,

8 Tsutomu Fujita, "Shin-kaisha-hō shikō de kabunushi sōkai wa issō jūyō ni" [The new Company Law is implemented: Toward a stronger general shareholders' meeting], *Ekonomisuto* (June 6, 2006): 78–80; "Hagetaka/hakuba no kishi ka, gaishi fando zenkaibō" [Vultures or white knights: A thorough analysis of foreign funds], *Shūkan Daiyamondo* (April 24, 2006).

9 Tatsuo Ushijima, "Understanding Partial Mergers in Japan," *Journal of Banking and Finance 34*, no. 12 (2010): 2941–53.

10 Schaede, *Choose and Focus*. These findings are supported by research on divestitures and acquisitions (though not reorganization) of 770 manufacturing firms during the 1999–2003 period; see Tatsuo Ushijima, "Evolving Market for Corporate Assets in Japan: Which Firms Enter and How?" paper presented at meeting of the Academy of Management, Philadelphia, 2007, who finds that 41 percent of firms made at least one acquisition, 24 percent made at least one divestiture, and 15 percent did both.

three-quarters of all companies is high by any measure. In a study of the United States, which underwent its own wave of refocusing in the 1980s, Markides found that by the most conservative estimate, 20 percent of the Fortune 500 firms refocused during that decade, and if underreporting were to be incorporated into the findings, the true number may be closer to 50 percent.[11] Studies on refocusing face great challenges in data identification, and cross-country comparisons are difficult. That said, these broad measures suggest that Japan's "choose and focus" wave was at least on par with the United States in the 1980s, making it a truly remarkable episode in global business history. Strategy literature provides evidence that it takes a long time—in large organizations, several decades—before the results of reorganization are reflected in corporate performance. Therefore, a full-fledged performance evaluation of Japan's "choose and focus" initiative will be left for future research.

To be sure, protected industries remained, and in many industries ossified laggards refused to "choose and focus." Over time, these Old Japan companies are becoming less and less influential in Japan's political economy. The leaders of New Japan's *zaikai* (business world) are the presidents of companies that have managed a successful strategic repositioning of their companies, such as Takeda Pharmaceuticals, SUMCO (semiconductor materials), or Toray (the world leader in carbon fiber), and the large trading houses. Furthermore, in this process of full-fledged strategic repositioning many of the former pillars of the postwar industrial architecture have been replaced with processes more conducive to aggressive global competition in a much more dynamic setting. Whereas Japan's industrial architecture in the postwar period had established strong incentives for managers to seek stability and market-share growth, the new system forces them to strive for profitability and competitive advantage.

System Change in Japan's Industrial Architecture

From the heyday of Japan business research in the late 1980s and early 1990s, we have established a perceived wisdom regarding Japan's business system. Government policies geared toward fast export-led economic growth formed the backdrop to the "industrial architecture"[12] that consisted

---

11 Constantinos C. Markides, "Diversification, Restructuring and Economic Performance," *Strategic Management Journal* 16, no. 2 (1995): 101–18; Constantinos C. Markides, *Diversification, Refocusing, and Economic Performance* (Cambridge: MIT Press, 1995).

12 James R. Lincoln and Michael L. Gerlach, *Japan's Network Economy: Structure, Persistance, and Change* (New York: Cambridge University Press, 2004).

of clearly specified relations among large firms as main pillars, small firms as supporting staff, and banks as central operators of finance. Supportive government policies included regulated interest rates to lower the costs of borrowing, subsidies, and tax measures to spur investments and trade policies to protect infant industries and to facilitate cooperative arrangements in innovation and technological catch-up. Because new entry was limited and technology policy managed such that all incumbents had access to new innovation streams, a stable competitive hierarchy developed with a set of clearly identified leaders in each market segment.

At the center of the industrial architecture were the so-called six horizontal *keiretsu* (inter-market business groups), whose preferential relations were cemented through cross-shareholdings and anchored by a main bank that fulfilled three important functions: to provide smooth access to finance even to the most highly leveraged firms; to monitor management based on superior insights into the company's operations; and to structure a coordinated workout should a company encounter trouble, so as to avoid bankruptcy and ensure the company's longevity (and thereby maintain Japan's competitive hierarchy as well as lifetime employment). Disclosure and bankruptcy rules were geared toward facilitating informal problem-solving. From this a peculiar setting for corporate governance emerged, based on internal processes with the stock and bond markets, as well as the courts, assuming roles of rarely used bit players.[13]

13 See, for example, ibid., on *keiretsu*; Takeo Hoshi and Anil Kashyap, *Corporate Financing and Corporate Governance in Japan: The Road to the Future* (Cambridge: MIT Press, 2001) and Masahiko Aoki and Hugh Patrick, eds., *The Japanese Main Bank System: Its Relevance for Developing and Transforming Economies* (New York: Oxford University Press, 1994) on the main bank system. On the policies of the "developmental state," see Chalmers A. Johnson, *MITI and the Japanese Miracle: The Growth of Industrial Policy, 1925–1975* (Stanford: Stanford University Press, 1984); Ryutaro Komiya, Masahiro Okuno, and Kotaro Suzumura, eds., *Industrial Policy of Japan* (Tokyo: Academic Press, 1988); Hugh Patrick and Henry Rosovsky, eds., *Asia's New Giant: How the Japanese Economy Works* (Washington, DC: Brookings Institution, 1976); Kent E. Calder, *Strategic Capitalism: Private Business and Public Purpose in Japanese Industrial Finance* (Princeton: Princeton University Press, 1993); Pempel, *Regime Shift*; and Ulrike Schaede, "The Japanese Financial System: From Postwar to the New Millennium," Harvard Business School Case 700-049 (October 20, 1999). Technology policies and R&D consortia are evaluated by Marie Anchordoguy, *Computers, Inc.: Japan's Challenge to IBM* (Cambridge: Council on East Asian Studies, Harvard University, 1989); Scott Callon, *Divided Sun: MITI and the Breakdown of Japanese High-Tech Industrial Policy, 1975–1993* (Stanford: Stanford University Press, 1995); Akira Goto and Ryuhei Wakasugi, "Technology Policy," in *Industrial Policy of Japan*, eds. Ryutaro Komiya, Masahiro Okuno, and Kotaro Suzumura (Tokyo: Academic Press, 1988), 183–204; L.H. Lynn, "The Commercialization of the Transistor Radio in Japan: The Functioning of an Innovation Community," *IEE Transactions on*

During the postwar period, industrial policy put strong pressure on managers of Japanese firms to pursue aggressive growth. Low costs of bank borrowing meant that in order to uphold a certain market share in a fast-growing market, firms had to invest at least as much as their competitors.[14] Moreover, the system of lifetime employment made labor a fixed cost, raising the average break-even point significantly. Every sale that earned positive income, however little, was desirable.[15] Banks, too, were more interested in steady sales than they were in profits because their main interest was to collect interest on the sizable amount of outstanding loans.

In this setting, the main vehicle for Japan's largest companies to reduce the risk of failure was to link up with a main bank and a business group through cross-shareholdings, and a governance mechanism that allowed group intervention only in times of failure. However, the strategic inflection point of the 1990s shifted the main goal of corporate management away from "no failure" to "high profitability." Moreover, for global success, firms needed to find new ways to compete, strategize, and organize. The Old Japan institutions that strived to preserve their venerable members were often an obstacle to this repositioning, and their inertia eventually pushed the firms in the direction of new modes of organization.

The Main Bank

The first significant break point with the past was the diversification of finance that began as early as the mid-1980s.[16] Financial deregulation allowed firms to also raise external funds through the issuance of stocks, bonds, and short-term notes. As a result, in the 1980s the portion of bank lending directed at large firms began to shrink, and the average financial

---

Engineering Management 45, no. 3 (1998): 220–29; Gregory W. Noble, "The Japanese Industrial Policy Debate," in *Pacific Dynamics: The International Politics of Industrial Change*, edited by Stephan Haggard and Chung-in C. Moon (Boulder, CO, Westview, 1989), 53–95; and Daniel J. Okimoto, *Between MITI and the Market: Japanese Industrial Policy for High Technology* (Stanford: Stanford University Press, 1989). Whether the industrial and technology policies were indeed successful has been debated; however, no one denies that these policies were attempted throughout the postwar period, and accordingly they formed the setting for large companies to formulate their corporate strategies.

14 James C. Abegglen and George J. Stalk, Jr., *The Japanese Corporation* (New York: Basic Books, 1985).

15 See Schaede, *Choose and Focus*, chaps. 3 and 9, for an in-depth analysis of corporate strategy in the postwar setting as well as a discussion of changing human resource practices with respect to performance pay and meritocracy.

16 Hoshi and Kashyap, *Corporate Financing and Corporate Governance in Japan*; Schaede, "The Japanese Financial System."

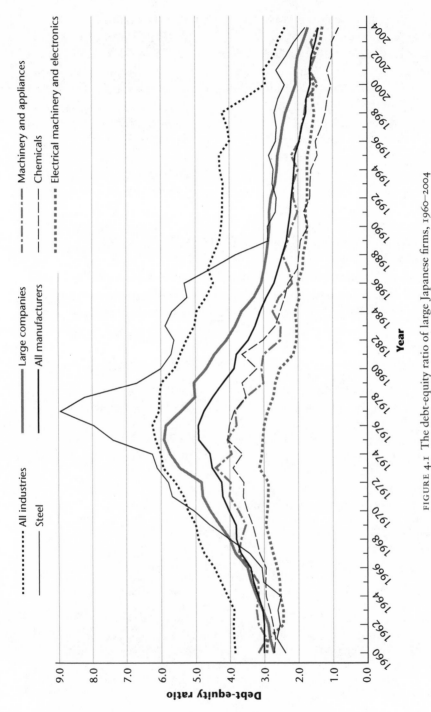

Legend:
- All industries
- Steel
- Large companies
- All manufacturers
- Machinery and appliances
- Chemicals
- Electrical machinery and electronics

FIGURE 4.1 The debt-equity ratio of large Japanese firms, 1960–2004

Source: Calculated from *Hōjin kigyō tōkei.*

Note: "Large companies" refers to firms with capital exceeding ¥1 billion.

leverage, expressed as the ratio of debt to equity (DER), was normalized. Figure 4.1 shows that for large firms with capital exceeding ¥1 billion, the DER peaked in the late 1970s at almost 6 (meaning that large firms had six times as much debt as they had equity). This ratio fell to less than 2 in the early 2000s, and in the chemical and electronics industries, which have been particularly aggressive in terms of "choose and focus," it fell to about 1. A lower debt-equity ratio also implies a much-reduced dependence on bank loans. The data suggest that beginning in 1998, companies increasingly began to finance projects through retained earnings, or to the extent they required external funds, through the issuance of stocks and bonds. For the latter, profitability is a critically important factor in determining the cost of financing.

Given all the research hailing the virtues of the main bank system in terms of patient capital and insurance, why would banks and companies part in this way? Two main reasons can be identified that demarcate an irreversible change in banking. First, for the relationship between companies and banks, the high leverage (debt-equity ratios) of the postwar period brought strict main bank oversight. Not all companies found this enjoyable, and many happily sought new venues for financing. During the 1980s, interest-rate regulation as well as restrictions on external funding, including from abroad, were being phased out. For the best companies, bank loans were no longer the cheapest way to secure funding. For the banks, a reduced loan volume translated into a much-reduced influence over companies, but also less financial interest in monitoring and supporting companies. This divergence of interests was extended by a strategic shift in the banking industry away from its previous reliance on lending (the predominant business model under regulated interest rates) and toward more reliance on fee-based income (such as the underwriting of securities issues or syndicated loans). Both banks and companies began to move toward more flexible means of funding that allowed them to react better and faster to the changing market situation. With loan activities reduced, banks saw fewer returns on their extensive monitoring activities, and relations became less tight. In the early 2000s, when the large banks began to consolidate from more than ten to four main players, companies used the opportunity to reduce their stockholdings in banks (see below).

Main bank relations were strained further when banks, struggling with financial difficulties, began to renege on their role as bailout agent. A study of cases of corporate restructuring between 1981 and 2007 finds that beginning in the mid-1990s being highly dependent on a main bank (measured by the ratio of loans from the main bank to all loans outstanding) no longer translated into an automated rescue event.[17] In 1997, after Fuji Bank announced that it was too financially stressed to rescue the group's flagship investment bank, Yamaichi Securities, some companies—facing financial challenges and the impending new mark-to-market accounting rules for their shareholdings—began to sell off cross-held shares that were a drag on profits. As the ultimate benefit of having a main bank, insurance against bankruptcy, became uncertain, the insurance premium of holding mutual shares became too expensive.

A 1999 Cabinet Office survey on the advantages of the main bank system supports this interpretation. Of the 1,361 listed companies that responded by ranking the three primary benefits of having a main bank in the past, the most frequent answers were about "stable access to funds" (60 percent), "having a stable shareholder" (49 percent), and "long-term relations" (32 percent). Looking forward, however, the responses referring to stability dropped by half. Instead, companies looked forward to increased creditworthiness due to the bank's reputation (20 percent), specialized advice on financial strategies (18 percent), and support for global business (11 percent).[18] This shift in demand for services from the main bank triggered a strategic response by the largest banks, including in human resources management (from generalists to specialists, and from seniority to meritocracy).

Overall, although the main bank system per se is still valued, its role and functions have begun to change. Instead of being a stable source of long-term credit and the designated rescue agent, the main bank is becoming a source of knowledge, information, and execution of unbundling strategies.

Moreover, the bank-company business relationship is no longer predicated on history or a long-term relationship, but rather it is increasingly determined competitively by who can provide the best services. The four main financial groups now cover all types of banking services. These groups are competing head-on with the foreign banks operating in Japan, and in order to be successful, they have to offer high-quality services, such as M&A advice, international financing, and initial public offerings. Old Japan's stodgy main bank lending institution that earned profits simply by lending no longer has a future.

17 Hoshi, Koibuchi, and Schaede, "Corporate Restructuring in Japan during the Lost Decade."

18 Cabinet Office, *Heisei 10-nen kigyō kōdō ni kan suru ankeeto chōsa* [1998 survey of corporate activities] (Tokyo, 1999), accessed June 14, 2013, http://www5.cao.go.jp/99/f/19990420ank/menu.html.

Business Groups

Throughout the postwar period, Japanese firms worked to shield themselves from the threats of competition, in particular from takeovers, through corporate tie-ups. These tie-ups came in three forms: large, inter-market groups; vertical line-ups of subcontractors and other suppliers; and vertical tie-ups with exclusive wholesalers and retailers for distribution. All three have undergone major transformations: supplier relations have become more diversified, and the retail revolution that began in the late 1990s has undermined exclusive wholesaler arrangements.[19] The focus here is on the "Big 6" horizontal groups.

Research on these groups provides important insights into the workings of the business groups during the postwar period. From data compiled in Toyo Keizai's annual *Kigyō keiretsu sōran*, we could measure cross-held ownership stakes, personnel dispatches, and within-group loans. The sheer size of these groups triggered regular impact surveys by the Japan Fair Trade Commission from 1977 through 2001. Sociologists have used these data for network analyses,[20] whereas economists have provided studies on the implications for corporate finance and industrial organization.[21]

From this research, four main insights have evolved. First, there were six "horizontal groups"—three descendants of the prewar *zaibatsu* reconstituted in the 1950s (Mitsubishi, Mitsui, and Sumitomo), and three anchored by postwar banks (Fuyō, Sanwa, and Dai-Ichi Kangyō [DIK]). Overall, the groups had 20–40 members, so that about 200 of Japan's largest firms in the postwar period belonged to the Big 6 horizontal *keiretsu*. Each of these groups had several core firms (such as a large bank, a general trading company, and perhaps a heavy machinery company), but no one company was dominant. Even though each member owned, on average, only 1–2 percent of shares in other group members, taken together this resulted

19 Schaede, *Choose and Focus*, chap. 8.

20 Michael L. Gerlach, *Alliance Capitalism: The Social Organization of Japanese Business* (Berkeley: University of California Press, 1992); Lincoln and Gerlach, *Japan's Network Economy*.

21 Hoshi and Kashyap, *Corporate Financing and Corporate Governance in Japan*; Takeo Hoshi, "The Economic Role of Corporate Grouping and the Main Bank System," in *The Japanese Firm: The Sources of Economic Strength*, eds. Masahiko Aoki and Ronald Dore (Oxford: Oxford University Press, 1994), 285–309; Iwao Nakatani, "The Economic Role of Financial Corporate Grouping," in *The Economic Analysis of the Japanese Firm*, ed. Masahiko Aoki (Amsterdam: North-Holland, 1984), 227–58; Richard E. Caves, and Masu Uekusa, *Industrial Organization in Japan* (Washington, DC: Brookings Institution, 1976).

in within-group ownership and a potential voting block of 15–30 percent of total outstanding shares of all group member firms.

The groups adhered to a concept called "one–setism": one group would include only one competitor in each industry, lest intra-group competition would create frictions. This also meant that in times of trouble it was important to support a member firm so as to avoid disruption of the network. With increasing diversification, the "one-set" rule loosened over time; for example, Mitsubishi Heavy and Mitsubishi Electric eventually began to compete in several product segments. Furthermore, the bank mergers of the early 2000s cut across group boundaries, thereby undermining the network logic. As the resultant large banks suddenly served several firms in one industry, it became more difficult to justify a generous bailout package for one of the competitors.

The most important purpose of the business groups was insurance. In the 1950s, companies attempted to shield themselves from hostile foreign takeovers. When the government proved it could effectively implement foreign exchange controls (through 1964, and in a different form after Japan joined the IMF and GATT), the emphasis of protection shifted to insurance against stock price fluctuations through an agreement that reciprocally held ownership stakes would not be sold, especially in times of crisis, and that dividends would be kept regular yet low (a custom was developed to cap them at 10 percent of a stock's face value, which was either ¥50 or ¥500).[22] For the largest firms, this made equity a cheap source of stable funding, even though it also meant low returns on their own stock portfolios. But this was considered to make economic sense as long as the insurance mechanism was fully intact.

Data suggest that group firms had lower average profitability than independent firms, but also lower variance in profitability over time.[23] Thus, group membership came at a cost, and the forgone profits could be regarded as an insurance premium against uncertainty. The lower profits may have been due to a more conservative attitude among companies that self-selected into groups. Over time, it is also possible that group firms were increasingly

22 The majority of stocks in the early postwar period had a par value of ¥50, so most companies paid dividends of ¥5 per share. James E. Hodder and Adrian E. Tschoegl, "Some Aspects of Japanese Corporate Finance," *Journal of Financial and Quantitative Analysis* 20, no. 2 (1985): 173–91 calculate for the 1960–83 period that the 1,500 largest firms listed on the 1st Section of the Tokyo Stock Exchange (TSE) paid an average of between ¥5.92 and ¥6.88 per share; during that same period, the TSE Index increased sevenfold, so that over twenty-five years average dividend yields declined to roughly a 1 percent share of the market value.

23 Nakatani, "The Economic Role of Financial Corporate Grouping"; Hoshi and Kashyap, *Corporate Financing and Corporate Governance in Japan*.

TABLE 4.1

Summary of the changing *keiretsu* roles and cohesion

Aspect of *keiretsu* role	Average for Big 6		Average for 3 "old zaibatsu" groups		Average for 3 "bank groups"	
1. Overall role in the economy	1970	1998				
Percent of total capital	18.9	13.2				
Percent of total assets	17.5	11.2				
Percent of total sales	15.0	10.8				
2. Measures of group cohesion	1981	1999	1981	1999	1981	1999
Intra-group shareholding ratio	25.5	20.1	32.2	25.0	19.1	15.2
Intra-group procurement ratio	11.7	6.4	14.8	8.1	9.1	4.9
Intra-group directorships	8.6	4.2	11.4	4.7	6.0	3.7
Intra-group lending	6.9	2.3	–	–	–	–

Source: Collated from *Tōyō Keizai* (various years) and Japan Fair Trade Commission (JFTC), *Kigyō shūdan no jittai ni tsuite: Dai-7-ji chōsa hōkokusho* [Survey on the state of horizontal business groups: Results from the seventh survey] (Tokyo, 2001).

"old industry" firms that began to decline with Japan's changing industrial structure after the oil crisis of the 1970s.[24] Another contributor to lower profits may have been the preferential trade agreements among group firms, which averaged between 4 percent and 12 percent of all sales by member firms. Although this was more relevant for intermediate products and equipment (e.g., steel, chemicals, or machine tools), it was visible even to the naked eye: at a Mitsubishi plant, only drinks from Kirin (a group member) would be served. When Mazda encountered a crisis in the 1970s, in addition to providing financial support and absorbing some surplus labor, Sumitomo Group firms suggested that employees purchase new Mazdas.[25] Preferential trade overrode cost considerations, and the system of "after-sales price adjustment" allowed group firms to smooth out income over time by post-negotiating prices for intermediate goods.[26] The important gain for a member firm from such preferential trades was to establish a minimum quarterly sales volume that served as a buffer against sales variations over the business cycle. Because major shareholders and managers were more interested in protection, long-term stability, and reducing uncertainty in the rapidly changing market than they were in profits, paying extra for group insurance was considered reasonable.

24 K. Suzuki, "Kabushiki sōgō mochiai no 'kishō' ni tsuite" [On the 'dissolution' of mutual *mochiai* shareholdings], *Osaka Keidai Ronshū* 55, no. 5 (2005): 7–23.

25 Richard Pascale and Thomas P. Rohlen, "The Mazda Turnaround," *Journal of Japanese Studies* 9, no. 2 (1983): 219–63.

26 Schaede, *Choose and Focus*, chap. 8.

Much of this changed in the 1990s when the strategic inflection point affected the cost-benefit calculations of the more successful member firms. Table 4.1 compares indicators of economic impact and cohesion for the six groups. From the upper part of the table, we realize that the economic role of the horizontal groups declined significantly, from almost one-fifth of total capital and assets and 15 percent of total sales in the 1970s to the low 10 percent range. The main reason for this decline is that Japan's largest firms were no longer members—either because they left, or because they are new firms (e.g., Softbank or Fast Retailing) that never joined a group. So clear is the evidence that horizontal groups no longer dominate Japan's economy that in 2001 the Japan Fair Trade Commission (JFTC) terminated its economic impact survey of the Big 6 groups.

The lower part of table 4.1 compares four measures of cohesiveness between 1981 and 1999. The first measure is the percentage of total outstanding shares of group firms owned by other group firms. On average, this ratio has fallen from 25 percent to 20 percent. A similar downward trend is also observable for preferential trade. On average, in 1999 group firms purchased but 6.4 percent of all inputs or goods from other group firms. This decline of 50 percent reflected a growing concern with costs at a time of market opening and globalization. The dispatch of senior executives to the boards

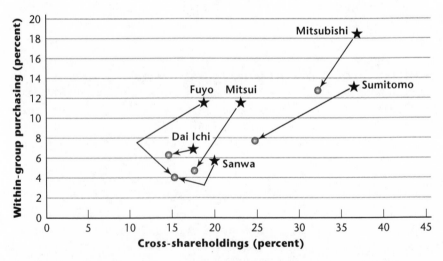

FIGURE 4.2 Changing *keiretsu* cohesion: the combined decline in cross-shareholdings and preferential trade in the big six *keiretsu*, 1981 and 2000

Notes: ★ = 1981; ◎ = 2000.

Source: Japan Fair Trade Commission (JFTC), *Kigyō shūdan no jittai ni tsuite: Dai-7-ji chōsa hōkokusho* [Survey on the state of horizontal business groups: Results from the 7th survey] (Tokyo, 2001).

of directors of other group firms also halved, from 8.6 percent of group directors sitting on other group boards to 4.2 percent. Finally, intra-group lending refers to the percentage of loans provided by the group's main bank to all loans outstanding for a group's member firms. It has always been the case that while the main bank was the largest single lender, it was rarely the only lender; instead it functioned as a delegated monitor for loans from other large banks.[27] Yet, beginning in the mid-1980s when large firms came to rely less on loans, the impact of the main bank on group finance has dwindled.

Figure 4.2 maps the two main categories of intra-group ownership and preferential trade from table 4.2 onto a two-axis repositioning chart comparing 1981 and 2000. The longest distance, reflecting the biggest loss in cohesion, was recorded for Sumitomo, and the smallest loss was for Dai-Ichi Kangyō. The Mitsui Group is no longer more cohesive than the DIK bank group, and Fuyō and Sanwa are least cohesive. The Mitsubishi Group, always the tightest and most conservative of all, remains the most cohesive, and its decline has been more in terms of purchasing than in shareholding. Overall, the cohesiveness of all groups has waned considerably.

Table 4.2 reports responses to a 1999 survey on the perceived costs and benefits of cross-shareholdings in the past and for the future. Note a four-fold increase, to 10 percent, in responses that see no merits in cross-share-holdings (more on this below). At the same time, reported costs include potential economic losses, lack of outside monitoring due to *keiretsu* domi-nance, and the fetters of preferential trade. Just as with the main banks, the valuation has shifted against stability, protection, and long-term relations; the inefficiencies are often considered too severe and the tie-ups too restric-tive for companies to compete successfully in the New Japan.

In Japan's new competitive environment, the previous value proposition of *keiretsu* networks is being challenged. This does not mean that all *keiretsu* are necessarily going to disappear. Rather, to survive and remain meaning-ful, these groups will have to offer new value. Stability was a major con-cern for the highly leveraged, market-share pursuing heavy industry firms of the postwar period, but in the twenty-first century profitability has become the critical variable. Thus, how does *keiretsu* membership help raise prof-its? Some survey respondents valued brand-name recognition and advanced

27 Paul Sheard, "The Main Bank System and Corporate Monitoring and Control in Japan," *Journal of Economic Behavior and Organization* 11, no. 3 (1989): 399–422; Paul Sheard, "Main Banks and the Governance of Financial Distress," in *The Japanese Main Bank System: Its Relevance for Developing and Transforming Economies*, eds. Masahiko Aoki and Hugh Patrick (New York: Oxford University Press, 1994), 188–230.

TABLE 4.2

Survey on costs and benefits of cross-shareholdings

	Important in the past	Important for the future
Advantages of cross-shareholdings		
Stable stock price due to long-term holdings	69.9	55.2
Long-term trade relations with stable shareholders	52.3	42.9
Protection from hostile takeovers	33.0	36.8
Easier issuances of new shares due to underwriting by stable shareholders	5.3	3.8
Long-term capital gains through stable holdings	4.8	0.9
Lower financing costs due to lower dividends	1.6	1.8
No advantage	2.2	9.3
Disadvantages of cross-shareholdings		
Hidden capital losses should share prices fall	58.6	41.1
Low liquidity of funds due to pressures to hold shares long term	37.8	40.8
Lower efficiency due to limited pressures on financing costs	11.5	19.4
Destabilized stock prices due to low liquidity	10.5	11.8
Limited choice and flexibility of trading partners	7.7	12.0
Reduced discipline over management due to limited shareholder influence	6.8	6.9
Increased interference in management by stable shareholders	5.4	7.2
No disadvantage	9.7	10.1

Note: Total n=1,361 listed companies. Up to 3 answers allowed.

Source: Cabinet Office, *Heisei 10-nen kigyō kōdō ni kan suru ankeeto chōsa* [1998 survey of corporate activities] (Tokyo, 1999), accessed June 14, 2013, http://www5.cao.go.jp/99/f/19990420ank/menu.html.

financial services.[28] Unless the groups define other new benefits—such as perhaps pooled labor (to reduce the high fixed cost component in employment), exchange of specialized knowledge in new technologies, or joint subsidiaries—they are unlikely to retain key members. Only groups that can help promote progress, reorganization, focus, and benefits toward competing in the dynamic and fast-changing global markets are likely to remain.

28 Japan Fair Trade Commission (JFTC), *Kigyō shūdan no jittai ni tsuite: Dai-7-ji chōsa hōkokusho* [Survey on the state of horizontal business groups: Results from the seventh survey] (Tokyo, 2001).

Cross-Shareholdings and the Advent of Hostile Takeover Attempts

Cross-shareholdings were the "insurance premium" to be paid and the glue that held the business groups together. The intent was to shield management from short-term stock market fluctuations in general, and from hostile takeovers in particular. This worked because until 2000 Japan had no clear rules that forced minority shareholders to surrender their shares in the event of a hostile takeover attempt. As eventually codified in the 2006 Corporation Law, Japan now has a "squeeze-out" mechanism that enables a raider to buy minority stakes at a fair price (sometimes contested in court, yet usually considered to be "fair" at a 20 percent premium over the current stock price). Theoretically, an ownership stake of 66 percent is sufficient to launch a squeeze-out, although legal advice suggests securing at least 80 percent before the launch, similar to that in other countries.[29] This means that even where business group companies combine to 20 percent of ownership in one member company and are united in their intent not to sell, they can no longer guarantee protection against a takeover. This brought a sea change in the benefit calculation of group membership. Without this insurance, the cost of carrying cross-shareholdings became very expensive relative to the benefits. As a result, cross-shareholdings have declined dramatically and the new composition of Japan's shareholder structure has brought great changes to Japanese business organization.

For the years 1987 through 2003 we have detailed data on cross-shareholdings from two annual surveys that combine corporate annual reports with survey responses on large shareholders: the annual survey of the Nihon Life Institute (NLI) and the Daiwa Research Institute survey. NLI also takes credit for introducing a strict distinction between "stable shareholders" (*antei kabunushi*, stock ownership that may be unilateral but is long term) and "mutual shareholders" (*mochiai kabunushi*, reciprocal commitments, even if unbalanced, to cement tighter corporate relations). Thus, reciprocal shareholdings constituted the superglue of group cohesion.

Figure 4.3 presents the percentage of stable shareholdings of total stocks outstanding. The top line shows that whereas stable shareholdings remained fairly unchanged at over 45 percent of all shares until 1995, this ratio dropped by half, to under 25 percent in 2003. The upright bars illustrate that the percentage of firms that identified themselves as having at least one

---

29 Norihiko Sekiguchi, Toshikazu Miyamoto, and Mihoko Ida, "Squeeze-Outs in Japan, Recent Developments," *B&M Newsletter* (Tokyo, Baker & McKenzie) 3 (2009); Ryutara Nakayama, "Japan Squeeze-Out Guide," *International Bar Association (IBA Corporate and M&A Law Committee), 2010,* accessed April 25, 2013, www.ibanet.org/Document/Defualt.aspx?DocumentUid.3736.

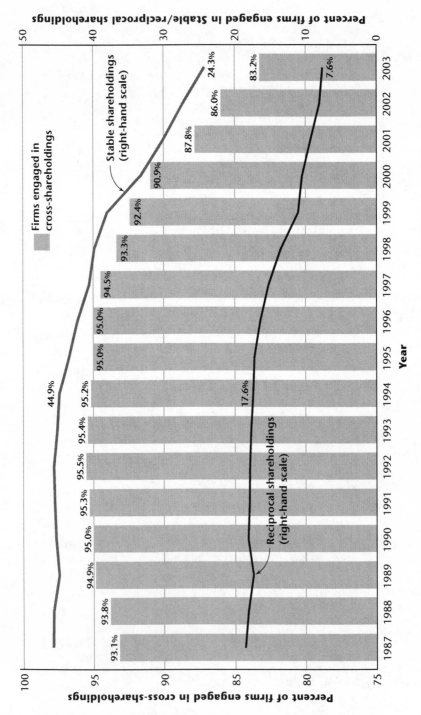

FIGURE 4.3 Stable shareholdings and reciprocal shareholdings, 1987–2003

Source: Adapted from Nihon Life Insurance (NLI), *Kabushiki mochiai jōkyō chōsa 2003 nenpan* [Survey on the state of *mochiai* shareholdings, 2003] (Tokyo: Nissei kisō kenkyūsho, 2004).

stable stock in their portfolio dropped from over 95 percent until 1996 to 83 percent in 2003.

The decline is even more remarkable for the superglue *(mochiai)* shareholdings. The second line in figure 4.3 shows that whereas in the 1980s and early 1990s more than 17 percent of listed firms were intertwined in mutual ownership, the ratio fell to 7.6 percent in 2003. Expressed in absolute terms for 2002, of a total market valuation of ¥237 trillion for all 2,674 listed firms, ¥17.6 trillion was identified by the survey respondents as being "mutual." This represents a decline of ¥10 trillion over a one-year period and the downward trend continued. The year 2003 was the seventeenth consecutive year that the percentage of *mochiai* declined. In 2005, NLI discontinued its survey on the grounds that the phenomenon had become too small to measure accurately.[30]

An important reason for the decline in cross-shareholdings is the 2001 Law Limiting Bank Stock Ownership. The law was designed to limit the banks' exposure to risky assets and thus improve the stability of the banking system. This was accomplished by limiting the total amount of corporate equity that one bank can own relative to its capital.[31] In fiscal year 2001, the largest four banks alone were estimated to face excess shareholdings of about ¥7 trillion. Remarkably, the banks sold off much more than required. In March 2001 commercial banks held ¥35.7 trillion shares, but their holdings declined to ¥18.2 trillion by March 2003. During this time, the stock market moved largely sideways, so that the banks halved the value of their stockholdings within a two-year period.[32]

30 Nihon Life Insurance (NLI), *Kabushiki mochiai jōkyō chōsa 2003 nenpan* [Survey on the state of *mochiai* shareholdings, 2003] (Tokyo: Nissei kisō kenkyūsho, 2004); Suzuki, "Kabushiki sōgō mochiai no 'kishō' ni tsuite." In an update extending to 2006, Keisuke Nitta, "Corporate Ownership Structure in Japan—Recent Trends and Their Impact," *NLI Research* (March 31, 2008): 1–7, confirms this trend, even when using a different methodology to estimate categories of cross-shareholdings; Keisuke Nitta, "On the Resurgence of Cross-Shareholding: Data from the Fiscal 2008 Survey of Corporate Ownership Structure," *NLI Research* (November 16, 2009): 1–8, shows that continuing and also newly forming cross-shareholdings are much more strategic in nature, as they are closer to business tie-ups bolstering strategic alliances than to simple insurance schemes.

31 Technically, the law limits equity holdings to the bank's "Tier 1 capital." This refers to terminology used in the Basel Accord at the time that required a capital adequacy ratio of at least 8 percent for internationally operating banks. In this calculation, there were two types (tiers) of capital: Tier 1, the bank's paid-in capital, shareholder's equity, and retained earnings not yet appropriated at the end of the fiscal year; and Tier 2 capital, the bank's stock portfolio, plus loan loss reserves and subordinated debt issued by the bank. Japan's new law stipulated that Tier 2 capital (ownership in other firms) must not exceed Tier 1 (the bank's own equity).

32 Tokyo Stock Exchange (TSE), ed., *Fact Book 2006* (Tokyo, 2006), accessed April 24, 2013, http://www.tse.or.jp/english/market/data/factbook/b7gje60000003032-att/fact_book_2006.pdf

Corporations, meanwhile, faced profitability pressures because of the 2001 shift to mark-to-market valuation of a company's shareholdings. Due to the recession in the 1990s, by 2002 the Nikkei Index had fallen to its 1982 level. Companies that had purchased cross-shareholdings during the 1987–91 bubble period suddenly had to report these stocks not at the price at which they were bought, but at the price they were worth. Facing new pressures to increase profitability, many companies simply sold off these stocks to avoid the negative effects on performance results due to losses in the stock portfolio.[33]

The above-mentioned 2000 "squeeze-out rule" means that underperforming Japanese companies may now become targets of hostile takeovers. To enable companies to defend themselves against a raider, in 2003 Japan introduced a takeover guideline (codified by inclusion in the 2006 Corporation Law) that allowed a "poison pill," i.e., a legal mechanism to make a hostile takeover difficult or prohibitively expensive. Japan's poison pill comes in the form of new, restricted warrants (bonds that can be turned into stocks) that are issued only to friendly owners, thereby diluting a raider's share to levels too low to carry through a takeover. However, management must receive a two-thirds majority vote from all shareholders before it can issue such warrants. In effect, this mechanism is similar to poison pills in the United States and Europe. The main difference may be a cultural aversion to being bought out, which is sometimes said to be more pronounced in Japan than elsewhere.

During the 2000s, several highly popularized takeover attempts—including Livedoor and U.S. Steel Partners—failed because the targets' shareholders allowed the company to issue these defensive warrants.[34] However, as of October 2007, only 10 percent of listed Japanese companies had either adopted or decided to adopt poison pills. More than half of those showed below-average performance (with an ROE of less than the average 8.3 percent at that time). Among those that decided against the adoption of poison pills, many felt that they were ineffective. Rather than structuring legal mechanisms, these firms aimed to attract long-term shareholders by improving their financial ratios.[35]

33 B. Kuroki, "Mochiai kaishō no miru kigyō to ginkō no kankei: 2002 nendo kabushiki mochiai jōkyō chōsa" [The relationship between banks and corporations from the viewpoint of *mochiai* dissolution], *Nissei kisōken REPORT* (October 2003).

34 See Schaede, *Choose and Focus*; and Curtis J. Milhaupt and Katharina Pistor, *Law and Capitalism: What Corporate Crises Reveal About Legal Systems and Economic Development Around the World* (Chicago: University of Chicago Press, 2008) for detailed accounts.

35 *Nikkei*, April 19, 2007; *Nikkei Weekly*, June 18, 2007; *Japan Times*, March 19, 2007; *Nikkei*, October 15, 2007. Some industries were more aggressive in seeking defense mechanisms; for example, 17.5 percent of Japan's steel companies adopted anti-takeover measures (in addition to rapid industry consolidation), followed by 13.6 percent of companies in land transportation (i.e., railways).

Clearly a new era has arrived for Japanese managers. For raiders, the objective behind a hostile takeover usually is to turn around a company that is performing below potential, by replacing management and improving performance, in order to sell it off at a higher price. The best defense for management against this threat is to make these changes themselves. No Japanese company president can afford to ignore this new reality.

The New Shareholders: Institutional Investors

The unraveling of cross-shareholdings begs the question of who bought the shares that were sold off. At the height of the postwar system in 1987, corporations and large banks together owned 71 percent of the shares traded (or held stable) on the Tokyo Stock Exchange. Figure 4.4 shows that the unraveling of these ownership positions gave rise to two new important groups of shareholders in Japan: Japanese institutional investors (in the form of trust banks) and foreigners. Given their investment strategies, the rise of these two shareholder groups further increased pressures on management to reform and focus on profitability.

Since 2005, one of the largest shareholder groups in Japan has been foreign investors, holding more than one-quarter of Tokyo Stock Exchange–traded shares (in comparison, the share of foreign investors on the New York Stock Exchange hovered around 7 percent at the time). Industries in which foreign investors held more than 30 percent in 2004 included transportation equipment, electronics, insurance, pharmaceuticals, and precision machinery, while holdings in financial services, chemicals, real estate, and petroleum were also above 24 percent.[36]

Although some of the foreign purchases were due to tie-ups among companies (such as Nissan and Renault), foreign investors also increased their ownership stakes through so-called "street name" trusts, such as Chase Manhattan Bank, London, or State Street Bank & Trust Co. During the 1990s, Japan became an investment opportunity for foreigners who were betting on a long-term devaluation of the U.S. dollar. This proved to be correct and the rising yen of the 2000s attracted more foreign capital. Another significant source of investment in the 1990s was acquisitions of Japanese firms by foreign equity funds. When banks accelerated the non-performing loan cleanup beginning in 1998, they increased pressure on their corporate clients to spin off business units that were either not profitable or not central to the core business. Many of these spin-offs were acquired by foreign turnaround funds. Finally, as Japan's market for mergers and acquisitions began

36 TSE, ed., *Fact Book 2006*, 8.

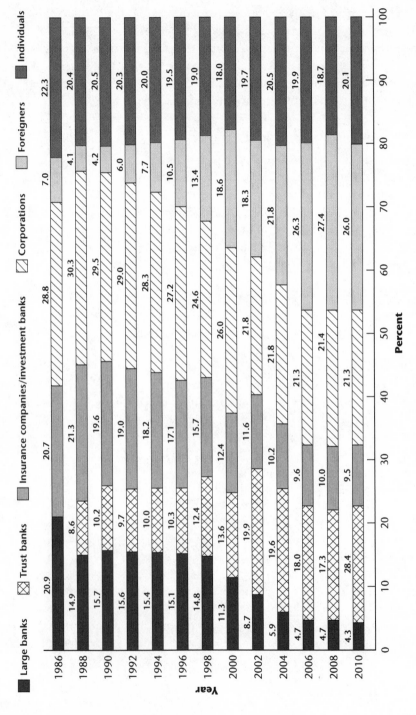

FIGURE 4.4 Ownership percentages, by type of investor, 1986-2010.

Note: In percentage of total market capitalization, as of March of each year.

Source: Tokyo Stock Exchange (TSE), ed., *Heisei 21 nendo kabushiki bunpu jōkyō chōsa no chōsa-kekka ni tsuite.*

to heat up, foreign investors and private equity funds arrived in Tokyo to buy out the underperforming firms.[37]

It is noteworthy that many of the foreign investments included Japanese money that had been diverted through Wall Street.[38] Japanese companies were interested in such diversions for two reasons. Many of the banks were cash-rich during the period of zero interest loans when they curbed their lending due to BIS constraints and the non-performing loan crisis. Yet, they did not want to appear to be unpatriotic "vultures" by buying up assets underlying their competitors' or their own bad loans. Whatever the cultural constraints in Japan, companies were keenly interested in higher returns on investments, and they relegated a portion of fund management to foreign institutions, precisely because these were not Old Japan stable investors. Yet again, no Japanese company president could afford to ignore owners that sought profits and strategic direction in management.

A second group of dominant shareholders emerged in the form of trust banks that administer large amounts of public and private pensions and other corporate funds as well as mutual funds. Figure 4.4 shows that as banks and insurance reduced their holdings, the category of "trust banks" grew from less than 10 percent in the 1980s to more than 18 percent in the late 2000s. This new category is dominated by three so-called "re-trusts," custodians that for almost every large Japanese company are now listed as major owners.[39] These trusts cut across financial and business groups; they vote on proxy at shareholder meetings; and in the final analysis they compete through services, and allow investors to trade anonymously and pursue higher returns on investment. Their creation and extension of business based on a legal revision in 2004 means that the institutional investor has arrived in Japan. In 2007, the Japan Pension Fund Association announced that it would sell off shares earning less than 8 percent in return on equity.[40] Regardless of

37 Schaede, *Choose and Focus.*

38 "Hagetaka/hakuba no kishi ka, gaishi fando zen-kaibō" [Vultures or white knights: A thorough analysis of foreign funds], *Shūkan Daiyamondo* [Diamond Weekly], April 24, 2005.

39 These three trusts are the Japan Trustee Services Bank, Ltd. (Nihon Turasuto Saabisu Shintaku Ginkō), founded in 2000 by Sumitomo Trust & Banking, Resona Bank, and Mitsui Trust Holding; the Trust & Custody Services Bank, Ltd. (Shisan Kanri Saabisu Shintaku Ginkō), founded in 2001 by the Mizuho Financial Group with four life insurance companies that became part of that financial group after the merger of the three original banks (Dai-Ichi, Asahi, Meiji Yasuda, and Fukuoka Mutual Life); and Nippon Master Trust (Nihon Masutaa Turasuto Shintaku Ginkō), founded in 2002 by the Mitsubishi UFJ Group, Nippon Life Insurance, Meiji Yasuda Life Insurance, and Nōchū Trust.

40 *Nikkei Weekly*, June 18, 2007.

whether subsequent stock market developments (especially the 2008 global financial crisis) allowed them to uphold this goal, the message was clear: suboptimal performance is no longer quietly tolerated. As a result of these reorganizations in fund management and the rise of foreign investors, almost one-half of the shares traded on the Tokyo Stock Exchange are administered by market-driven investors. Old Japan business strategies of market share expansion at the expense of profitability that were so valued by the main banks of the postwar era are not tolerated by these new dominant shareholders.

Corporate Governance: New Managerial Incentives

As the main banks assumed a new role offering differentiated fee-based services, and as the relevance of many of the *keiretsu* declined and new institutional shareholders became more prominent, a fundamental shift occurred in the process of management oversight, and with it came changes in the incentives for senior management. Together with the legal changes that greatly strengthened the rights of shareholders and the rise of the market for hostile takeovers, Japan has witnessed the onset of a revision of its corporate governance system.

In the Old Japan, the board of directors consisted of inside executives, and perhaps several "Old Boys" from friendly companies, resulting in an overlap of management and monitoring. While the old Commercial Code was rather restrictive in terms of spin-offs, divestitures, and other matters of organizational design, it granted the board of directors power to change the bylaws without a shareholder vote.[41] The main bank observed the client but took action only when a company defaulted. As long as regular interest payments were made, the bank would not intervene even if companies operated below their potential for years on end. Thus, managers were constrained by laws in terms of strategic positioning, but they were not monitored in their routine managerial decision-making.

The successive revisions of business laws have changed this. A 2003 revision of the Commercial Code gave companies a choice to alter their board structure by adding outside directors and by adopting a "committee system" for auditing, nomination, and compensation committees, with the majority of members being outside directors (defined as never having been directly affiliated with the company or its subsidiaries). This system is even stricter

41 T. Wakasugi, "'Kantoku to keiei no bunri' ga sekai no gabanansu no chōryū" [Separation of management and monitoring follows global practices], *Ekonomisuto* (April 11, 2006): 28–29.

than that in the United States where a company may have one or all such committees; in Japan, a company adopting the "committee system" must introduce all three. Together with the simultaneous introduction of different types of shares, stock options, and increased possibilities for corporate reorganization through mergers and acquisitions, these changes opened the door to new processes of governance.[42]

Even though the committee system initially did not have the expected impact, it paved the way for a reorganization of the internal monitoring processes.[43] The 2006 Corporation Law revised the legal logic of management rights and responsibilities. Although executives are now afforded greater freedom and new flexibility to reform, restructure, or reposition the company, they also face more stringent outside monitoring processes through a vastly empowered shareholders' meeting. For example, any change in the bylaws now requires a two-thirds majority vote from the owners (this is stricter than that in the United States, where a simple majority suffices). Other measures now in need of shareholder approval include: (1) balance sheets and budgets; (2) dividends; (3) executive compensation and stock options; (4) mergers and acquisitions, both as raiders and as targets; (5) appointment of directors; and (6) defense mechanisms against hostile takeovers. Although this may appear to be fairly standard, except for the appointment of director all of these previously could be decided upon by the board of directors, i.e., management itself, without shareholder input.

The 2007 FIEL introduced the Japanese version of the U.S. Sarbanes-Oxley Act, which makes board members legally liable for the accuracy of their financial reporting. It is more likely for companies to be sued, and if found guilty, the members of the board of directors may face jail sentences. This has quietly changed the incentives of board members and thus has enhanced the internal mechanisms of corporate oversight. Old Japan companies—such as in the infamous case of Olympus in 2012—that act as if the old rules were still in place are increasingly exposed as being simply dysfunctional, and suffer from great valuation losses.

---

42 Motomi Hashimoto, "Commercial Code Revisions: Promoting the Evolution of Japanese Companies," *NRI Papers*, no. 48 (2002); Christina Ahmadjian, "Changing Japanese Corporate Governance," in *Japan's Managed Globalization: Adapting to the Twenty-first Century*, eds. Ulrike Schaede and William Grimes, 215–24 (Armonk, NY: M.E. Sharpe, 2003).

43 Hiroyuki Itami, "Revision of the Commercial Code and Reform of the Japanese Corporate Governance," *Japan Labor Review* 2, no. 1 (2005): 4–25.

From "Contingent" to "Continuous" Governance

All this combines into a change in the basic logic of corporate governance in Japan that is best described as a shift away from the previous "contingent monitoring" by banks to a new "continuous monitoring" by a variety of actors. In the contingent system of the postwar period, the main bank, relying on inside information gathered through years of repeated financial interactions with a company, extended loans and provided financial services. In the event of impending collapse, it substituted for the market for corporate control.[44] Although the main bank might have dispatched an employee to a struggling company to gather more information, it would step in to rescue only after a client had fallen into negative net worth and needed a debt restructuring. In that case, a turnaround team replaced incumbent managers and refinancing schemes were worked out with other lenders. Naturally, the main bank's prime motivation in a rescue was to avoid losses in its loan portfolio in the long run, and therefore it focused on reorganizing the failing company's finances. The bank was much less interested in improving the client's business model, and over time a herd of "zombies"—companies considered "too big to fail" and kept alive artificially even though they had no viable business model—were created.[45] The main economic cost associated with this system of governance contingent on bankruptcy was that a company could operate below its potential for many years before action was taken, creating losses in economic efficiency. These losses not only resulted in underperformance but also had an effect on the overall economy as resources (labor and capital) were tied up in suboptimal usage.

As a result of the changes described in this chapter—including, importantly, the new incentive structure for banks after the 1998 crisis—Japan changed to a system of "continuous" governance. Monitoring now occurs through ongoing sampling by many different actors that are constantly checking up on the firm. These monitoring agents include institutional investors (domestic and foreign), equity funds, securities analysts, rating agencies, and competing firms. These new players arrived in Japan because the banks' previous monopoly over corporate information was replaced by quarterly earnings statements, stricter accounting rules, and readily available corporate information. As monitors, the focus of the new agents is different from that of the former main banks. Rather than waiting until a company goes bankrupt, they are activated at the first indication of suboptimal performance. If a company underperforms, the new investors may

44 Sheard, "The Main Bank System and Corporate Monitoring and Control in Japan."
45 Ricardo J. Caballero, Takeo Hoshi, and Anil K. Kashyap, "Zombie Lending and Depressed Restructuring in Japan," *American Economic Review* 98, no. 5 (2008): 1943–77.

"exit" (i.e., sell, thus driving down the stock price, which in turn may invite a takeover) or practice "voice" (i.e., intervene in management); rarely are these new investors quiet and loyal. The highest costs of this continuous system are legal, consulting and time expenses incurred in defending against hostile takeover bids, and economic waste created in cases where a corporate raider tears apart a healthy firm. The greatest gain is that underperformance is made public at a very early stage, allowing management and owners alike to take action before the net worth of the company becomes negative.

In the early twenty-first century Japan's system began to move away from its former almost exclusive reliance on contingent governance and in the direction of continuous monitoring. This is evidenced not only by the reduced role of banks, but also by the decline, by half, of intra-group dispatches of senior executives to the boards of other group firms. The new system subjects even those companies that choose not to change to a committee system to scrutiny by shareholders. Over time, as the stock market reacts negatively to mismanagement, more and more companies will realize that pressures for higher profitability may be best answered by exposing management to a market of corporate information and early intervention.

Conclusions: Competition in New Japan

The 1990s have sometimes been described as "Japan's lost decade"—a period of recession and crisis. An alternative interpretation is that the decade marked a strategic inflection point, in that the changes, reforms, and reorientation of the rules, regulations, and markets resulted in a fundamentally and irreversibly different system. These changes were brought about by a confluence of factors. The severity of the crisis reduced resistance to change—especially in the business sector—and invited an unprecedented reconstitution of the legal setting for business. Globalization became "real" for Japan after 1998, when the new Foreign Exchange Law removed the remaining restrictions on cross-border transactions, greatly facilitating foreign investments in Japan. Furthermore, the new accounting and disclosure rules made Japan's market much more transparent, and political leadership added the willpower to push for change. Japan's new political entrepreneurship is discussed elsewhere.[46] For Japan's business organization, the proactive stance of "toward the market" by Prime Minister Hashimoto and Prime Minister Koizumi between 1996 and 2006 brought a fundamental reorientation, including a change in the role of law in adjudicating business disputes.

---

46 Yves Tiberghien, *Entrepreneurial States: Reforming Corporate Governance in France, Japan, and Korea* (Ithaca, NY: Cornell University Press, 2007).

Given the changed incentives, "New Japan" companies have begun to adjust their corporate strategies to compete in the new, open, and much more dynamic markets. These companies are the most successful and profitable, and their actions have led to a revision of the strategic logic of Japan's industrial architecture, as they are no longer interested in Old Japan practices. As these companies threaten to leave their main banks and business groups, they force these groups to reposition, thus pushing Japan's business organization in a new direction. Where Old Japan institutions—including reciprocal trade, "wet" subcontractor relations based on long-term obligations rather than price, and inefficient processes to uphold those relations—continue in their old form, they constrain the competitive strategies needed for survival in a globalized setting. The best firms have begun to leave such constrained settings, thus further reducing their relevance. Corporate incentives in the New Japan are directed toward profitability and competitive advantage. Companies strive to accomplish these through "choose and focus" restructuring, by shedding non-core operations and competing more actively in clearly defined core businesses. Overall change may well take a generation, and Old Japan laggards still remain. However, as of 2010 the results were already clearly visible for the trailblazers in this movement, including the electronics, components, materials and fine chemicals, and the pharmaceutical industries. Leading companies in these sectors no longer operate according to Old Japan rules.

For these new, highly charged companies, the previous value proposition of membership in a horizontal business group, a main bank, or stable cross-shareholdings has become an obstacle. Stability through insurance has become an undesirable drag on profits. The fetters of business groups and preferential trade have proven too costly in responding to the new demands created by greater transparency and stricter disclosure rules that make poor performance immediately apparent. For New Japan firms, the value of group membership will lie in benefits that make members more competitive and profitable than non-members. While it is too early to say exactly how the various groups will reposition themselves, in order to remain meaningful for their most important members they will have to offer services that help members compete. The stock market, meanwhile, is beginning to reflect these ongoing changes, with new institutional investors taking over where cross-shareholdings have begun to become untangled. The new investors, both foreign and domestic, are evaluated based on returns on investment, and they often trade actively.

These changes make companies and banks more interested in the new governance processes, and the new Corporation Law of 2006 reflects such an interest. In the New Japan, managing a successful corporation means transparency, profitability, and accountability. Some of the Old Japan companies may continue their previous practices, but their fate is preordained. Either they will soon become irrelevant and their practices will be inconsequential, or—to the extent their business is still viable—they will be subject to an acquisition bid. Either way, knowingly or unwittingly, the dinosaurs that resist Japan's new market realities have begun their long march out. Proactive restructuring has resulted in a new system of business organization in Japan.

References

Abegglen, James C., and George J. Stalk, Jr. *Kaisha: The Japanese Corporation*. New York: Basic Books, 1985.

Ahmadjian, Christina L. "Changing Japanese Corporate Governance." In *Japan's Managed Globalization: Adapting to the Twenty-first Century*, edited by Ulrike Schaede and William Grimes, 215–40. Armonk, NY: M.E. Sharpe, 2003.

Amyx, Jennifer A. *Japan's Financial Crisis: Institutional Rigidity and Reluctant Change*. Princeton: Princeton University Press, 2004.

Anchordoguy, Marie. *Computers, Inc.: Japan's Challenge to IBM*. Cambridge: Council on East Asian Studies, Harvard University, 1989.

Aoki, Masahiko, and Hugh Patrick, eds. *The Japanese Main Bank System: Its Relevance for Developing and Transforming Economies*. New York: Oxford University Press, 1994.

Burgelman, Robert A., and Andrew S. Grove. "Strategic Dissonance." *California Management Review* 38, no. 2 (1996): 8–28.

Caballero, Ricardo J., Takeo Hoshi, and Anil K. Kashyap. "Zombie Lending and Depressed Restructuring in Japan." *American Economic Review* 98, no. 5 (2008): 1943–77.

Cabinet Office (CO). *Heisei 10-nen kigyō kōdō ni kan suru ankeeto chōsa* [1998 survey of corporate activities]. Tokyo, 1999. Accessed June 14, 2013. http://www5.cao.go.jp/99/f/19990420ank/menu.html, .

Calder, Kent E. *Strategic Capitalism: Private Business and Public Purpose in Japanese Industrial Finance*. Princeton: Princeton University Press, 1993.

Callon, Scott. *Divided Sun: MITI and the Breakdown of Japanese High-Tech Industrial Policy, 1975–1993*. Stanford: Stanford University Press, 1995.

Caves, Richard E., and Masu Uekusa. *Industrial Organization in Japan*. Washington, DC: Brookings Institution, 1976.

Daiwa Institute of Research (DIR). '*Mochiai' jidai no shūen* [The end of the *mochiai* era]. *Daiwa Sōken* (Tokyo), February 4, 2004.

Fujioka, Bunshichi. "Wagakuni kigyō no M&A katsudō: chiiki kasseika ni mukete" [M&A activities by Japanese firms: Toward regional revitalization]. Tokyo: Cabinet Office.

Fujita, Tsutomu. "Shin-Kaisha-hō shikō de kabunushi sōkai wa issō jūyō ni" [The new Company Law is implemented: Toward a stronger general shareholders' meeting]. *Ekonomisuto* (June 6, 2006): 78–80.

Gerlach, Michael L. *Alliance Capitalism: The Social Organization of Japanese Business*. Berkeley: University of California Press, 1992.

Goto, Akira, and Ryuhei Wakasugi. "Technology Policy." In *Industrial Policy of Japan*, edited by Ryutaro Komiya, Masahiro Okuno, and Kotaro Suzumura, 183–204. Tokyo: Academic Press, 1988.

"Hagetaka/hakuba no kishi ka, gaishi fando zen-kaibō" [Vultures or white knights: A thorough analysis of foreign funds]. *Shūkan Daiyamondo* [Diamond Weekly], April 24, 2005.

Hashimoto, Motomi. "Commercial Code Revisions: Promoting the Evolution of Japanese Companies." *NRI Papers* (Nomura Research Institute), no. 48 (2002).

Higashino, Dai. "Corporate Reorganization Picks Up Steam in Japan: Part 1, Improved Legal Provisions." *Japan Economic Monthly* (November 2004).

Hodder, James E., and Adrian E. Tschoegl. "Some Aspects of Japanese Corporate Finance." *Journal of Financial and Quantitative Analysis* 20, no. 2 (1985): 173–91.

Hoshi, Takeo. "The Economic Role of Corporate Grouping and the Main Bank System." In *The Japanese Firm: The Sources of Economic Strength*, edited by Masahiko Aoki and Ronald Dore, 285–309. New York: Oxford University Press, 1994.

———. "Economics of the Living Dead." *Japanese Economic Review* 57, no. 1 (2006): 30–49.

Hoshi, Takeo, and Anil Kashyap. *Corporate Financing and Corporate Governance in Japan: The Road to the Future*. Cambridge: MIT Press, 2001.

Hoshi, Takeo, Satoshi Koibuchi, and Ulrike Schaede. "Corporate Restructuring in Japan During the Lost Decade." In *Japan's Bubble, Deflation, and Long-Term Stagnation*, edited by Koichi Hamada, Anil K. Kashyap, and David E. Weinstein, 343–73. Cambridge: MIT Press, 2011.

Itami, Hiroyuki. "Revision of the Commercial Code and Reform of the Japanese Corporate Government." *Japan Labor Review* 2, no. 1 (2005): 4–25. Accessed April 24, 2013. http://www.jil.go.jp/english/JLR/documents/2005/JLR05_itami.pdf.

Japan Fair Trade Commission (JFTC). *Kigyō shūdan no jittai ni tsuite: Dai-7-ji chōsa hōkokusho* [Survey on the state of horizontal business groups: Results from the seventh survey]. Tokyo, 2001.

Johnson, Chalmers A. *MITI and the Japanese Miracle: The Growth of Industrial Policy, 1925–1975*. Stanford: Stanford University Press, 1982.

Komiya, Ryutaro, Masahiro Okuno, and Kotaro Suzumura, eds. *Industrial Policy of Japan*. Tokyo: Academic Press, 1988.

Kuroki, B. "Mochiai kaishō no miru kigyō to ginkō no kankei: 2002 nendo kabushiki mochiai jōkyō chōsa" [The relationship between banks and corporations from the viewpoint of *mochiai* dissolution]. *Nissei kisōken REPORT* (October 2003).

Lincoln, James R., Christina L. Ahmadjian, and Eliot Mason. "Organizational Learning and Purchase-Supply Relations in Japan: Hitachi, Matsushita, and Toyota Compared." *California Management Review* 40, no. 3 (1998): 241–64.

Lincoln, James R., and Michael L. Gerlach. *Japan's Network Economy: Structure, Persistence, and Change*. New York: Cambridge University Press, 2004.

Lincoln, James, Michael L. Gerlach, and Christina L. Ahmadjian. "Keiretsu Networks and Corporate Performance in Japan." *American Sociological Review* 61, no. 1 (1996): 67–88.

Lynn, Leonard H. "The Commercialization of the Transistor Radio in Japan: The Functioning of an Innovation Community." *IEEE Transactions on Engineering Management* 45, no. 3 (1998): 220–29.

Markides, Constantinos C. *Diversification, Refocusing, and Economic Performance*. Cambridge: MIT Press, 1995.

———. "Diversification, Restructuring and Economic Performance." *Strategic Management Journal* 16, no. 2 (1995): 101–18.

Milhaupt, Curtis J. "In the Shadow of Delaware? The Rise of Hostile Takeovers in Japan." *Columbia Law Review* 105, no 7 (2005): 2171–216.

Milhaupt, Curtis J., and Katharina Pistor. *Law and Capitalism: What Corporate Crises Reveal about Legal Systems and Economic Development Around the World*. Chicago: University of Chicago Press, 2008.

Nakatani, Iwao. "The Economic Role of Financial Corporate Grouping." In *The Economic Analysis of the Japanese Firm*, edited by Masahiko Aoki, 227–58. Amsterdam: North-Holland, 1984.

Nakayama, Ryutaro. "Japan Squeeze-Out Guide." *International Bar Association* (IBA Corporate and M&A Law Committee). 2010. Accessed April 25, 2013. http://www.ibanet.org/Document/Defualt.aspx?DocumentUid.3736.

Nihon Life Institute (NLI), ed. *Kabushiki mochiai jōkyō chōsa 2003 nenpan* [Survey on the state of *mochiai* shareholdings, 2003]. Tokyo: Nissei kisō kenkyūsho, 2004.

Nitta, Keisuke. "Corporate Ownership Structure in Japan: Recent Trends and Their Impact." *NLI Research* (March 31, 2008): 1–7.

―――. "On the Resurgence of Cross-Shareholding: Data from the Fiscal 2008 Survey of Corporate Ownership Structure." *NLI Research* (November 16, 2009): 1–8.

Noble, Gregory W. "The Japanese Industrial Policy Debate." In *Pacific Dynamics: The International Politics of Industrial Change,* edited by Stephan Haggard and Chung-in C. Moon, 53–95. Boulder, CO: Westview, 1989.

Okimoto, Daniel J. *Between MITI and the Market: Japanese Industrial Policy for High Technology.* Stanford: Stanford University Press, 1989.

Pascale, Richard, and Thomas P. Rohlen. "The Mazda Turnaround." *Journal of Japanese Studies* 9, no. 2 (1983): 219–63.

Patrick, Hugh, and Henry Rosovsky, eds. *Asia's New Giant: How the Japanese Economy Works.* Washington, DC: Brookings Institution, 1976.

Pempel, T. J. *Regime Shift: Comparative Dynamics of the Japanese Political Economy.* Ithaca, NY: Cornell University Press, 1998.

Schaede, Ulrike. "The Japanese Financial System: From Postwar to the New Millennium." Harvard Business School Case 700-049 (October 20, 1999).

―――. *Choose and Focus: Japan's Business Strategies for the 21st Century.* Ithaca, NY: Cornell University Press, 2008.

―――. "From Developmental State to the 'New Japan': The Strategic Inflection Point in Japanese Business." *Asia Pacific Business Review* 18, no. 2 (2012): 167–85.

Sekiguchi, Norihiro, Toshikazu Miyamoto, and Mihoko Ida. "Squeeze-Outs in Japan, Recent Developments." *B&M Newsletter* (Tokyo, Baker & McKenzie) 3 (2009).

Sheard, Paul. "The Main Bank System and Corporate Monitoring and Control in Japan." *Journal of Economic Behavior and Organization* 11, no. 3 (1989): 399–422.

Sheard, Paul. "Main Banks and the Governance of Financial Distress." In *The Japanese Main Bank System: Its Relevance for Developing and Transforming Economies,* edited by Masahiko Aoki and Hugh Patrick, 188–230. New York: Oxford University Press, 1994.

Suzuki, K. "Kabushiki sōgō mochiai no 'kishō' ni tsuite" [On the 'dissolution' of mutual *mochiai* shareholdings]. *Osaka Keidai Ronshū* 55, no. 5 (2005): 7–23.

Tiberghien, Yves. *Entrepreneurial States: Reforming Corporate Governance in France, Japan, and Korea.* Ithaca, NY: Cornell University Press, 2007.

Tokyo Stock Exchange (TSE), ed. *Fact Book 2006.* Tokyo, 2006. Accessed April 24, 2013. http://www.tse.or.jp/english/market/data/factbook/b7gje60000003.32-att/fact_book_2006.pdf.

————, ed. *Heisei 21nendo kabushiki bunpu jōkyō chōsa no chōsa-kekka ni tsuite* [Results of the 2009 survey on shareholdings]. Tokyo, 2010.

Tōyō Keizai. *Kigyō Keiretsu Sōran* [Data on corporate groups]. Tokyo.

Ushijima, Tatsuo. "Evolving Market for Corporate Assets in Japan: Which Firms Enter and How?" Paper presented at the meeting of the Academy of Management, Philadelphia, 2007.

————. "Understanding Partial Mergers in Japan." *Journal of Banking and Finance* 34, no. 12 (2010): 2941–53.

Vogel, Steven K. *Japan Remodeled: How Government and Industry are Reforming Japanese Capitalism*. Ithaca, NY: Cornell University Press, 2006.

Wakasugi, T. "'Kantoku to keiei no bunri' ga sekai no gabanansu no chōryū" [Separation of management and monitoring follows global practices]. *Ekonomisuto* (April 11, 2006): 28–29.

5 Koizumi's Complementary Coalition for (Mostly) Neoliberal Reform in Japan

Gregory W. Noble

More than two decades after the bursting of the financial bubble in 1990, Japan's economy remains weak, with accumulated public debt exceeding 200 percent of GDP and a series of short-lived prime ministers struggling to address the many challenges facing Japan's aging society. Nevertheless, the situation has actually improved since the late 1990s and early 2000s, when a mountain of non-performing loans (NPLs) paralyzed the economy, a seemingly inexorable deflation settled in, and government budget deficits exploded. Much of that improvement can be traced to the structural reforms introduced by Prime Minister Koizumi Junichirō (2001–6), who made good use of the new political and administrative structures crafted by Prime Minister Hashimoto Ryūtarō in the late 1990s. Though momentum slowed at the end of Koizumi's term and his successors were unable to introduce many additional innovations, few of Koizumi's reforms were reversed (though postal privatization remained frozen) and budgetary expenditures remained relatively restrained, despite the mounting pressures for public pensions and health care posed by the aging population.

The scope and persistence of reform under Koizumi are best explained as the result of a tripartite coalition of three complementary elements:

1. *Political leadership* by Prime Minister Koizumi provided direction and maintained high levels of popular support, enabling Koizumi to convince an often-reluctant Liberal Democratic Party (LDP) to acquiesce to policy changes, even when the changes threatened the immediate electoral interests of many party members.

2. The big business community, particularly Keidanren and Keizai Doyukai, provided *support* in the form of campaign funds, policy proposals and feedback, and legitimacy.

3. Academic economists provided *ideas, expertise, and legitimacy* for Koizumi's program.

In general, this coalition promulgated neoliberal reforms, but under the constraints imposed by Koizumi's main constituents, business and the middle classes, neither of which was consistently dedicated to unfettered competition and both of which still preferred that government and society absorb some of the economic risk facing individuals and companies. Equally important was Koizumi's ability to balance the intensity and focus necessary to achieve change and to hold together the coalition with pragmatism and persistence in the face of widespread opposition from the "forces of resistance," as Koizumi astutely dubbed his opponents within the LDP.

Dilemmas of Reform

Japan is hardly alone in facing difficulties in implementing reform, but in some ways its situation is particularly severe. Several possible explanations have been offered for the reforms some advanced economies have managed to achieve in recent years. Analysts have attributed the decentralization of wage bargaining in Scandinavia and recovery of fiscal balance in Italy, for example, to the effects of global, and especially regional, integration that pressed national governments, unions, and employer associations to accept changes to existing arrangements.[1] Japan is relatively immune to the effects of globalization and regionalization, though, since it has a huge, well-established economy with a very low reliance on trade and especially investments, and at most minimal regional commitments. Thus, whereas structural reforms in Europe frequently can be justified in terms of pressing international forces or overriding political and security goals, in Japan they must rely on strictly domestic arguments.

An alternative approach emphasizes the effects of partisan transitions. Parties advocate different positions, and once in power surprisingly they are likely actually to implement those different policies,[2] though the effects are far from uniform[3] and they often require accompanying changes in ideology, institutions, and bureaucratic personnel.[4] In the Japanese case, partisan change

1 Torben Iversen, *Contested Economic Institutions: The Politics of Macroeconomics and Wage Bargaining in Advanced Democracies* (Cambridge: Cambridge University Press, 1999).

2 Hans-Dieter Klingemann, Richard I. Hofferbert, and Ian Budge, *Parties, Policies and Democracy* (Boulder, CO: Westview, 1994).

3 Robert J. Franzese, Jr., "Electoral and Partisan Cycles in Economic Policies and Outcomes," *Annual Review of Political Science*, no. 1 (June 2002): 369–421.

4 Peter A. Hall, "Policy Paradigms, Social Learning, and the State: The Case of Economic Policymaking in Britain," *Comparative Politics* 25, no. 3 (April 1993): 275–96.

occurred slowly and in muted form. For half a century the LDP remained by far the most dominant party in the House of Representatives (the more powerful Lower House of Japan's Diet) but it lost control of the House of Councillors in 1989 and never fully recovered it. The LDP surrendered control of the House of Representatives to a motley coalition of opposition parties for just less than a year in 1993–94, but then, with the help of small coalition partners, largely recovered it until the Democratic Party of Japan (DPJ) finally defeated the LDP in the 2009 Lower House elections. Partisan change in Japan was crucial in making electoral reform possible in 1993–94, and the LDP's co-alition partners did occasionally overcome its reluctance to carry out various reforms,[5] but on balance the influence of partisan change in spurring structural reform was much weaker in Japan than in Europe or the United States.

A third perspective emphasizes variations in the strength and patterns of cooperation among domestic coalitions of interest groups. For example, it has been argued that the wide variance in patterns of corporate governance across the advanced capitalist democracies can be explained by the shifting composition and balance of power among managers, workers, and owners (investors).[6] The "varieties of capitalism" approach emphasizes the strategies of companies, particularly how they affect labor training and social policies.[7] This approach is even more cautious about the prospects for change because it sees finance, labor, pensions, and other policy areas as deeply intertwined. Sabatier's version of the coalitional approach focuses on ideas and expertise, claiming that significant policy change generally requires a decade or more of sustained advocacy.[8] Thus, not only interest groups but experts and academics are also crucial parts of reform coalitions. Even in the coalitional approaches, policy arrangements are not entirely immune to change, but one or more severe and sustained shocks seems to be required, such as a long period of weak performance, a series of scandals, or major changes in the political and economic environments, such as war, oil shocks,

5 Koichi Nakano, "The Politics of Administrative Reform in Japan, 1993–1998: Toward a More Accountable Government?" *Asian Survey* 38, no. 3 (1998): 291–309.

6 Peter Alexis Gourevitch and James J. Shinn, *Political Power and Corporate Control: The New Global Politics of Corporate Governance* (Princeton: Princeton University Press, 2005).

7 Peter A. Hall and David Soskice, eds., *Varieties of Capitalism: The Institutional Foundations of Comparative Advantage* (New York: Oxford University Press, 2001). For comparative review and application to Japan, see Gregory W. Noble, " Review Essay: Recent Trends in Comparative Political Economy and their Implications for Japan," *Japanese Journal of Political Science* 4, no. 1 (2003): 135–51.

8 Paul A. Sabatier, "The Need for Better Theories," in *Theories of the Policy Process*, ed. P. A. Sabatier, 3–17 (Boulder, CO: Westview, 1999).

or outbursts of inflation.[9] In the "varieties of capitalism" schema, Japan occupies an intermediate position, implying that structural reforms should be difficult but not impossible.[10]

The Japanese Recovery

Continuing economic weakness notwithstanding, a broad array of indicators indicates that Japan largely overcame many of its most frustrating problems during Koizumi's tenure. Deflation in both consumer prices and key assets such as land eased off. After several years of deflation, the consumer price index leveled off in 2006 and thereafter maintained equilibrium.[11] National land prices continued to decline, but at only about half the rate that had persisted in the years leading up to Koizumi's term.[12] Real estate prices in the six major metropolitan areas actually began a sustained rise until the international financial crisis of 2008–9 pushed them back down to Koizumi-era levels.[13]

The end of consumer price deflation and the bottoming-out of real estate prices also helped the corporate sector regain its financial keel. By the latter part of Koizumi's term corporations had finally reduced the triple burden of excessive facilities, bloated workforces, and oppressive debt.[14] At first, the reduction of excess capacity led to increased unemployment, but with recovery the situation improved; the unemployment rate, only 2.1 percent in 1990, steadily climbed to 5.4 percent in 2002, but with the end of the nonperforming loans crisis, it began to decline. Despite the sharp shocks due to the global financial crisis of 2008–9 and the Fukushima tsunami and nuclear power crisis of 2011, the rate of financial leveraging of Japanese companies

9 James Q. Wilson, *Bureaucracy: What Government Agencies Do and Why They Do It* (New York: Basic Books, 1989); Martha Derthick and Paul J. Quirk, *The Politics of Deregulation* (Washington, DC: Brookings Institution, 1985).

10 For France, another intermediate case, see Bob Hancké, "Revisiting the French Model: Coordination and Restructuring in French Industry," in *Varieties of Capitalism*, ed. Hall and Soskice, 307-35.

11 Ministry of Internal Affairs and Communications (MIC). "17-6 Shōhisha bukka shisū" [Consumer price index], accessed June 16, 2013, http://www.stat.go.jp/data/nenkan/zuhyou/y1706a00.xls.

12 Japan Real Estate Institute (JREI). "Shigaichi kakaku shisū" [Urban area land price index], accessed June 16, 2013, http://www.stat.go.jp/data/nenkan/zuhyou/y1712000.xls.

13 JREI, "Rokudai toshi" [Six major cities], 2011, accessed June 16, 2013, http://www.reinet.or.jp/pdf/report/shigaiti201106/6toshi.pdf.

14 Cabinet Office Economic and Social Research Institute, *Kappatsuka suru kigyō no M&A katsudō to shokadai: Heisei 17 nen M&A kenkyūkai chūkan hōkoku sho* [Corporate M&A activity rising, issues they face: Heisei 17 M&A research group interim report], 2005.

steadily improved, suggesting that structural reform has had a lasting impact. The net worth ratio of Japanese companies was only 25.2 percent in 2001; by 2006 the figure had grown to 32.8 percent, and by mid-2011 it hit 36.9 percent. Particularly striking and encouraging was a sustained recovery in the rate of return. Historically, Japanese companies did not earn high profits even when economic growth was rapid. Ironically, corporate profitability began to improve after the bursting of the bubble. In 2001, the first year of Koizumi's prime ministership, the ratio of recurring profits to sales stood at only 2.1 percent. But when Koizumi left office in 2006, the ratio was 3.5 percent, a level sustained through 2010.[15]

To be sure, much of the recovery followed traditional lines and cannot be attributed solely to structural reforms. Massive government spending helped prop up demand after the drop in asset prices, giving companies time to repair their balance sheets.[16] Highly productive industries such as steel and autos utilized traditional methods to maintain their international competitiveness. The five major integrated steelmakers merged into just two groups, thereby increasing their market power. By refraining from major investments, steel companies greatly improved their balance sheets, though at the cost of forgoing extra demand that was gobbled up by their competitors in China and other developing countries.[17] After a mini-slump in the mid-1990s, the Japanese automobile industry followed a somewhat similar trajectory of using rationalization to wring out record profits. In contrast to steel, however, the auto industry balanced stagnant domestic demand and output with a rapid increase in production in Japan's overseas markets, particularly the United States and later China.

The electronics industry showed somewhat greater signs of structural transformation. In computers, memory devices, and consumer electronics, Japanese firms made tentative moves away from the old "one-set" approach of trying to compete with similar products in each sub-market to a more focused approach of trying to develop scale and dominance in particular product markets,[18] though as yet there is not yet much sign that Japanese

15 Ministry of Finance (MOF), "Shuyō sangyōbetsu kaisha eigyō jōkyō (zen kigyō) 2000–2011" [Corporate performance by major industry (all industries) 2000–2011], 2011, accessed June 16, 2013, http://www.stat.go.jp/data/getujidb/zuhyou/j01-1.xls.

16 Richard C. Koo, *Balance Sheet Recession: Japan's Struggle with Uncharted Economics and its Global Implications* (Singapore: John Wiley, 2003).

17 Ministry of Economy, Trade, and Industry (METI), "Sangyō katsudō bunseki: Heisei 17nen 7-9gatsuki happyō" [Industry activities analysis: Heisei 17 July-September], 2005, *Wedge* (April 2006): 34–36.

18 Ulrike Schaede, *Choose and Focus: Japanese Business Strategies for the 21st Century* (Ithaca, NY: Cornell University Press, 2008).

companies can fundamentally increase their innovative capability, much less determine global standards and product architectures.[19] Thus, much of the recovery reflects extensions of relatively traditional approaches. Weak industries such as textiles and food processing remain mired in low productivity, whereas Japan's strongest industries are (mostly) still quite effective and somewhat more focused. After the financial shock of the 1990s and the reforms of the Koizumi era, both stronger and weaker industries managed to reduce excessive debts and improve profitability.

One area in which a quantitative change approached a qualitative transformation was inward foreign investment. In the late 1990s, a wave of direct foreign investment, both greenfield and via mergers and acquisitions, swept into Japan. This marked a major change in a country long known as the least receptive of any of the OECD member states to foreign investment. In some cases, such as the transformation of the failed Long-Term Credit Bank of Japan into Shinsei Bank (literally "new life bank") and Renault's takeover of troubled Nissan Motor Company, the results were dramatic. Nissan's Brazilian-born French boss Carlos Ghosn engineered a remarkably effective and rapid "v-shaped" recovery. In other cases, however, direct foreign investment proved less successful. Walmart, for example, struggled to make good on its investment in Seiyu, while the French giant Carrefour eventually pulled out of Japan, selling its operations to the local retailer Aeon. In January 2003, Prime Minister Koizumi announced a plan to double incoming foreign investment within five years. Foreign investment did indeed surge, thereafter, though its share of GDP remained far lower than that in the other developed economies.[20] Moreover, in Japan, unlike the case in virtually all other developed countries, investment in existing firms was overwhelmingly restricted to financially distressed firms like Nissan or Seiyu; throughout Koizumi's tenure, no foreign company succeeded in carrying out a hostile takeover in Japan,[21] and there was only one hostile takeover in the following half decade (the acquisition of wig maker Aderans by Steel Partners in 2009), and even that proved to be a pyrrhic victory.[22]

In sum, Japan experienced a genuine structural transformation after the Koizumi structural reforms, not just a cyclical recovery, even if the

19 Marie Anchordoguy, *Reprogramming Japan: The High Tech Crisis under Communitarian Capitalism* (Ithaca, NY: Cornell University Press, 2005).

20 United Nations Conference on Trade and Development (UNCTAD), *World Investment Report* (including Country Fact Sheet: Japan), 2001, accessed April 24, 2013, http://www.unctad.org/Templates/Page.asp?intItemID=2441&lang=1.

21 U.S.–Japan Business Council, "Expanding FDI in Japan: M&A is the Key" (Tokyo, September 28, 2005): 12–15, 19.

22 *Nihon Keizai Shinbun*, February 18, 2011; March 24, 2011.

transformation took place in many ways due to surprisingly traditional efforts by companies. Japan became more focused on profitability and financial rigor, more open to imports (as seen in the textile and footwear industries) and even somewhat more accepting of inward foreign investment, at least when it came on friendly terms. The Koizumi reforms did not spark a business revolution, but they accelerated significant changes in business practices and facilitated improvements in economic performance.

Policy Reform

Restricting Budgetary Expenditures

Despite the relatively homegrown character and wide industrial variation in Japan's transformation, the Koizumi reforms played a significant role in the recovery. A prudent but measured tightening of fiscal policy provided a crucial backdrop. After the collapse of Yamaichi Securities, Hokkaido Takushoku Bank, and other financial companies further depressed asset prices in 1997 and sent a shock of panic throughout the country, the Obuchi and Mori governments resorted to massive deficit spending to prop up the economy. When public works, in particular, proved to be less effective in stimulating demand than in the past, the new Koizumi government cut public investment and held aggregate expenditures flat. Unlike the Hashimoto administration in 1996, the government did not take hasty actions to increase taxes to begin the painful task of fiscal reconstruction, but neither did it pour good money after bad by further increasing the deficit, despite an ongoing clamor from the public and the backbenches of the LDP for a more aggressive stimulus. The weakness of the economy and the reliance of Japan's fiscal system on direct taxation depressed tax revenues to the lowest level in twenty years, preventing Prime Minister Koizumi from achieving his pledge to hold deficit spending to 30 trillion yen. The Koizumi team proved tenacious, however, restricting expenditures year in and year out and cutting spending in the infamous Fiscal Investment and Loan Program (FILP), or "second budget," by almost one-half.[23] Koizumi also passed, in the face of considerable opposition, legislation to cut future pension benefits, implement piecemeal increases in health-care premiums, and allow some temporary tax cuts to expire.

23 Gregory W. Noble, "Front Door, Back Door: The Reform of Postal Savings and Loans in Japan," *The Japanese Economy* 33, no. 1 (2005): 107–23; Gregory W. Noble, "Seijiteki rīdāshippu to kōzōkaikaku" [Japanese political leadership and structural reform], in *"Ushinawareta 10 nen" o koete (2) Koizumi kaikaku he no jidai* [Beyond the "lost decade," volume 2: The Koizumi reforms], ed. Institute of Social Science, Tokyo University (Tokyo: University of Tokyo Press, 2006).

Overcoming Deflation and Non-performing Loans

Perhaps the most notable achievement of Koizumi and his chief economic lieutenant Takenaka Heizō was to overcome the deflationary spiral into which Japan had fallen. A crucial element of the anti-deflationary program was the revival of lending and consumer confidence by getting the banks out from underneath the mountain of bad debts that had paralyzed the credit system. NPLs soared in 2001, just as Koizumi came into office. But Koizumi's first finance minister, Yanagisawa Hakuo, was reluctant to pressure the banks to take decisive action. In September 2002 Koizumi reorganized the Cabinet, putting the Financial Services Agency (FSA) under Takenaka, who unveiled a major financial revitalization program. Takenaka combined financial support in the form of injections of public funds and special loans from the Bank of Japan with a number of tough measures to force banks to acknowledge and deal with their bad loans. Takenaka ordered that banks apply standard discounted cash-flow accounting to establish realistic prospects for repayment, decreased the allowance for future "tax-deferred assets" against total capital and reserves, and undertook a series of intrusive inspections to force banks to end dubious accounting practices aimed at making dicey loans appear sound. He instructed banks to cut their NPL rate from the 8 percent level in March 2002 to less than 4 percent by March 2005. When the mid-sized Resona Bank neared collapse, the government effectively nationalized it and replaced its top managers. Within six months, the banks were reporting sharply lower NPLs, but the government still did not relent. The FSA under Takenaka ordered banks to take even more aggressive actions against bad loans and to cut costs and hike profitability.

The government also increased pressure on the most egregious borrowers, particularly in real estate and retailing. The climax came with the rehabilitation of the overextended retail giant Daiei. The Ministry of Economy, Trade, and Industry (METI), the primary regulatory authority for the retail sector, proved unwilling to force Daiei's management to carry out a sweeping reorganization of underperforming outlets. Initially, even Prime Minister Koizumi reluctantly backed a multi-billion dollar bailout for Japan's most famous zombie company. The government threatened to nationalize financial institutions that did not reduce NPLs, and in October 2004 creditors finally forced Daiei to accept rehabilitation under the new Industrial Revitalization Corporation of Japan (IRCJ). The IRCJ developed basic principles for reorganization, forced the entire board of directors to resign without the usual retirement benefits,[24]

24 Press Release, "IRCJ Approves Application for Assistance for Daiei Group Companies," IRCJ, December 28, 2004, at www8.cao.go.jp/sangyo/ircj/en/pdf_aa_20041228 .pdf, accessed June 16, 2013.

and chose a private-sector team to run the company. The IRCJ, established in 2003 with a limited mandate and lifespan (it expired in 2007 after processing over forty cases), succeeded in setting new precedents for corporate rehabilitation and in convincing the markets that the government was committed to forcibly rehabilitating zombie companies and cleaning up the balance sheets of banks so that they could resume prudent commercial lending.

Monetary Policy

The government also pressed a reluctant Bank of Japan (BOJ) to adopt a more accommodative monetary policy. In March 2003, with the completion of the five-year term of the first governor appointed following legal revisions giving the BOJ greater independence from the Ministry of Finance, Koizumi had the opportunity to appoint new executives to the Bank's board. The Koizumi Cabinet appointed as governor Fukui Toshihiko, a former BOJ executive known to be willing to take active steps to combat deflation. He also appointed two deputies from outside the bank. One hailed from the Ministry of Finance, which favored a more aggressive monetary stance, and the other was from the University of Tokyo. Representatives of foreign financial firms praised the financial revitalization plan and the new BOJ officials:

> With those appointments, the prime minister put in place a team to cast aside Japan's decade-long obsession with steady fiscal expansion and budget exuberance, coupled with tight money and banking policy. By April 2003, Japan was running with a hyper expansionary monetary and banking policy, while fiscal policy had become modestly restrictive. And that change in macro policy direction is working—slowly but surely the Japanese economy is being pulled out of deflation, toward growth and inflation."[25]

Locals agreed. In response to the new policies, the corporate sector's expectations for future growth, which had declined relentlessly for over a decade with only a brief respite in response to the massive but unsustainable fiscal stimulus of the late 1990s, turned around sharply, a crucial prerequisite for ending asset deflation.[26]

At the microeconomic level, the Koizumi administration continued the effort to eliminate or streamline regulations so as to reduce Japan's high cost structure and improve the efficiency of the Japanese economy. Entry,

25 Jesper Koll, "Koizumi's Third Anniversary," *Wall Street Journal*, April 23, 2004, accessed June 16, 2013, http://online.wsj.com/article/O,,SB108267418451291294,00. html. See also *Financial Times*, July 8, 2003.

26 Mizuho Research Institute, "Nihonkeizai no asu o yomu 2005" [Reading the tomorrow of Japan's economy 2005] (Tokyo: Toyo Keizai, 2004).

exit, pricing, and approval of new products became easier in a variety of sectors. Competition from new entrants brought price cuts to trucking and air transport. Venture firms transformed the telecommunications business, shaking up the old Nippon Telegraph and Telephone Corporation (NTT) monopoly and giving Japan one of the most widely diffused and inexpensive broadband infrastructures in the world. Prices of gas and electricity came down. Discount taxis and self-service gas stations appeared, and convenience stores were allowed to carry liquor and nonprescription drugs.[27]

Perhaps the regulatory change of most immediate benefit to business was the relaxation of regulations governing the hiring of workers dispatched from temporary employment agencies. The Worker Dispatch Law, first passed in 1985, was revised in 1999 to move to a "negative list" system, expanding the range of eligible industries. In 2003, following principles laid down by the Council on Economic and Fiscal Policy (CEFP), the Diet passed further revisions that expanded worker dispatch to include manufacturing and construction, and lengthened the permissible period to as many as three years.

The Koizumi reforms focused heavily on the public sector, including privatization of the postal savings system, quasi-privatization of the highway system, and reorganization of many public policy companies. Pressure on the private sector was limited to key areas and was generally delayed until the peak of unemployment had passed. The administration walked a tightrope between demonstrating a serious commitment to reform without unnecessarily scaring business and consumers in a fragile economy. This business-friendly approach reflected the ideology and interests of the backers of the Koizumi coalition. As the case of the NPLs suggests, however, solicitude for business was not unlimited. The Koizumi administration did press the business community in a few crucial areas, particularly accounting, auditing, and finance.

The Koizumi Reform Coalition

The LDP Crisis and the Unlikely Ascent of Koizumi

A major factor leading to (mostly) neoliberal reform under Koizumi and his allies in business and academics was the weakening of the "old" LDP's ruling coalition of farmers, small business owners, social conservatives, and the elderly. International pressures were not the most important factors. Japan is a large country with a low level of trade to GDP and an excess

27 Gregory W. Noble, "1990 nendai no keizai kisei kaikaku: Ushinawareta jūnen ka, yuruyaka na zenshin ka" [Reforming economic regulation in the 1990s: Lost decade or slow progress?], *Shakai kagaku kenkyū* 53, no. 2/3 (2002): 173–217.

of savings that allows it largely to ignore international financial markets. Comparisons with the vigorous recovery of the United States or the rapid growth in the other East Asian countries did exert some impact on the thinking of Japanese policy elites and business people, and the IMF, the OECD, and other international organizations did try to push Japan to reform. On balance, though, with the exception of several brief periods in 1997 and 2001 when turmoil in the Japanese financial system led local banks to face a "Japan premium," international forces had relatively little direct effect.

Much more important was a series of domestic developments in the 1990s that weakened the old LDP coalition. After losing the majority of seats in the Upper House in 1989, the LDP could no longer simply maximize the interests of its own constituents, and the opposition interim of 1993–94 provided space for a number of initiatives, including electoral reform, that weakened the factions and increased the focus on the prime minister. These political setbacks, in turn, reflected not only economic and other policy problems but also a long-term weakening of old party loyalties, forcing the LDP to think more seriously about appealing to "floating voters."

In the mid-1990s, economic weakness and somewhat greater openness in government and politics brought to light a number of scandals and examples of government incompetence—from the government's slow response to the Kobe earthquake of 1995, to the "*jūsen*" housing finance company scandal and revelations of unconscionable cover-ups of AIDS-tainted blood transfusions. The failure of attempts by the Obuchi and Mori cabinets to use massive expenditures on public works to stimulate economic recovery was also important in undermining support for the old LDP modus operandi.

To be sure, the key reformer, Hashimoto Ryūtarō (prime minister from 1996 to 1998), was not neoliberal, yet he paved the way for Koizumi. Hashimoto's greatest area of policy concern was health and welfare, and in his belief in the necessity of rationalizing and reinvigorating government so that it could meet social needs, he resembled Clinton or Blair more than Reagan or Thatcher.[28] The Hashimoto government pursued a number of reforms that strengthened the institutional basis of the Cabinet and the prime minister. Most of these reforms took effect in 2001, just before Koizumi assumed office.[29]

Renewed economic weakness and Prime Minister Mori's repeated verbal gaffes diminished the remains of LDP support by early 2001. Backbenchers faced a classic dilemma: continue along traditional lines and risk being thrown

---

28 Hideo Otake, *Nihon seiji no tairitsujiku: 93 nen ikō no seikai saihen no naka de* [Axes of cleavage in Japanese politics in the political reorganizations after 1993] (Tokyo: Chuko Shinsho, 1999).

29 Noble, "Seijiteki rīdāshippu to kōzōkaikaku."

out en masse by the newly energized floating voters, or promote genuine reforms and risk undermining the traditional coalitions of support in individual electoral districts. The party compromised, attempting to create an image of openness by settling on an electoral plan for choosing the party president (and thus the prime minister) that somewhat tipped the balance away from sitting members of parliament (MPs) and toward individual party members in the constituencies. To everyone's surprise, the voters overwhelmingly rejected rejuvenated Hashimoto and other party stalwarts in favor of "odd man" Koizumi, who had never held any of the major party or government posts previously thought to be necessary prerequisites for a would-be prime minister.

Ideology and Strategy

Despite Koizumi's tense relations with the majority of his own party, the Koizumi coalition proved remarkably determined. One key element was a moderate but persistent neoliberal ideology that guided reform and held the coalition together. Koizumi might not have been an intellectual or a policy maven, but he consistently held to a neoliberal doctrine of "smaller government" and supported "shifting responsibility from the government to the private sector" via deregulation, privatization, or delegation to quasi-independent agencies, which was quite consistent with the prescriptions of Britain's *Economist* magazine or Washington's Cato Institute. He encouraged free trade initiatives (but did not attempt the monumental task of liberalizing imports of rice) and shifted some tax revenues to the localities (though cutting local subsidies even more). Koizumi's rhetoric emphasized personal responsibility, acceptance of risk, and the glories of entrepreneurship, while expressing relatively little concern about equality or stability.

Despite this neoliberal approach and Koizuimi's insistence on visiting the Yasukuni Shrine in defiance of the sensibilities of China and the Koreas and his willingness to support the American occupation of Iraq with a modest contingent of Japanese military forces, he was not a conservative in the American or British sense. As revealed by his limited military budgets and repeated attempts to forge diplomatic relations with North Korea despite provocations by Pyongyang, Koizumi was not inclined toward an aggressive foreign policy and he was not committed to the view that the advanced countries should try to convert authoritarian regimes to democracy by force. Nor was Koizumi, a divorced man who favored elegant suits and Italian opera, a forceful advocate for traditional Japanese family values. He declined to support a proposal championed by conservatives in the LDP to strengthen the teaching of patriotism in the schools, and he favored (albeit only tepidly) increased immigration.

Stylistically, Koizumi combined a tenacious commitment to the idea of neoliberal reform with a pragmatic willingness to accept compromises on the details. Though a clear and forceful communicator and a skilled debater, he eschewed theorizing and moralizing and generally appeared to the public as neither extreme nor threatening. As a third generation politician with little experience abroad and only a modest command of English, he was able to champion Anglo-American ideas without coming across as slick and alien. In the case of his signature issue of corporatizing and eventually privatizing the postal savings and insurance systems, Koizumi accepted drastic limitations on the freedom of the new system to rationalize operations in order to make the conceptual and legal breakthroughs necessary for privatization.

Koizumi was particularly adept at timing and packaging, balancing subservience to the United States with trips to Yasukuni and hard and soft approaches to North Korea. On several occasions Koizumi seemed to be on the verge of losing control of the agenda and of public support, particularly after dumping his popular but erratic ally, Foreign Minister Tanaka Makiko, in February 2002, and also after the failure of his bold attempt to normalize relations with North Korea. Yet in large part due to the unprecedented frequency and skill of his media appearances, Koizumi left office with higher support ratings than his long-serving predecessors Yoshida, Ikeda, and Nakasone.

Economists and the CEFP

For policy direction and formulation, Koizumi relied primarily on the new Council on Economic and Fiscal Policy. To head the Council he brought in Professor Takenaka Heizō of Keio University. By statute, as many as half of the Council's members were to come from the private sector, while the remainder were to be ministers and heads of agencies, such as MOF, METI, and the BOJ. When the Council first came into existence in January 2001, Prime Minister Mori appointed four private members: prominent economists from Osaka and Tokyo universities (Honma Masaaki and Yoshikawa Hiroshi); Ushio Jiro, founder of the innovative lighting company Ushio; and Okuda Hiroshi, chairman of Toyota. Whereas previous councils typically included representatives of the mass media, labor unions, and women's groups, CEFP members only represented business, and particularly the more open internationally and more competitive sectors such as electronics and autos. The four private members quickly formed a bloc, regularly issuing reports bolder than the Council as a whole was willing to support.

Heading the Council was Takenaka, who had worked for a number of years as a researcher at the Japan Development Bank and at MOF, as well as stints at Harvard and the University of Pennsylvania, where he imbibed the emerging libertarian doctrines of supply-side economics, monetarism, and rational expectations, before Professor Honma lured him to a position as professor of economics at Osaka University.[30] Takenaka vowed to apply the "common sense of economics"[31] to policymaking. In that effort, he was able to call on the assistance of a wide range of policy-oriented economists whom he had cultivated in academia and during his service on advisory committees to Prime Ministers Obuchi and Mori. Many of them came together in the Tokyo Foundation, a new think tank that Takenaka had helped to establish.

Takenaka was the only person to serve in all of the Koizumi cabinets, sometimes in multiple positions. When outraged backbenchers in the LDP attacked the "civilian" Takenaka for a lack of political legitimacy, Koizumi placed Takenaka on the top of the party list for the 2004 House of Councillors election; Takenaka garnered twice as many votes as the next candidate, largely silencing his critics. In 2006, when Koizumi moved Takenaka from the position of minister for economic and fiscal policy (and thus the CEFP) to the internal affairs ministry in order to push through a set of administrative reforms, including the selling off of government assets and cutting the number of bureaucrats, policy leadership on budgets and overall economic policy shifted away from the CEFP and back to the LDP.[32]

If Takenaka Heizō served as the key link between Prime Minister Koizumi and the community of academic economists, he was hardly alone. Japan's economic fraternity, once dominated by Marxists and Keynesians, had moved steadily toward Anglo-American orthodoxy. By the 1980s and 1990s, they were able to provide the ideological rationale and technical expertise for reform. An influx of economists preceded Takenaka, but under

---

30 Masato Shimizu, *Kantei shudō: Koizumi Jun'ichirō no kakumei* [Cabinet leadership: Koizumi Junichirō's revolution] (Tokyo: Nihon Keizai Shinbunsha, 2005); Masato Shimizu, *Keizai zaisei senki: Kantei shudō Koizumi kara Abe he* [Battle stories of the Council on Economic and Fiscal Policy: Cabinet leadership from Koizumi to Abe] (Tokyo: Nihon Keizai Shinbun Shuppansha, 2007).

31 Ushio Shiota, "Takenaka Heizō no chōsen: Seiji o mezashita gakusha no kiseki (chū): Seisaku no ketteiken o meguru Kasumigaseki to no kōbō sen" [Takenaka Heizō's challenge: The trail of a scholar who aimed at politics. Part 2: Battles with Kasumigaseki over the power to determine economic policy], *Ronza* (2005): 111–21, at 114.

32 *Asahi Shinbun*, May 16, 2006.

him reform accelerated. Economists influenced elite and public opinion through both scholarly works and numerous semi-popular writings. Most economists focused on public policy issues, such as the economic consequences of deficit spending and the aging population, or the costs of regulatory barriers to market entry and exit, and economic analysis provided considerable leverage, as many government programs were clearly highly inefficient. Until about 2000, far fewer economists focused on corporate governance, where there was less academic consensus about the economic consequences of alternative forms of organization and where the business community was largely skeptical and resistant rather than supportive.

In addition to the two positions on the CEFP, many academic economists served in the newly expanded Cabinet Office, the think tanks of various ministries, and especially in the ubiquitous advisory councils reporting to each agency and ministry as well as to the Cabinet and the prime minister. Once seen as ideal institutional loci for "veto players" in each policy sub-arena, a series of reforms in the late 1990s (many led by economists) transformed the advisory councils. Ex-bureaucratic *amakudari* appointments declined (especially for chair positions) while representation by industry insiders was bypassed or diluted. Academic experts and "figures of experience," among whom economists and business people were dominant, became ever more prominent. Traditionally, bureaucrats had served as key staff and wrote the drafts of almost all reports, but now academics and experts increasingly took on the task of writing the reports on their own.[33] In the case of the Fiscal Investment and Loan Program, for example, pressure from Prime Minister Hashimoto led a crucial advisory commission under the Ministry of Finance to establish an "informal" advisory subcommittee headed by Professor Honma of Osaka University (and later of the CEFP) that incorporated a number of economists known for their vociferous criticisms of MOF and the FILP program.[34]

Big Business: Keidanren and Keizai Doyukai

The third major element in the Koizumi reform coalition was the big business community, a crucial source of political and economic support, cooperation, and legitimacy. The most famous and important peak business organization in Japan is Nippon Keidanren, an alliance of industry

---

33 Gregory W. Noble, "Reform and Continuity in Japan's Shingikai Deliberation Councils," in *Japanese Governance: Beyond Japan Inc.*, ed. Jennifer Amyx and Peter Drysdale, 113–33 (London: RoutledgeCurzon, 2003).

34 Noble, "Seijiteki rīdāshippu to kōzōkaikaku."

associations and leading firms. Founded in 1947, Keidanren has long enjoyed the highest profile and the best access of any business group in Japan, but it has also been hobbled by diversity and internal conflicts of interest. Structurally, its leadership has been biased toward older, more domestically focused industries, including finance, utilities, and heavy industry, and it has traditionally been inclined toward caution.

By the mid-1990s, however, the recession, spikes in the value of the yen, and political instability resulted in Keidanren and the rest of the business community casting a much tougher eye on cutting costs and competing internationally. In 1997, as part of its fiftieth anniversary, Keidanren established a new think tank, the 21st Century Public Policy Institute, headed by Tanaka Naoki, an Asian Development Bank economist from the University of Tokyo and a frequent author of neoliberal policy prescriptions.

In 2002, Okuda Hiroshi, chairman of Toyota and already a member of the CEFP, took over as chair of Keidanren. Okuda and Toyota had earned overwhelming respect for triumphing in international competition while maintaining Japanese-style techniques of business management and labor organization. Okuda was noted especially for his close relations with Prime Minister Koizumi. Under Okuda's leadership, Keidanren resumed its role of organizing and allocating political donations by major companies, a tradition it had suspended for a decade in response to the scandals and political instability of the early 1990s. By the end of 2003 Keidanren had developed a set of guidelines and criteria for evaluating political parties, evaluations that were often critical (like Koizumi) of traditional LDP methods, but invariably were even more critical of the center-left Democratic Party of Japan.

In 2006 Okuda was succeeded by Mitarai Fujio of camera and electronics maker Canon, another company that had succeeded spectacularly under Japanese-style management. Ultimately, however, neither Mitarai nor his company was as traditional as Toyota. Canon focused more on research and innovation than most Japanese companies (it had among the most patents in the United States), and Mitarai, who had spent twenty-three years working in the United States, was actually somewhat less solicitous of the interests and solidarity of employees than his rhetoric would suggest. The choice of Mitarai pushed Keidanren further in the neoliberal direction.

Japan's second-most influential business group, the Japanese Association of Corporate Executives, or Keizai Doyukai, has always been both more neoliberal and more outspoken than Keidanren. Unlike Keidanren, with its blue-chip firms and industry associations, Keizai Doyukai is based on the principle that each member sheds his (or, rarely, her) corporate identity and participates as an individual. Unlike Keidanren, Keizai Doyukai long took corporate governance seriously. In 2006 it published its fifteenth annual

White Paper on Corporations, publicly calling on Prime Minister Koizumi to end his visits to Yasukuni Shrine.

In contrast to Keidanren (before Mitarai), the leadership of Keizai Doyukai featured a strikingly high proportion of foreign-trained and foreign-oriented leaders from companies with large foreign ownership stakes. Among the most prominent, and the most aggressive in promoting neoliberal approaches to economic problems, were:

1. Ushio Jiro (Ushio Corporation), chair 1995–99: graduate work in political science at University of California, Berkeley, 1956; member of the influential Second Administrative Reform Committee (Daini Rinchō), 1981–83; one of two private-sector executives on the Council on Economic and Fiscal Policy, 2001–6; chairman of the National Institute for Research Advancement (2007–). Under Ushio, Doyukai issued its famous "Declaration of Market Principles."[35]

2. Kobayashi Yotaro (Fuji Xerox), chair 1999–2003: born in England; Wharton School MBA, 1958; Pacific Asia chair of the Trilateral Commission; head of a commission on improving bilateral relations with China. As head of Doyukai, he issued the policy paper "Beyond the Declaration of Market Principles" (April 22, 1999), outlining a vision for establishing four pillars of governance—corporate, social, global, and individual—for which full implementation of market principles and bold action on reform constituted an immediate challenge.

3. Kitashiro Kakutaro (IBM Japan), chair 2003–7, lifetime officer 2007–; MSc in Electrical Engineering and computer science, University of California, Berkeley, 1972.

4. Miyauchi Yoshihiko (founding director, chairman and chief executive officer of Orix Corporation, a multinational leasing and financial services company), vice-chair; MBA, University of Washington, 1960; chairman of the Regulatory Reform Committee of the Cabinet Headquarters for Administrative Reform; joined the Deregulation Subcommittee of the Administrative Reform Commission in April 1995; inaugural chair of the Deregulation Committee (1998–99) and of the Regulatory Reform Committee (1999–2006); director of Keidanren.

By the time Koizumi became prime minister, leaders of Keidanren and especially Keizai Doyukai were less willing than their predecessors to put up with explicit and implicit cross-subsidies to inefficient sectors of the economy.

35 Keizai Doyukai, "Shijōshugi sengen" [Declaration of market principles], January 9, 1997.

At the same time, both (especially Keidanren) were more interested in furthering the interests of big business than in markets per se, and they were both reluctant to intervene in the internal workings of Japanese companies.

Internal Disagreements and Limits of Influence

The interests, orientations, and political weight of the members of the reform coalition help explain the accomplishments and limits of economic restructuring under Koizumi. In areas of substantial agreement, such as the need to cut back or to privatize inefficient government programs, or to promote deregulation to improve freedom of entry, exit, and pricing, the coalition achieved significant reform. In some other cases, the members of the coalition agreed, but their proposals foundered due to resistance from the LDP rank-and-file. When it came to agricultural liberalization, for example, Koizumi only nibbled at the edges, though some initiatives, such as the creation of small agriculture deregulation zones around the country, may have had a significant long-term impact in creating constituencies for agricultural reform. In the case of highway liberalization, Koizumi pushed hard, but in the end he was forced to make large concessions; even so, he kept actual spending on roads low and he used some revenue to pay back old loans rather than to continue building highways that no one used. A similar dynamic applied to postal privatization, where Koizumi made a key breakthrough via corporatization, but where further reform will take years.

In other cases, the reform coalition was split over the details of the reform. All three elements agreed, in principle, on the desirability of cuts in expenditures and restraint in taxes, but they often disagreed over the specifics. Taxes, in particular, raised thorny issues of incidence and timing. Neoliberal supply-sider Takenaka tended to advocate postponement of tax increases in favor of further expenditure cuts and a firmer recovery of the economic momentum, while some in the business community were more open to the possibility of increasing consumption taxes (though not taxes on personal or corporate income) in order to begin filling the yawning budget deficit.

On immigration, the private members of the CEFP were positive, whereas the ministries of labor and justice, reflecting widespread popular concern about "foreigner crime" and employment competition, insisted on stringent limitations. Koizumi compromised, supporting immigration in principle, but displaying no inclination to expend political capital on increasing intakes of real, live immigrants.[36]

---

36 For the inclination to restrict immigration even in areas where the government in principle developed a more liberal policy, see *Asahi Shinbun*, May 10, May 15, and May 31, 2006.

Even two prominent cases of potential privatization led to dissension among the coalition members. An advisory panel headed by Takenaka originally inclined toward the privatization of the national broadcaster NHK. Ironically, the private broadcasters opposed because a privatized NHK would compete with them for the same advertising dollars rather than rely on the governmentally mandated license fees. Also, the LDP had traditionally enjoyed the opportunity to exercise political influence over NHK, whose budget required approval by the Diet.[37] In the face of resistance from the private broadcasters and the LDP, Prime Minister Koizumi ruled out privatization, instead supporting a more modest plan to eliminate three of NHK's eight television and radio channels and to cut licensing fees without moving toward privatization.[38]

In the case of the national telecommunications carrier NTT, neither neoliberal theory nor Anglo-American experience provided an unambiguous answer as to how best organize a utility that still exercised a virtual monopoly on the "last mile" of phone service to individual customers. Faced with increasing competition in broadband and cellular phones and a transition from switching to routing technologies that progressively rendered much of NTT's infrastructure obsolete, NTT drafted a plan to slough off a large chunk of its workforce to lower-paying subsidiaries. When the Ministry of Labor blocked the plan on the grounds that NTT had not shown sufficiently compelling distress, NTT took the highly unusual step of suing the ministry. Japan has actually proved to be more aggressive than either Britain or the United States in forcing incumbent utilities to make their wires and conduits available to competitors on the grounds that they constitute "essential facilities,"[39] but the CEFP generally refrained from the NTT thickets.

On defense and diplomacy, too, the neoliberal coalition was not entirely united. The firmly neoliberal Keizai Doyukai publicly opposed Koizumi's controversial visits to the Yasukuni Shrine, whereas Keidanren under Koizumi's close ally Okuda maintained a restrained posture. When it came to defense technology and production, however, Keidanren actively supported the efforts of Japanese firms to capture new budget allocations and to gain authorization to export "dual-use" technology, whereas Keizai Doyukai expressed little interest.

37 Ellis S. Krauss, *Broadcasting Politics in Japan: NHK and Television News* (Ithaca, NY: Cornell University Press, 2000).

38 *Asahi Shinbun*, May 18, 2006.

39 Noble, "1990 nendai no keizai kisei kaikaku"; Kenji E. Kushida, "Entrepreneurship in Japan's ICT Sector: Opportunities and Protection from Japan's Telecommunications Regulatory Regime Shift," *Social Science Japan Journal* 15, no. 1 (2012): 3–30.

Finally, in a number of policy areas, the reform coalition was not so much divided or blocked as it was purposely restrained. Koizumi, the economists, and the business community expressed concern about Japan's rapidly declining birth rate, but they were reluctant to take serious steps to change the situation, such as by expanding public funds on child care or intervening in corporate managerial practices that imposed long hours on employees and severely penalized workers who broke their employment continuity for child-rearing or other family obligations.

A similar caution can be observed in the case of corporate governance. From the neoliberal perspective, corporate governance is not as ideologically suspect as government programs, and neither economic theory nor Anglo-American practice proves the absolute superiority of any particular approach to corporate governance. Moreover, proposing reforms in corporate governance requires specialized expertise in law, accounting, and other disciplines far less well represented than economics in the neoliberal coalition.

Traditionally, the Ministry of Justice carried out periodic revisions to the Commercial Code on the basis of reports by advisory commissions dominated by law professors. Starting in the mid-1990s, METI and the business community proposed a series of legal revisions to give Japanese managers freedom to match the flexibility and innovation available to British and American companies, including liberalization of stock options, lifting the ban on holding companies, and the addition of outside auditors. In 1997, a private member bill, introduced due to urging from the business community, led to the liberalized use of stock options. A bill proposed by the LDP at the same time but not passed until 2001 strengthened the role of corporate auditors and limited the liability of company directors. A major revision of the Commercial Code in 2002, after Koizumi assumed office, gave firms the choice of retaining the old insider-dominated approach or of creating auditing, compensation, and nominating committees in which outsiders constituted a majority.

The theme linking most of the revisions promoted by Keidanren and METI was the enhancement of options for corporate managers to exercise strategic choice.[40] Orix's Miyauchi, a committed neoliberal, pushed for stronger outside oversight, but Keidanren heads Okuda and Mitarai resisted mandatory impositions on corporate autonomy. Actual firm behavior was consistent with this policy stance. Although surveys of firms listed on the

40 Curtis J. Milhaupt and Mark D. West, *Economic Organizations and Corporate Governance in Japan: The Impact of Formal and Informal Rule*s (New York: Oxford University Press, 2004); Pepper D. Culpepper, *Quiet Politics and Business Power: Corporate Control in Europe and Japan* (Cambridge: Cambridge University Press, 2011).

first section of the Tokyo Stock Exchange revealed steady improvement in transparency and clarity of management systems and corporate objectives, led by large firms with a large share of foreign ownership, the number of companies adopting a "board with [outsider-dominated] committees" system remained very low (26 out of 395 respondent firms in 2005).[41] A small but increasing number of firms, particularly those with persistently weak performance, used the new provisions in the Commercial Code to fend off hostile acquisitions.[42]

Similarly, attitudes toward inward direct foreign investment turned sharply negative. As noted above, when the Japanese economy weakened in the 1990s, inward investments surged due to active encouragement from METI (at that time called the Ministry of International Trade and Industry [MITI]). Mergers and acquisitions increased, but most involved "in-in" investments by one Japanese company in another. Direct investments by major Western multinationals lost prominence to the inflow of foreign indirect (portfolio) investment. Investments to and from China created particular disquiet in Japan.[43] The advisory commission convened by the Cabinet's Economic and Social Research Institute to analyze mergers and acquisitions was dominated by business executives and professors of law, politics, and management, along with a large contingent of "advisers" from the bureaucracy, but it included few economists. The commission's report acknowledged the valuable role M&As can play in corporate restructuring and in the maximization of asset values, but also emphasized the risks and systemic incompatibilities caused by cross-border acquisitions.[44] Mergers, acquisitions, and new public offerings all peaked just as Koizumi was stepping down from office, and thereafter declined sharply.[45]

If internal tensions within the reform coalition and the centrality of the business community as a constituency blunted the impact of many efforts to reform corporate governance, particularly attempts to encourage acceptance of outside directors or owners, on key financial and auditing issues

41 Japan Corporate Governance Research Institute (JCGR), "JCGR Corporate Governance Survey 2005: Final Report," December 1, 2005, accessed April 24, 2013, http://www.JCGR/eng/survey/index.html. See also *Wedge* (May 2004): 40–42.

42 *Asahi Shinbun*, May 22, 2006.

43 Ibid., May 17, 2006.

44 Cabinet Office Economic and Social Research Institute, "Kappatsuka suru kigyō no M&A katsudō to shokadai."

45 Gregory W. Noble, "Changing Politics of Japanese Corporate Governance: Party Dynamics and the Myth of the Myth of Permanent Employment," paper prepared for the Joint Conference of the Association for Asian Studies and the International Convention of Asia Scholars, Honolulu, March 31–April 3, 2011.

the government adopted a somewhat tougher line. Beginning in 2000, the government required firms to report the value of their holdings in terms of market levels rather than costs at the time of acquisition, and to report consolidated financial results for all companies in which they had a large ("controlling") stake, making it far more difficult to hide losses by sloughing them off to subsidiaries (some of which were unlisted and therefore previously immune from most disclosure requirements).

Under Koizumi, the FSA also took an increasingly hard line on auditing, as seen in the stiff treatment accorded to PricewaterhouseCoopers' Japanese affiliate Chuo Aoyama, one of the four main auditing firms in Japan. In October 2004, the cosmetics and textile maker Kanebo admitted that it had systematically inflated its earnings, leading prosecutors to indict its executives. The Industrial Revitalization Corporation of Japan took control of the company and eventually sold Kanebo's assets to rival Kao. Prosecutors then indicted three accountants from Chuo Aoyama for conspiring with Kanebo executives to falsify the accounts. The FSA imposed a two-month suspension and in 2007 Chuo Ayoyama was dissolved.[46] The Koizumi coalition focused on eliminating rather than improving regulation, but it did pressure companies to improve the openness and accuracy of their financial accounts.

What About the Bureaucracy?

As the numerous references above to METI, MOF, and FSA suggest, the vital role of the Koizumi reform coalition should not obscure the enduring importance of the bureaucracy. In all political systems, the bureaucracy enjoys a huge structural advantage in terms of size, expertise, information, and continuity of institutional mission. Despite a sharp decline in the prestige of the Japanese bureaucracy, it is still chiefly responsible for drafting both legislation and the specific rules of implementation putting meat on the often-skimpy legal bones.

As even advocates of bureaucratic influence admit, however, often the power of the bureaucracy is in the making the best of a bad situation by protecting core powers at the expense of peripheral ones,[47] as when the Ministry of Finance relinquished authority over bank supervision when the FSA was hived off, in order to save MOF's central role in compiling budgets. A decade of scandals, debacles, and institutional reform had clearly weakened the position of the bureaucracy. When Prime Minister Koizumi

46 *The Times*, May 31, 2006.
47 Junko Kato, *The Problem of Bureaucratic Rationality: Tax Politics in Japan* (Princeton: Princeton University Press, 1994).

and the neoliberals attacked the "forces of resistance," the bureaucracy was one of their major targets. In many cases, the bureaucracy clearly lost, as when METI failed to keep Daiei out of the hands of the IRCJ or when Prime Minister Koizumi overrode stiff resistance by MOF (and METI) to close or merge a passel of government-affiliated banks.

On specific issues, the bureaucracy is often split, and many of the younger and more elite bureaucrats have accepted some of the neoliberal critique. Many look to a stint serving in the Cabinet as an important part of forging a path to the top of their agencies. On balance, the still-powerful yet sharply challenged bureaucracy, always on the lookout to protect institutional privilege but increasingly sensitive to the direction of the Cabinet, probably accentuates the broad tendency coming from the neoliberal coalition: cautious, incremental, yet persistent reform that is gradually transforming Japanese economic policy.

What About the Opposition?

Many voters shared Prime Minister Koizumi's outrage at the pork barrel politics and policy failures of the Japanese government, but they were by no means uniformly supportive of neoliberal reforms. Most voters were far more interested in upholding stability than in increasing the risks and burdens on individual households. That is, they were more inclined to an attenuated version of social democracy than to full-blown neoliberalism. So why did the opposition parties fail to present an effective counter-advocacy coalition? The 1994 reforms, creating an electoral system dominated by single-member districts, gradually fostered the emergence of a two-party dominant political system with greater focus on party leaders. The consolidation of the parties, in turn, forced them to develop and defend more substantive policy platforms and electoral manifestos.

In the first five years of Koizumi's term, however, the opposition parties failed to provide a clear and compelling alternative to the neoliberal line. The gigantic fiscal black hole bequeathed by "the LDP before Koizumi" made any proposals to move in a more social-democratic direction appear to be irresponsible. With the decline of organized labor, the opposition lost one of its most important sources of electoral mobilization. And while many academic specialists in law and sociology were critical of Koizumi's neoliberalism, they lacked the combination of intellectual consensus, technical expertise, and social prestige wielded by the economists supportive of Koizumi and neoliberalism. In fact, the opposition struggled to develop a consistent approach to reform. In some cases, such as during the 2005 Lower House election fought over privatization of the postal savings system, they adopted a more neoliberal line than that of the LDP, allowing Koizumi to position himself as the true reformer between the recalcitrant LDP rebels and the idealistic but less-than-entirely-credible opposition.

Has (Broadly) Neoliberal Reform Petered Out?

Contrary to Mulgan's emphasis on crisis as a motivator for change, the greatest difficulty in general-interest policy reform is maintaining momentum and preventing relapse.[48] Prime Minister Koizumi managed to pull out a spectacular political and policy victory electoral triumph in the fall of 2005, but by early 2006 ominous signs were accumulating. A series of scandals, including falsification of reports on earthquake-resistance standards for buildings and on inspections of nuclear power plants, raised doubts about the honesty and commitment to transparency of the business community and the advisability of continuing the "regulatory reform" that seemed to remove the only oversight over crafty and dishonest business executives.

In a number of cases, the scandals cut closer to home, casting doubt on the integrity of the neoliberal reformers and their business buddies. For example, after the FSA issued a temporary business suspension order against Mitsui Sumitomo Bank for forcing loan clients to buy financial derivative products, journalists pointed out that at the time of the offending behavior Takenaka Heizō had personally chosen Nishikawa Yoshifumi, head of Mitsui Sumitomo, to serve as the first head of the privatized postal agency.[49]

Similarly, the LDP informally but clearly supported Horie Takafumi, the founder of Internet pioneer Livedoor, as a candidate in the 2004 Upper House elections. The controversial Horie had used furtive trading methods to gain control of the radio company Nippon Broadcasting, thus obtaining a major indirect share in the Fuji Sankei Media Group, before he was arrested on charges of insider trading. A close business contact, Murakami Yoshiaki, a former METI official who had founded his own investment fund and lived and worked in the same glitzy Tokyo development as Horie, was then indicted on similar charges. Next, it turned out that Bank of Japan governor Fukui Toshihiko had invested 10 million yen (roughly US$100,000) in the Murakami Fund, selling his shares several months before the Livedoor-Murakami scandal became public. Though he apparently broke no laws, there was a storm of criticism because

48 Aurelia George Mulgan, *Japan's Failed Revolution: Koizumi and the Politics of Economic Reform* (Canberra: Asia Pacific Press, 2002); Eric M. Patashnik, *Reforms at Risk: What Happens After Major Policy Changes are Enacted* (Princeton: Princeton University Press, 2008).

49 *Mainichi Shinbun*, June 6, 2006.

he profited from a buccaneering investment fund to which no one knew he was connected. The DPJ capitalized on this issue during the Diet debates.

These various scandals erupted against a background of increasing concern that Koizumi's coalition was creating an unequal, unjust, and unstable society, similar to that of the neoliberal pioneers Britain and America. The *Asahi Shinbun* published a long series of articles on the apparent growth of inequality. Prime Minister Koizumi cited respected academic works contending that growing structural inequality was nothing but an "illusion" created by the increasing share of elderly with relatively low incomes, though these same works also suggested that inequality might well begin to increase.[50] Moreover, to the extent that Koizumi's policies contributed to the recovery of economic growth and the drop in unemployment rates, they may well have improved income distribution, because the incomes of the poor are disproportionately sensitive to employment rates.

A more plausible interpretation focuses on perceptions. Although disparities in the distribution of income in Japan were already slightly worse than the average in the twenty-seven OECD countries in 2000, on the eve of Koizumi's ascent to power, the gap between actual inequality (fairly high) and perceived inequality (very low) was tied with New Zealand for the second widest among the OECD countries, trailing only the United States, whose deluded citizens were the most likely to consider income distribution in their country to be equal, even though it actually trailed Mexico, Turkey, and Poland. Survey evidence from the OECD study also shows that the willingness to accept a role for government to reduce inequality was significantly influenced by the perceived level of inequality. Japanese citizens were among the more neoliberal in their reluctance to embrace a government role to reduce inequalities, but this was mostly because they perceived that income in Japan was more equally distributed than it really was; relative to that perception, they were actually slightly more likely than average to accept an active governmental role.[51] Thus, although it is far from clear that neoliberalism had a significant impact on inequality in Japan, it appears that by the beginning of the scandals in 2006, cuts in public works and government expenditures and the emergence of extremely wealthy and flashy figures, particularly in financial circles, were reviving concerns about inequality that

50 Fumio Otake, *Nihon no fubyōdō: Kakusa shakai no gensō to mirai* [Japan's inequality: The illusion and future of a stratified society] (Tokyo: Nihon Keizai Shinbun Sha, 2005).

51 Michael Förster and Marco Mira d'Ercole, "Income Distribution and Poverty in OECD Countries in the Second Half of the 1990s," OECD Social, Employment and Migration Working Paper No. 22 (Paris, 2005): 10–12.

had not been felt in Japan since the peak of the economic bubble in the late 1980s, when soaring housing and stock prices simultaneously created hordes of nouveaux riches and raised fears that younger and poorer Japanese would never be able to afford to own their own homes. To the concern about the scandals and perceived inequalities must be added the natural tendency for agenda fatigue. None of Koizumi's three LDP successors shared his enthusiasm for neoliberalism and they all fell from power within a year, eventually leading to the takeover by the DPJ in 2009.

Nonetheless, it is by no means a given that the neoliberal wave crested with Koizumi and will never return. Fiscal pressures and the aging society suggest that reforms to cut expenditures and increase returns on investments will almost always appear to be preferable to raising taxes, as vividly attested to by the long and difficult campaign to raise the consumption tax to plug the gaping hole in Japan's budget. New norms against the domination of advisory commissions by insiders seem relatively set, and neoliberal, or at least reformist, ideas have made big inroads, not least because the advisory commissions are increasingly dominated by economists.

Conclusion

Significant policy reforms occurred under the auspices of a persistent and (generally) neoliberal coalition led by Prime Minister Koizumi and his economic czar Takenaka Heizō, with support from academic economists and big business, especially its more open and Western-oriented elements. Within five years, the Koizumi-Takenaka team managed to resolve the banking crisis and end deflation; hold expenditures to almost zero growth despite the aging of society and the weakness of the economy; sharply cut inefficient spending on public works and many programs in the Fiscal Investment and Loan Program; corporatize the postal delivery and savings system; consolidate or privatize the main government-affiliated banks; and increase expectations for transparency, provision of information, and prudential operations in both the public and private sectors.

Policy reforms, in turn, contributed to sharp improvements in the finances and profitability of the corporate sector, though changes in business behavior were generally cautious and incremental. Even though scandals, concerns about inequality, and agenda fatigue slowed the progress of the neoliberal reform after 2006, an ideological transformation has affected much of the populace, and especially the policy-attentive public, and the pressure of huge fiscal imbalances is likely to militate against the development of a new social democratic vision, despite widespread preferences in Japan for social stability.

At first glance, these results might seem to support the case for globalization and neoliberal convergence, but the main causal links are domestic rather than international, as we should expect in a huge, mature country that has had relatively little exposure to the world economy and regularly featured an excess of savings. The forces for convergence show up most strongly where we would expect them, in finance and high tech, but even there the effects are limited. The high-tech industries constitute a relatively small part of the economy, and companies can and do move some of their most innovative financial and technological operations to the centers of flexibility in the United States and the United Kingdom rather than change their domestic operations, despite the fact that they may as a result sacrifice the economic advantages.[52]

One vital question is whether the financial sector will serve as a lever forcing change in other parts of the economy: Is it possible for a liberal financial sector focused on immediate returns to coexist with a labor system oriented toward stability and long-term accretion of skills? As head of Keidanren, Canon's Mitarai maintained that labor policy would continue to vary from country to country, despite the globalization of finance. To some extent, though, finance *is* likely to serve as a driver for change. Japanese managers are now significantly more attuned to the need to achieve acceptable returns on investments and equity (even if not as intense or short term as in the United States) and they are aware that financial weaknesses will leave them vulnerable to challenges and takeovers. The key driver, however, is not the influx of international financial institutions or hot money, but rather pressures to pay for a rapidly aging society: higher returns mean more rapid growth, higher tax revenues, and less of a need to raise taxes or to cut benefits.

The major elements of the postwar Japanese political economy are already changing under financial pressures. With the recurrent cuts in spending on public works since Koizumi, Japan is no longer a "construction state." Massive changes in the FILP and government banks have reduced much of the cosseting of small and medium enterprises that has long characterized Japan. Significant modifications to agricultural policy will take longer, but generational change is already under way and the LDP and DPJ are now much less reliant on farmers and other traditional social groups to mobilize the vote.

Even in the United States and the UK, neoliberalism has not (so far, anyway) destroyed social security or public health care, and as the risks facing individuals have grown, resistance to neoliberalism has also grown.

52 Hall and Soskice, eds., *Varieties of Capitalism.*

Neoliberalism has served as an important source for change, especially when countries have fallen into fiscal imbalances, but it is has not occurred solely or primarily for international reasons and it has not dictated the final agenda. Japan is unlikely to prove to be an exception.

References

Anchordoguy, Marie. *Reprogramming Japan: The High Tech Crisis under Communitarian Capitalism*. Ithaca, NY: Cornell University Press, 2005.

Cabinet Office Economic and Social Research Institute. *Kappatsuka suru kigyō no M&A katsudō to shokadai: Heisei 17 nen M&A kenkyūkai chūkan hōkoku sho* [Corporate M&A activity rising, issues they face: Heisei 17 M&A research group interim report], 2005.

Culpepper, Pepper D. *Quiet Politics and Business Power: Corporate Control in Europe and Japan*. New York: Cambridge University Press, 2011.

Derthick, Martha, and Paul J. Quirk. *The Politics of Deregulation*. Washington, DC: Brookings Institution, 1985.

Förster, Michael, and Marco Mira d'Ercole. "Income Distribution and Poverty in OECD Countries in the Second Half of the 1990s." OECD Social, Employment and Migration Working Paper No. 22. Paris, 2005.

Franzese, Robert J., Jr. "Electoral and Partisan Cycles in Economic Policies and Outcomes." *Annual Review of Political Science*, no. 1 (2002): 369–421.

Gourevitch, Peter Alexis, and James J. Shinn. *Political Power and Corporate Control: The New Global Politics of Corporate Governance*. Princeton: Princeton University Press, 2005.

Hall, Peter A. "Policy Paradigms, Social Learning, and the State: The Case of Economic Policymaking in Britain." *Comparative Politics* 25, no. 3 (1993): 275–96.

Hall, Peter A., and David Soskice, eds. *Varieties of Capitalism: The Institutional Foundations of Comparative Advantage*. New York: Oxford University Press, 2001.

Hancké, Bob. "Revisiting the French Model: Coordination and Restructuring in French Industry." In *Varieties of Capitalism: The Institutional Foundations of Comparative Advantage*, edited by Peter A. Hall and David Soskice, 307–37. New York: Oxford University Press, 2001.

Iversen, Torben. *Contested Economic Institutions: The Politics of Macroeconomics and Wage Bargaining in Advanced Democracies*. New York: Cambridge University Press, 1999.

Japan Corporate Governance Research Institute. "JCGR Corporate Governance Survey 2005: Final Report," December 1, 2005. Accessed April 24, 2013. http://www.JCGR/eng/survey/index.html.

Japan Real Estate Institute (JREI). "Rokudai toshi" [Six major cities], 2011. Accessed June 16, 2013. http://www.reinet.or.jp/pdf/report/shigaiti201106/6toshi.pdf.

Japan Real Estate Institute (JREI). "Shigaichi kakaku shisū [Urban area land price index], 2011. Accessed June 16, 2013. http://www.stat.go.jp/data/nenkan/zuhyou/y1712000.xls.

Kato, Junko. *The Problem of Bureaucratic Rationality: Tax Politics in Japan.* Princeton: Princeton University Press, 1994.

Klingemann, Hans-Dieter, Richard I. Hofferbert, and Ian Budge. *Parties, Policies and Democracy.* Boulder, CO: Westview, 1994.

Jesper Koll, "Koizumi's Third Anniversary," *Wall Street Journal*, April 23, 2004. Accessed June 16, 2013. http://online.wsj.com/article/O„SB108267418451291294,00.html.

Koo, Richard C. *Balance Sheet Recession: Japan's Struggle with Uncharted Economics and its Global Implications.* Singapore: John Wiley, 2003.

Krauss, Ellis S. *Broadcasting Politics in Japan: NHK and Television News.* Ithaca, NY: Cornell University Press, 2000.

Kushida, Kenji E. "Entrepreneurship in Japan's ICT Sector: Opportunities and Protection from Japan's Telecommunications Regulatory Regime Shift." *Social Science Japan Journal* 15, no. 1 (2012): 3–30.

Milhaupt, Curtis J., and Mark D. West. *Economic Organizations and Corporate Governance in Japan: The Impact of Formal and Informal Rules.* New York: Oxford University Press, 2004.

Ministry of Economy, Trade, and Industry (METI). "Sangyō katsudō bunseki Heisei 17 nen 7–9 gatsuki happyō" [Industry activities analysis Heisei 17 July-September], 2005. *Wedge* (April 2006): 34–36.

Ministry of Finance (MOF). "Shuyō sangyōbetsu kaisha eigyō jōkyō (zen kigyō) 2000–2011" [Corporate performance by major industry (all industries) 2000–2011], 2011. Accessed June 16, 2013. http://www.stat.go.jp/data/getujidb/zuhyou/j01-1.xls.

Ministry of Internal Affairs and Communications (MIC). "17-6 Shōhisha bukka shisū" [Consumer price index] , 2010. Accessed June 16, 2013. http://www.stat.go.jp/data/nenkan/zuhyou/y1706a00.xls.

Mizuho Research Institute. *Nihon keizai no asu o yomu 2005* [Reading the tomorrow of Japan's economy 2005]. Tokyo: Toyo Keizai, 2004.

Mulgan, Aurelia George. *Japan's Failed Revolution: Koizumi and the Politics of Economic Reform.* Canberra: Asia Pacific Press, 2002.

Nakano, Koichi. "The Politics of Administrative Reform in Japan, 1993–1998: Toward a More Accountable Government?" *Asian Survey* 38, no. 3 (1998): 291–309.

Noble, Gregory W. "1990 nendai no keizai kisei kaikaku: Ushinawareta jūnen ka, yuruyaka na zenshin ka" [Reforming economic regulation in the 1990s: Lost decade or slow progress?]. *Shakai Kagaku Kenkyū* 53, no. 2/3 (2002): 173–217.

———. "Reform and Continuity in Japan's *Shingikai* Deliberation Councils." In *Japanese Governance: Beyond Japan Inc.*, edited by Jennifer Amyx and Peter Drysdale, 113–33. London: RoutledgeCurzon, 2003.

———. "Review Essay: Recent Trends in Comparative Political Economy and their Implications for Japan." *Japanese Journal of Political Science* 4, no. 1 (2003): 135–51.

———. "Front Door, Back Door: The Reform of Postal Savings and Loans in Japan." *The Japanese Economy* 33, no. 1 (2005): 107–23.

———. "Seijiteki rīdāshippu to kōzōkaikaku" [Japanese political leadership and structural reform]. In *"Ushinawareta 10 nen" o koete (2) Koizumi kaikaku he no jidai* [Beyond the "lost decade," volume 2: The Koizumi reforms], edited by Institute of Social Science, University of Tokyo, 73–105. Tokyo: University of Tokyo Press, 2006.

———. "Changing Politics of Japanese Corporate Governance: Party Dynamics and the Myth of the Myth of Permanent Employment." Paper presented at the Joint Conference of the Association for Asian Studies and the International Convention of Asia Scholars, Honolulu, March 31–April 3, 2011.

Otake, Fumio. *Nihon no fubyōdō: Kakusa shakai no gensō to mirai* [Japan's inequality: The illusion and future of a stratified society]. Tokyo: Nihon Keizai Shinbun Sha, 2005.

Otake, Hideo. *Nihon seiji no tairitsujiku: 93 nen ikō no seikai saihen no naka de* [Axes of cleavage in Japanese politics in the political reorganizations after 1993]. Tokyo: Chūō Kōron Shinsha, 1999.

Patashnik, Eric M. *Reforms at Risk: What Happens after Major Policy Changes are Enacted*. Princeton: Princeton University Press, 2008.

Press Release, "IRCJ Approves Application for Assistance for Daiei Group Companies," IRCJ, December 28, 2004. Accessed June 16, 2013. http://www8.cao.go.jp/sangyo/ircj/en/pdf_aa_20041228.pdf.

Sabatier, Paul A. "The Need for Better Theories." In *Theories of the Policy Process*, edited by Paul A. Sabatier, 3–17. Boulder, CO: Westview, 1999.

Schaede, Ulrike. *Choose and Focus: Japanese Business Strategies for the 21st Century*. Ithaca, NY: Cornell University Press, 2008.

Shimizu, Masato. *Kantei shudō: Koizumi Jun'ichirō no kakumei* [Cabinet leadership: Koizumi Junichiro's revolution]. Tokyo: Nihon Keizai Shinbunsha, 2005.

————. *Keizai zaisei senki: Kantei shudō Koizumi kara Abe he* [Battle stories of the Council on Economic and Fiscal Policy: Cabinet leadership from Koizumi to Abe]. Tokyo: Nihon Keizai Shinbun Shuppansha, 2007.

Shiota, Ushio. "Takenaka Heizō no chōsen: Seiji o mezashita gakusha no kiseki (chū): Seisaku no ketteiken o meguru Kasumigaseki to no kōbō sen" [Takenaka Heizō's challenge: The trail of a scholar who aimed at politics. Part 2: Battles with Kasumigaseki over the power to determine economic policy]. *Ronza* (2005): 111–21.

United Nations Conference on Trade and Development (UNCTAD). *World Investment Report* (including Country Fact Sheet: Japan), 2001. Accessed April 24, 2013. http://www.unctad.org/Templates/Page. asp?intItemID=2441&lang=1.

U.S. –Japan Business Council. "Expanding FDI in Japan: M&A is the Key." Tokyo, September 28, 2005: 12–15, 19.

Wilson, James Q. *Bureaucracy: What Government Agencies Do and Why They Do It*. New York: Basic Books, 1989.

6 The Survival of Regional Banks and Small and Medium Enterprises
MAINTAINING LOW UNEMPLOYMENT UNDER ECONOMIC STRESS

Kay Shimizu

Chapter 1 on syncretism in Japan's financial system introduces regional banks as a sector that has seen little change in its basic business practices since its establishment in the immediate postwar period. For regional banks, non–fee-based retail banking remains their primary source of income; in contrast, their global counterparts and larger city banks have greatly diversified their income sources by offering a myriad of financial services and products and by generating income through service fees. This chapter seeks to understand why sectors such as regional banks have retained such seemingly outdated features and practices despite being surrounded by significant forces of change. Why and how does resistance to change survive and what are the institutional and systemic factors that support this resistance?

The answer to this question lies with regional banks' primary customers, small and medium enterprises (SMEs). Regional banks have largely retained their original forms and have remained in business due to the numerous policies that support and protect Japan's 4.2 million SMEs. Such policies exist because SMEs and their employees are a critical source of votes and provide a large source of employment in a system with minimal welfare provisions for the structurally unemployed. For their part, SMEs have retained their strong political influence by fully utilizing their organizational structures to ensure continued protection. As demand in Japan's domestic market continues to remain weak, however, Japan's inefficient SME policies have begun to reach their limits. So-called "zombie" firms can no longer be propped up solely by public funds and more competitive firms have turned to markets outside of Japan. In recent years, public support for SMEs has diminished, putting the future of their primary funders, the regional banks, into question.

During the two decades following the 1990 burst of the economic bubble, SMEs, which were once the target of compensation for industrial policies that favored large firms, became polarized along two dimensions. First, SMEs themselves split into inefficient zombie firms that are largely dependent on public funds and protective policies for survival, whereas competitive global firms became innovative and resilient. Second, the labor force supplying SMEs also bifurcated into regular and non-regular workers, with the latter growing rapidly. Japan's SME policies have come to reflect this reality by propping up noncompetitive firms that remain a source of employment and serve as a substitute for welfare policies for the structurally unemployed, while, at the same time, a number of new policies have been implemented in the hopes of stimulating growth of the more innovative and globally competitive firms. This chapter closely examines this overall trend in SME policies, paying particular attention to policies regarding financing, the most critical resource for SMEs.

The chapter begins by taking a comparative approach to the role of SMEs in Japan, demonstrating the particularly strong emphasis that Japan placed on SME survival and employment during its high-growth years. But numbers alone cannot explain SME survival, especially during the last two decades of slower economic growth when SMEs should have been among the hardest hit. The chapter next opens the black box of SMEs to uncover their organizational structure and how it functions to successfully promote their interests. Doing so shows SMEs cooperating and organizing along different interests to ensure their survival. The chapter pays special attention to policies regarding funding and employment. Although impeding market efficiency and competition for capital and labor, these policies help keep unemployment low, thus serving as a social safety net in lieu of a more fluid labor market and a sound welfare system. Finally, the chapter connects the survival of regional banks to the political savvy of the SMEs. It shows that regional banks have continued to survive by earning a majority of their profits from lending to SMEs, but with the associated risks significantly reduced due to the help of public funds. The conclusion examines the viability of Japan's SME policies and, by extension, the continued survival of regional banks in their current form.

What are SMEs and Why are They Influential?

Strength in Numbers

Past studies of Japan's political economy have largely focused on big businesses and the mega-banks that serve them; much less attention has been given to the remaining 99 percent of Japanese firms that are SMEs. SMEs have long served as the workhorses for Japan's most politically vociferous industries, such as construction and manufacturing, where SMEs constitute 99.9 percent and 99.5 percent of the firms respectively.[1] Yet SMEs have been largely left out of the literature and scholarship on Japan because by design they were not the designated engines of Japan's spectacular postwar growth. Instead, Japan's postwar industrial policies channeled the nation's energy and resources into large firms in export-oriented industries while treating SMEs as the targets of compensatory policies to mitigate such biases.[2] Japan's powerful postwar economic organizations such as Keidanren are dominated by large corporations, as are the chambers of commerce and other industry-based organizations. In contrast, many SMEs have historically worked under larger corporations as *shita-uke*, or dedicated suppliers, striving to meet the demands of their parent companies in exchange for relative stability and longer-term predictability in the supply chain relationship.

By all accounts, SMEs should be facing far greater difficulties in a country like Japan in part due to its high labor costs and scarce raw materials. This is especially true in sectors like manufacturing, where neighboring countries with much lower labor costs and more abundant supplies of raw materials and energy resources have quickly improved their manufacturing skills and technological know-how. In non-traded sectors, such as services and construction, large firms should also have the advantage of greater buying power and economies of scale. Under certain conditions, some SMEs may be more resilient to economic stress than their larger corporate counterparts since their daily overhead is smaller and they tend to have more flexibility in terms of labor costs due to their relatively low dependence on full-time employees. However, under the conditions during Japan's prolonged economic slowdown, SMEs should have been the least likely to survive. Why then have SMEs, together with their regional bank funders, survived and how have they protected their interests?

1 *Chūshō kigyō hakusho 2011* [Small and medium enterprise white paper 2011] (Tokyo: Okurasho Insatsukyoku), accessed June 16, 2013, http://www.chusho.meti.go.jp/sme_english/whitepaper/whitepaper.html. Based on data from the Ministry of Internal Affairs and Communications, *2009 Economic Census—Basic Survey.*

2 SME policies during the postwar period are discussed in a dedicated chapter in Kent E. Calder, *Crisis and Compensation: Public Policy and Political Stability in Japan, 1949–1986* (Princeton: Princeton University Press, 1988), which, in the appendix, includes a timeline of SME policies. Margarita Estévez-Abe, *Welfare and Capitalism in Postwar Japan* (New York: Cambridge University Press, 2008) also discusses SMEs in the context of Japan's welfare policy. Japanese-language scholarship typically examines specific aspects of SME policy. For work on SME funding, see Nobuyoshi Yamori, *Chiiki kinyū sisutemu no kiki to chūshō kigyō kinyū* [The crises in regional financial systems and financing to small and medium enterprises] (Tokyo: Chikura Shobo, 2004), among others.

The secret to SMEs' success comes in part from their numerical dominance. SMEs in Japan include all firms with less than 300 million yen[3] in capital or fewer than 300 employees.[4] According to the 2009 economic census, Japan had a total of 4.21 million enterprises,[5] of which 4.20 million (99.7 percent) were considered to be SMEs. Among them, 3.67 million (87.0 percent) were considered small enterprises with fewer than twenty employees (five or fewer employees in the wholesale, retail, and service industries).[6] In short, all but a handful of firms in Japan are SMEs. Even by international standards, Japan has a relatively large number of SMEs per capita; while the United States has 5.9 million SMEs, or .019 SMEs per capita, and Germany has 1.7 million SMEs, or .020 SMEs per capita,[7] Japan has .033 SMEs per capita. These numbers suggest that Japanese SMEs could have a considerable amount of influence in policymaking, but to even further strengthen their case they are more often portrayed as powerless and at the mercy of larger corporations and/or industrial bureaucrats for their survival.

One reason why SMEs today are seen as the underdog is because after two decades of economic slowdown, their numbers are far below their peak. The total number of SMEs increased rapidly during the high-growth era (1955–73), but has now returned to 1960s levels. In 1963, there were roughly 3.99 million establishments, peaking at 6.64 million establishments in 1991, before declining to 5.80 million establishments (constituting 4.19 million enterprises, or a 12.8 percent decrease) in 2009.[8] The number of employees

3 Roughly US$3.7 million in 2012.

4 Exceptions to this definition, as stated in the revised Small and Medium-sized Enterprise Basic Act, include wholesalers (less than 100 million yen in capital or fewer than 100 employees); retailers (less than 50 million yen in capital or fewer than 50 employees); and services (less than 50 million yen in capital or fewer than 100 employees). The more typical definition of SMEs used globally is fewer than 250 employees.

5 Note that the term "enterprise" (kigyō) differs from "establishments" (jigyōsho) or "company" (kaisha). Any given enterprise can have one or more establishments. Data on SMEs often use establishments as the base unit and are then agglomerated into enterprises. Companies are a subset of enterprises.

6 As defined in Small and Medium Enterprise Agency, Statistics on Small and Medium Enterprises in Japan 2012, accessed June 15, 2013, http://www.chusho.meti.go.jp/pamflet/hakusyo/H24/download/2012hakusho_eng.pdf.

7 Data for the United States 2008 are found in United States Census Bureau, Statistics About Business Size (Including Small Business) from the U.S. Census Bureau, accessed June 28, 2013, http://www.census.gov/econ/smallbus.html. Data for Germany 2008 are found in European Commission Enterprise and Industry, SBA Fact Sheet Germany, accessed June 28, 2013, http://ec.europa.eu/enterprise/policies/sme/facts-figures-analysis/performance-review/files/countries-sheets/2008/germany_en.pdf

8 Here, establishments are used as the unit of analysis, since in the immediate postwar period the vast majority of SMEs had just one establishment and data were collected per establishment.

(*jūgyōin*) has witnessed similar trends, with the 23.6 million employees in 1963 increasing to 48.2 million employees in 1996 before declining to 28.3 million employees in 2010 (a 41.2 percent decrease). However, SME employees still make up 66.0 percent of all employees, and this strength in numbers, which both stabilizes the economy and directly translates into votes, is a key source of influence for SMEs.

SMEs as a Source of Employment

Despite nearly two decades of economic stagnation, one of the surprising forces of stability in Japan's political economy has been the relatively low level of unemployment, which reached a peak of 5.4 percent in 2002 and has since hovered around 5 percent. Unlike other developed nations, such as the United States, France, and Spain, that have experienced political upheavals in response to spiking levels of unemployment, Japan's unemployment rate has remained manageable. Indicators of firm profitability and other measures of economic health, however, would suggest much higher levels of unemployment for Japan. What explains this discrepancy?

One reason behind Japan's relatively low unemployment rates is the employment demand created by SMEs. As early as 1953, 73.5 percent of Japan's entire workforce in manufacturing was employed in firms with fewer than 300 employees.[9] In 1972, shortly before the first oil shock, 78.4 percent of the total nonagricultural labor force worked for SMEs. This number peaked at 81.7 percent in 1981 despite the slowdown in economic growth after the two oil shocks of the 1970s that hit SMEs especially hard.

Over the last two decades of slower economic growth, SME employment in Japan has remained unusually high relative to that in other developed countries, constituting 66.0 percent of the nonagricultural labor force in 2010. Among Japan's 42.97 million full-time workers, 28.34 million work for SMEs, of which 9.12 million work for small firms. In the manufacturing and service sectors, each of which employ roughly one-quarter of Japan's workers, the share of the labor force working for SMEs is much larger than the shares in other major industrialized nations.

This relatively large ratio of employment in SMEs underscores the critical role SMEs play in mitigating an otherwise rigid labor market that provides few opportunities for horizontal movement or temporary adjustments for both employees and employers. As Calder notes, many SMEs serve as a "labor reservoir" from which both large and small employers can hire as many workers as they need for as long as required.[10] During the first half

9 Calder, *Crisis and Compensation*, 314.
10 Ibid., 315.

of the high-growth period (1955–62), non-traded sectors such as services and construction increased SME employment at a rapid rate. In the following years, these domestically oriented sectors were not only shielded from global competition, but they also benefited from legal constraints on the expansion of large-scale businesses, particularly in the retail and service sectors. Admittedly, such protections led to growing inefficiencies and redundant employment in the non-traded sectors, but the rapid economic growth and growing affluence, which increased demand for specialty shops and services, were able to absorb part of this growth in employment. Even during the 1980s when mechanization and automation expanded rapidly, large firms took the brunt of the labor cuts whereas the SMEs, which typically are slower to incorporate new technology and less able to afford the large capital investments necessary for labor-cutting, retained their role as Japan's labor-sponge. In 1986, unemployment in Japan was only 2.8 percent, compared to 6.9 percent in the United States and 11.7 percent in Europe.[11]

The role of SMEs as a sponge for excess labor has similarly allowed Japan to maintain relatively low levels of unemployment in the post-bubble era. However, along with the slowdown in the economy, the labor-adjustment mechanism has evolved from redundant employment in protected sectors to an increase in non-regular employment, shifting the costs of maintaining lower unemployment from employers to workers. Non-regular employment includes part-time and temporary workers, dispatched workers from temporary labor agencies, and contract workers. During the last two decades, non-regular employment has increased rapidly, from 20.2 percent of total employment in 1990 to 35.7 percent in 2011.[12] Among firms with fewer than thirty employees, over 37 percent were non-regular workers.[13]

Relative to large firms, SMEs have always relied more heavily on non-regular workers, but a surge in non-regular hires occurred in the post-bubble years. Between 1987 and 1993, during the latter bubble years, large firms expanded their workforce by hiring full-time regular workers, pushing many SMEs out of the competition for the best employees. Due to such pressures, SMEs increasingly began to hire non-regular workers. After the bubble burst, large firms cut back on hiring regular workers to save on labor costs, making way

11 Ibid., 316.

12 Calculated from Ministry of Internal Affairs and Communications, Statistics Bureau, *Rōdōryoku chōsa 2011* [Labor force survey 2011], various years; Ministry of Internal Affairs and Communications, Statistics Bureau, *Rōdōryoku chōsa tokubetsu chōsa* [The special survey of the labor force survey], accessed June 15, 2013, http://www.stat.go.jp/english/.

13 Ministry of Health, *Annual Health, Labour and Welfare Report, 2010–2011*, accessed April 24, 2013, http://www.mhlw.go.jp/english/wp/.

for some SMEs to increase their regular workforce. However, by 1997, with the onset of the Asian Financial Crisis, the hiring of all workers ground to a halt, with firms of all sizes rapidly decreasing the hiring of regular workers. When the economy began its slow recovery in 2002, new hires were primarily non-regular employees. By 2009, even among large firms, more than 30 percent of the labor force was made up of non-regular workers.

For both large and small employers, hiring non-regular workers has several benefits that become increasingly attractive as the economy sours. The most important advantage is the low cost of non-regular workers, who typically earn much lower wages. Whereas the average regular SME worker earned about 286,000 yen per month in 2005, the average for non-regular workers was 128,000 yen, or less than one-half that of regular workers.[14] Additional cost savings come from the absence of benefits paid to most non-regular workers. Employers also favor non-regular workers for their flexibility, allowing short-notice adjustments to hiring according to need.

One of the keys to success for SMEs in maintaining such favorable labor conditions has been their shared interests with big business. In times of economic plenty, SMEs and big business often stand in conflict over labor issues. Whereas large firms hire more regular, full-time workers who stay with the same firm for many years, SMEs, with their more volatile business environments, place greater value on flexibility and lower costs. As such, SMEs will lobby for minimal benefits for non-regular workers, seeking to keep regulations pertaining to their workforce largely separate from those pertaining to workers in larger firms. In contrast, larger firms are more able and willing to bear the costs of employee benefits and pensions in exchange for long-term employee loyalty. But the post-bubble economy changed the labor outlook for many large firms who now needed to drastically cut back on labor costs. Under these new economic conditions, SMEs were able to partner with big business in a successful effort to oppose demands for greater benefits for non-regular workers. The deregulation of human resource outsourcing, as well as businesses built around the market for non-regular workers (such as temporary employment agencies), further facilitated such efforts.

Thus, despite two decades of economic slowdown, SMEs continue to play an important social security role by continuously providing jobs for workers who would otherwise be structurally unemployed. These jobs are often temporary and they come with little to no benefits. Traditionally, Japan has paid comparatively low welfare payments, and retirement comes early relative to the potential working years of the average Japanese

14 "Chart 3-3-7: Wage Changes of Regular and Irregular Workers, 1990-2005," in *Chūshō kigyō hakusho 2007*.

worker.[15] But Japan's labor market for mid-career hires still remains extremely tight, with the vast majority of full-time regular employees hired upon graduation. Thus, the flexible work opportunities in SMEs fill an important gap in the labor market. Although Estévez-Abe shows that Japan has augmented low welfare payments with the "functional equivalents" of welfare payments,[16] SMEs and their non-regular positions have provided much-needed employment opportunities to further make up for unmet needs, especially for the young, the elderly, and women.

In short, although both the number of SMEs and the number of their employees reached their peak shortly after the burst of the economic bubble, SMEs still have a large influence in the Japanese political economy due to their dominant size in terms of numbers and employment, especially in some of the more politically influential non-traded sectors. However, numbers alone do not guarantee political influence since collective action problems abound and internal conflicts of interest are sure to emerge.[17] Many other potential interest groups with large numbers, such as labor unions or consumers, have had varying levels of influence whereas smaller groups have had a disproportionately large impact.[18] The ability to provide jobs in a slow economy certainly keeps politicians interested in the plight of SMEs, but it is the organizational structure of SMEs that amplifies their voice on the political stage.

SME Organization

In order to overcome the collective-action problems that often limit the influence of large interest groups, SMEs deftly use a nationally hierarchical but locally mobilized organizational structure to protect and defend their

15 Calder, *Crisis and Compensation*, 316.

16 Estévez-Abe, *Welfare and Capitalism in Postwar Japan*.

17 According to collective-action theories, large groups with diffuse interests such as SMEs cannot compete against smaller groups with better-defined interests, such as large corporations in the export sector. Mancur Olson, *The Logic of Collective Action: Public Goods and the Theory of Groups* (Cambridge: Harvard University Press, 1971).

18 Daniel I. Okimoto, *Japan's Economy: Coping with Change in the International Environment* (Boulder, CO: Westview Press, 1982) and Frances McCall Rosenbluth, *Financial Politics in Contemporary Japan* (Ithaca, NY: Cornell University Press, 1989) have characterized consumers as a politically weak interest group in Japan. However, Steven K. Vogel, "When Interests Are Not Preferences: The Cautionary Tale of Japanese Consumers," *Comparative Politics* 31, no. 2 (1999): 187–207, argues that consumers in Japan are a group whose assumed interests are not necessarily their preferences, and, in fact, consumers have been satisfied with many of the policies assumed to be anti-consumer, including the continued protection of the agricultural and retail sectors.

diffuse interests. Furthermore, their organizations cut across a wide range of industries with varying interests, making them effective at gaining concessions in broad policy areas including financing, taxation, labor, and welfare regulation. Their coordination mechanisms have three distinct features that together have proven extremely successful in promoting their interests.

First, SMEs organize and mobilize locally based on shared interests to invigorate the local economies. These shared interests often involve local infrastructure such as shopping districts and transportation routes that almost exclusively benefit those SMEs with a physical presence in the locality. As such, these SME groups often have names that include the name of the infrastructure, for instance, "The SME Organization for the Promotion of Tatehashi Shopping District." Such types of locally based organizations are effective in harnessing the cooperation of local politicians whose electoral futures depend heavily on the support of local organizations. Prefectural and municipal assemblymen who are typically elected from small communities are particularly responsive to such overtures. Elections for local assemblymen continue to follow the multi-member system whereby multiple politicians are selected from each electoral district, greatly reducing the share of votes necessary to win a seat. This institutional feature of the local electoral system has also influenced how locally based SME organizations mobilize. Many SMEs belong to local industry groups, for instance, hospitality services or retail stores. These local groups provide electoral support for local assemblymen in exchange for promises to promote projects and policies favorable to their group. SMEs find this kind of mobilization effective precisely because SMEs know that their limited but reliable votes make a difference in local elections.[19]

Second, SMEs also organize vertically, with local groups falling under nationally hierarchical organizations. These vertical organizations mobilize to lobby central-level bureaucrats and politicians. This vertical hierarchy facilitates the funneling of necessary resources, including manpower and funds, to lobby for national policies such as trade restrictions and tax exemptions. Although this type of lobbying in the nation's capital may be commonly observed in other countries, Japan's SMEs are particularly keen to organize nationally in order to influence central-level bureaucrats as much as, if not more than, their own Diet representatives. This is because bureaucrats in Japan have long been responsible for drafting legislation, and this is especially true for detailed policies that involve SMEs. In particular, SME policies are dominated by the SME Agency, which falls under the Ministry

19 Author interview at a municipal-level chamber of commerce, Aichi Prefecture, 2011 (Interview No. 110915).

of Economy, Trade, and Industry, with minimal input from the regional offices, making it imperative that the SME organizations have a tightly controlled, national hierarchical organization in order to effectively influence
bureaucrats at the national level.[20]

Third, and perhaps most importantly, SMEs also organize horizontally,
creating broad networks both locally and nationwide. At their base, SME
networks are organized by industry. Within broader categories, such as manufacturing, more specific industry groups, such as textile producers or electronics manufacturers, form their own networks across the country. What
makes SMEs politically effective, however, is another horizontal layer of organization that cuts broadly across a much wider range of interests and industry groups. One such example is the Japan Association of Life Sanitation
Industries (Zenkoku Seikatsu Eisei Dōgyō Kumiai Rengō), or Seiei for short.
This association brings together eighteen different businesses with shared
interests in "sanitation" broadly defined. They include seemingly unrelated
industries, such as bathhouses, restaurants, ice makers, hotels, and even the-
aters. Each of these business categories has its own industry-specific organizations, but they come together under one organization, Seiei, to lobby for
policies that involve the shared concerns of the broader group.[21] A prime example of a shared interest among this group of primarily service providers
is to keep part-time workers flexible, both in terms of the number of hours
they work per day and in terms of the length of their contracts. By focusing
on common goals to agglomerate interests across a range of industries, associations like Seiei allow SMEs to overcome collective-action problems that
often cripple similarly diverse groups.

Furthermore, associations like Seiei have become adept at using size to
their advantage. In 2001, the latest year for which data are available, SME
members of Seiei together employed 6.50 million employees, out of a total of
53.58 million employees nationwide, that is, 12 percent of all SME employees.[22] Through its organization, Seiei promotes national policies favorable

20 Author interview at the Small and Medium Enterprise Agency, 2011 (Interview
No. 110924).

21 Seiei also provides a number of services that make the organization attractive to
member SMEs. Members have access to a wide range of information through a dedicated
database, receive information on loans and other financial matters, and, most importantly, gain access to a broad network of other SMEs.

22 Data on the number of workers from Zenkoku Seikatsu Eisei Eigyō Shidō Sentaa
[National Environmental Health Business Guidance Center], "Number of Enterprises
and Workers (Private Sector) in Life Sanitation Industries (by Industry), 1996 and 2001,"
http://seiei.or.jp. Data on the total employees from Ministry of Internal Affairs and Communications, Statistics Bureau, *Rōdōryoku chōsa tokubetsu chōsa.*

to its members by creating its own standards and rules that are first put into action by member SMEs. Calorie-count indicators and recycling regulations for food containers are two examples.[23] These standards and rules are often adopted wholesale as national regulations for all firms, large and small, owing primarily to the strength of Seiei as a consolidator of interests across numerous SMEs in various industries. By taking advantage of their large membership, horizontal organizations like Seiei are especially influential and effective at promoting and protecting policies that are favorable to SMEs.

Support for and Protection of SMEs

Still, dominance in numbers and effective organization alone do not adequately explain the nature of support and protection given to SMEs in Japan. The survival of Japan's SMEs despite nearly two decades of economic slowdown owes much to the actual design and content of SME policies.

Calder shows that among the major industrialized nations, Japan is unique in systematically designing policies that serve the interests of small firms.[24] During the high-growth period, SME policies compensated SMEs for many of the disadvantages that came from a national industrial policy focused on promoting big business. Since such compensatory policies were designed as a safety net for hard times rather than as incentives for innovation or high performance, Japan's SME policy was comprehensive and multifaceted so as to reach the widest range of SMEs.[25]

Historically, small businesses worldwide have been politically influential, overcoming problems of collective action particularly during times of economic or political crises. Examples include Germany and the United States in the early 1930s, when small businesses became a critical swing group in national politics.[26] However, even in times of relative stability and economic growth, Japan's public policies have strongly favored SMEs along multiple dimensions, including subsidized loans,[27] tax policies, export policies, and

23 Author interview, Seiei official, 2011 (Interview No. 110912).

24 Calder, *Crisis and Compensation*.

25 A 1978 survey by the Organisation for Economic Co-operation and Development that compared SME policies among the industrialized nations shows that Japan had the most extensive range of policy tools, using all major means of support covered in the survey. Organisation for Economic Co-operation and Development, *Industrial Adjustment Policies* (Paris, 1978), as cited in Calder, *Crisis and Compensation*, 317.

26 Arno J. Mayer, as cited in Calder, *Crisis and Compensation*.

27 According to Japanese government unpublished data, in 1982 Japanese government agencies for small business finance disbursed 17.5 times the volume of loans and undertook 13.3 times the volume of loan guarantees compared to that of the American Small Business Administration. Calder, *Crisis and Compensation*.

competition policies. Such policies not only overshadowed the policy stances of other major conservative administrations, such as those of Reagan and Thatcher, but also those of the socialist governments in France and Italy.[28] Key among all of the policies in place to protect SMEs are policies and institutions that help SMEs gain access to capital. SMEs in Japan, like SMEs everywhere, are at an inherent disadvantage in terms of raising funds. Their small size makes them more sensitive to economic ups and downs, creating greater uncertainty in their profitability and consequently their risk profile. Thus SME policies tend to focus on sources of funding, and, among them, on regional banks. While regional banks are not the only financial institutions through which SMEs can raise capital, regional banks themselves rely heavily on the continued existence of preferential policies for SMEs to remain in business. In short, regional banks and SMEs have a symbiotic relationship, assuring each other's survival.

Giving SMEs Access to Capital

One of the main reasons why regional banks have retained their traditional business style is due to the continued dependence of SMEs on bank loans. The average SME receives over 50 percent of its capital in the form of loans from financial institutions and other sources.[29] In general, the smaller the firm, the more it depends on borrowing. In 2001, firms with less than twenty employees received 66.9 percent of their capital in loans, whereas firms with more than 300 employees received only 24.2 percent of their capital from loans.[30] Larger firms can raise funds through financial markets by issuing corporate bonds or equity. In contrast, raising funds through equity capital remains a challenge for SMEs, even though their equity ratio has increased in recent years.[31] SME reliance on bank loans for funding is worrisome in light of the significant decline in outstanding loans to both SMEs and large enterprises. For large firms, this is less worrisome since, as noted above, they are better able to raise funds on domestic or international financial markets.

28 Ibid., 313.

29 *Chūshō kigyō hakusho 2001.*

30 By 2003, these numbers had decreased to 55.7 percent and 21.9 percent respectively (*Chūshō kigyō hakusho 2005*, 92; original data from the annual Ministry of Finance, *Financial Statements Statistics of Corporations by Industry*, accessed June 15, 2013, http://www.mof.go.jp/english/pri/reference/ssc/).

31 In 2003, large enterprises had an equity ratio of over 30 percent, whereas SMEs had an average equity ratio of 20 percent. The ratio of corporate bonds for large enterprises was over 5 percent, whereas for SMEs the ratio was less than 1 percent (*Chūshō kigyō hakusho 2005*, 92); original data from the annual Ministry of Finance, *Financial Statements Statistics of Corporations by Industry*.

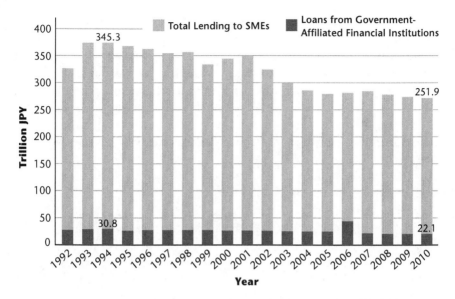

FIGURE 6.1 Lending to small and medium enterprises, 1992–2010

Sources: Chūshō kigyō hakusho [Small and medium enterprise white paper] (Tokyo: Okurasho Insatsukyoku, 1992–2000; Gyosei, 2000–8; Keizai Sangyo Chosakai, 2009; Nikkei Insatsu, 2010; Koyukan, 2011) accessed June 15, 2013, http://www.chusho.meti.go.jp/sme_english/whitepaper/whitepaper.html. Original data compiled by the Small and Medium Enterprise Agency from the Bank of Japan, Financial and Economic Statistics Monthly, and others.

For SMEs, however, the decline in loans is a direct reflection of their financial health. Loans to SMEs from all types of financial institutions peaked in 1994 at 345.3 trillion yen, but they declined to only 251.9 trillion yen in 2010, a 27 percent reduction in outstanding loans (see figure 6.1). Whereas the total number of SMEs also declined by 13 percent during this period, the 27 percent decline in loans can be considered much more steep.

Even though the amount of outstanding loans to SMEs is declining, SME lending remains vitally important not only for the SMEs that take out the loans, but even more so for the financial institutions that provide them. In the mid-1990s, loans to SMEs became the largest portion of the overall loan portfolio of private banks. Whereas in 1965, just 41 percent of all bank loans went to SMEs, by 1997 the ratio had risen to 70 percent.[32] This ratio remained stable in the following years, reaching 71.3 percent in 2005 but declining slightly to 68.0 percent by the first quarter of 2012.[33] Today, regional

32 Bank of Japan, Keizai tōkei nenpo [Annual statistics on the economy] (Tokyo, 1999).

33 Data available from Tokyo Shōkō Research, various years, accessed July 1, 2012, http://www.tsr-net.co.jp/english/.

banks, such as Suruga Bank and Kinki Osaka Bank, top the list of banks with the largest ratio of loans to SMEs, at 95.2 percent and 92.7 percent respectively. City banks have a smaller ratio, with Mizuho Corporate Bank the lowest ratio at 37.3 percent, but their average remains at about 60 percent.[34] In contrast, in the United States, the ratio of lending to SMEs falls as bank assets increase, and banks with assets of US$10 billion or more[35] have an SME lending ratio of only 24.0 percent.[36] The dominance of SMEs in their loan portfolios helps explain why Japan's regional banks have steadfastly retained their traditional forms of banking whereas other financial institutions have undergone significant changes in the face of global competition and other external pressures.

Several factors have contributed to the high ratio of lending to SMEs by financial institutions in Japan. First, large enterprises successfully shifted away from borrowing as their primary source of funds. Instead, they raised funds on financial markets by issuing corporate bonds and shares, which left retail-oriented banks more dependent on profits from loans to SMEs. Second, the development of direct financial markets for SMEs, both in Japan and abroad, was stymied by a lack of necessary information and know-how and consequently higher risks. Lastly, and perhaps most importantly, banks are able to earn a higher profit margin by lending to SMEs rather than to large enterprises, making SMEs more attractive as customers. As will be discussed later, competition for loans to high-paying SME customers has become an increasing source of concern for regional banks, which are being crowded out by both larger city banks and smaller credit cooperatives seeking a larger piece of the SME loan market.

Government-affiliated Financial Institutions

From the viewpoint of overall SME policy, however, government-affiliated financial institutions have long been the central pillar of SME financing. During the high-growth period when SME policy was best characterized as compensatory, Japan created several government-affiliated financial institutions[37] to

34 Ibid.

35 In fiscal year 2011, the average Japanese regional bank had assets of US$50 billion (calculated from data available on the Web site of the Regional Bank Association, at www.chiginkyo.or.jp, accessed June 23, 2012).

36 *Chūshō kigyō hakusho* (1986–2011).

37 These included the People's Finance Corporation (Kokumin Seikatsu Kinyū Kōko), the Agriculture, Forestry and Fisheries Finance Corporation (Noringyogyō Kinyū Kōko), and the Japan Finance Corporation for Small and Medium Enterprise (Chūsho Kigyō Kinyū Kōko), established in 1953.

exclusively fund SMEs and micro businesses that did not have access to ad-equate private bank loans. The main targets of these institutions were SMEs that did not have enough collateral (typically real estate) to secure loans from private banks or lacked sufficient financial information for satisfactory evaluations. At its peak (2004), government-affiliated financial institutions provided 10.4 percent of all funding to SMEs, and 70 percent of all SMEs used such funds.[38]

Government-affiliated financial institutions benefited many SMEs that otherwise would have gone bankrupt during the last two decades due to the slow economic growth. By providing direct loans to SMEs with public funds, thereby bypassing the more stringent requirements of the profit-seeking pri-vate banks, these institutions allowed SMEs to survive during tough economic times. In so doing, they indirectly helped to keep unemployment and bank-ruptcy numbers relatively low. Preventing SMEs from going out of business has been a particularly big concern for government-affiliated financial institutions that operate under direct government control and are subject to directives to keep businesses alive and within Japanese borders, thereby stopping business flight overseas. Bankruptcies among SMEs peaked during the years following the Asian Financial Crisis from 1998 to 2002, but they have since declined.[39]

At the same time, however, the direct distribution of public funds to prop up weaker firms has met with criticism for allocating valuable funds to inefficient sectors of the economy. Opponents are concerned that by in-jecting public funds into the marketplace via government-affiliated financial institutions, the laws of supply and demand no longer determine the price and allocation of funds. The use of public funds to keep firms afloat also invites accusations of unfair competition from both domestic and foreign firms that do not have access to such funds. Such criticisms, and the govern-ment's own realization of the decline of competitiveness among SMEs, have led to a gradual downsizing of such programs.

In recent years, as has been the case for SME loans from regional banks, the post-bubble economic slowdown has led to a decline in funding via government-affiliated financial institutions. The total amount of such loans peaked in 1992 at 30.9 trillion yen but it has since been declining, and by 2010 it was 22.1 trillion yen, a 28 percent reduction. The amount of loans from

38 Data on loans from government-affiliated financial institutions from *Chūshō kigyō hakusho 2005*. Data on the percentage of SMEs that used funds from government-affiliated financial institutions from Agency for Small and Medium Enterprises, *Waga kuni kigyō keiei jittai chōsa* [A survey of Japan's firm performance] (Tokyo, December 2009), Graph 4-2-1.

39 Tokyo Shōkō Research, Ltd., *Business Failure News* (monthly), various years.

government-affiliated financial institutions as a share of total loans given to SMEs remained steady at roughly 9 percent throughout this period, but the absolute amount declined significantly. These trends suggest that although the government can justify shouldering a certain share of SME loans, the actual amount of loans must be in line with the broader economic decline.[40]

Furthermore, there have been additional signs that suggest the government's growing sensitivity to the excessive influence of public funds in the SME loan market. One such example was the move to merge, privatize, or abolish several government-affiliated financial institutions. Of greatest impact to SMEs was the creation of the Japan Finance Corporation (JFC) in 2008. Established by the merger of four policy-based financing institutions, the JFC has greatly reduced the overall operations of government-affiliated financial institutions by reducing personnel and the number and amount of publicly funded loans. Between 1999 and 2008 the JFC reduced total funding for SMEs from just under 8 trillion yen (under the former Japan Finance Corporation for Small and Medium Enterprise) to 5.6 trillion yen (under the SME unit of the JFC).[41] There were similar reductions at the People's Finance Corporation, another government-affiliated financial institution established in the postwar period, and its successor, the JFC.[42] Other institutions such as the Japan Finance Corporation for Municipal Enterprises (Kōei Kigyō Kinyū Kōko) and the Shōkō Chūkin Bank (Shōkō Kumiai Chuō Kinko) were either abolished or privatized.[43] Today, the JFC accounts for 5.6 percent of all loans to SMEs and the Shōkō Chūkin Bank accounts for another 3.9 percent, leaving the bulk of loans (90.5 percent) in the hands of private financial institutions.[44]

Credit Guarantees

As opposed to government-affiliated financial institutions that primarily distribute public funds directly to SMEs through loans, the government can also facilitate the distribution of loans from private banks by using public funds to guarantee the loans. These credit guarantees help reduce the lenders' risks associated with loans to SMEs and also serve to help fill the

40 Author's interview with a veteran loan officer at a government-affiliated financial institution, December 2011.

41 Japan Finance Corporation, accessed July 15, 2012, http://www.jfc.go.jp. Funding increased somewhat following the 2011 Tohoku earthquake.

42 The People's Finance Corporation had outstanding loans of 7.2 trillion yen in 2006. By 2010, outstanding loans had declined to 6.5 trillion yen.

43 The Shōkō Chūkin Bank began its transition toward privatization on October 1, 2008 and it is expected to be fully privatized by 2022, accessed June 28, 2012, http://www.shokochukin.co.jp.

44 Japan Finance Corporation, accessed June 15, 2012, http://www.jfc.go.jp.

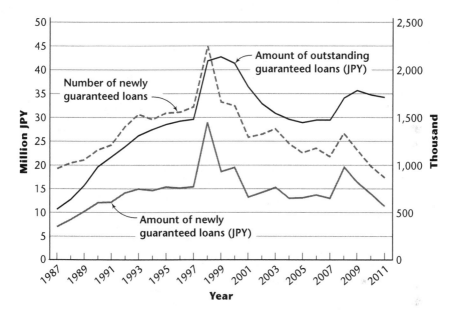

FIGURE 6.2 Use of credit guarantees by small and medium enterprises, 1987–2011
Source: Japan Small Business Research Institute, accessed June 15, 2013, http://www.jsbri.or.jp/new-hp-e/.

so-called middle-risk gap left by the private market. The middle-risk gap refers to the hole in the interest-rate structure of the loan market between lower rates for proper loans given to healthy firms and much higher rates for risky loans from loan sharks and other informal money lenders. Schaede argues that Japan suffers from this middle-risk gap due to a confluence of systemic reasons, including the shift away from using real estate as collateral and political pressures. As a result, private banks are neither willing to take on the higher risks of direct loans to SMEs nor do they have the information necessary to accurately assess the associated risks and to set an appropriate price.[45] Thus, for SMEs with higher risks, one of the only ways to obtain a loan from a private bank is to make use of the publicly funded credit guarantees.

During the years following the burst of the economic bubble, the use of credit guarantees gradually increased, and it increased even more rapidly after the Asian Financial Crisis in 1997. Between 1990 and 2000, the total amount of outstanding loans to SMEs using credit guarantees nearly doubled, from 20 trillion yen to over 40 trillion yen (see figure 6.2).[46]

45 Ulrike Schaede, "The 'Middle Risk Gap' and Financial System Reform: Small Firm Financing in Japan." Institute for Monetary and Economic Studies, Bank of Japan, 2004, accessed April 24, 2013, http://www.imes.boj.or.jp.

46 Japan Small Business Research Institute, accessed June 15, 2013, http://www.jsbri.or.jp/new-hp-e/.

The proportion of total borrowing backed by credit guarantees also rose, peaking in about 1998–99. In 1990, just 5.3 percent of all outstanding loans to SMEs from private financial institutions were backed by credit guarantees.[47] By 1999, the ratio of loans covered by credit guarantees had more than doubled to 12.9 percent; for outstanding loans to SMEs from regional banks, this ratio was even higher, at 18.2 percent.[48]

From the perspective of the lenders, however, the number and amount of loans covered by credit guarantees were insufficient. Although up until 2007 credit guarantees covered 100 percent of the loans they guaranteed, leaving lenders with no risks from these loans, the criteria for qualifying for credit guarantees set by the credit-guarantee agency remained difficult, granting guarantees to only a fraction of the SMEs that applied. Furthermore, many SMEs requested multiple loans, only some of which were approved. Thus, despite the reduction in risk afforded by these publicly funded credit guarantees, private financial institutions still had to shoulder the risks for the vast majority of their loans. This reality contributed to the continued difficulties many SMEs faced in obtaining loans despite the large amount of public funds that was poured into credit guarantees. In fact, between 1990 and 2000, the decade during which the use of credit guarantees nearly doubled, SME lending by private financial institutions declined rapidly. For regional banks, loans to SMEs were growing at 6.1 percent in 1990, but the growth rate was down to −2.6 percent by 1999, the peak year for credit guarantee coverage. This decline in loans was even more acute for larger city banks, which were much less dependent on SMEs, falling to −12.0 percent in 1999.[49]

Although credit guarantees provided limited security for private financial institutions, they were crucial to many SMEs that were partially or fully dependent on such guarantees to obtain funds. According to a 2005 survey by the National Conference of Association of Small Business Entrepreneurs, as many as 57.4 percent of all SMEs had used or were using credit guarantees to receive loans from private financial institutions.[50] This number is consistent with several other estimates revealed in interviews with SME own-

---

47 Data from the monthly report of the predecessor to the Chūshō Kigyō Sōgō Jigyōdan [Organization for Small and Medium Enterprises and Regional Innovation], *Shinyō hoken geppō* [Monthly report on credit guarantees], accessed June 15, 2013, http://www.smrj.go.jp/fsw/cgi-bin/fsclient.cgi?andor1=0&category1=1&dispnum=20 &matchlv=0.8&keyword1=monthly+report+of+credit+guarantees&x=0&y=0.

48 *Chūshō kigyō hakusho 2000*, Graph 213-2.

49 Ibid., Graph 211-5.

50 National Conference of Association of Small Business Entrepreneurs, "Survey of 1005 Firms," 2005, http://www.doyu.jp/research/theme/data/option200505.html.

ers and regional bank loan officers. Moreover, about two out of every three enterprises relying on credit guarantees had access only to guarantee-backed loans.[51] These numbers suggest the critical role of credit guarantees in giving many weaker SMEs access to credit, especially in times of need.

As was the case for government-affiliated financial institutions, however, criticism came from those who saw publicly funded credit guarantees as an inefficient use of increasingly scarce funds. In a study of large Japanese banks, Caballero, Hoshi, and Kashyap examine the effects of extending credit to otherwise insolvent borrowers.[52] They show that keeping so-called zombie firms alive reduces the profits for healthy firms, thus discouraging their entry and investment. Furthermore, zombie-dominated industries exhibit more depressed job creation and more job destruction, as well as lower productivity. Even though credit guarantees may prolong the lives of weaker SMEs with little risk to their financial lenders, defending the cost performance of these valuable public funds became increasingly difficult. That credit guarantees covered 100 percent of the risk, leaving the lending financial institutions and the SMEs with very little, if any, risk also raised concerns about potential moral hazard problems. The credit-guarantee agency tried to overcome this problem by setting strict qualification standards for credit guarantee approvals, but lenders had weak incentives to monitor borrowers. SME loan policy thus came under increasing pressure to reconsider its focus on protecting older SMEs at the cost of forgoing loans to new, innovative firms in emerging industries. With the revision of the Basic Law Governing SMEs (Chūshō Kigyō Kihon Hō) in 1999, Japan's overall SME policy slowly began to move away from a compensatory and protective stance geared toward saving weaker firms to one more focused on strengthening and expanding profitable firms and encouraging the birth of new firms.[53]

The Decline of Credit Guarantees

In response to these growing concerns regarding the use of public funds and the overall decline in their availability, the use of credit guarantees began to decline in the 2000s. The number of newly guaranteed loans declined from 2.24 million loans in 1998 to 0.87 million loans in 2011, a decline of 61 percent; the amount of newly guaranteed loans declined from 29.0 trillion yen to 11.6 trillion yen, a decline of a similar proportion, during this same

51 *Chūshō kigyō hakusho 2005*, 95.
52 Ricardo J. Caballero, Takeo Hoshi, and Anil K. Kashyap, "Zombie Lending and Depressed Restructuring in Japan," *American Economic Review* 98, no. 5 (2008): 1943–77.
53 *Chūshō kigyō hakusho 2011*, Column 2-2-1.

period.[54] The total amount of outstanding loans using credit guarantees, however, declined from 43.0 trillion yen in 1998 to only 34.4 trillion yen in 2011, a much smaller decline of only 20 percent due to the loans carried over from the surge in the use of credit guarantees during the 1990s (see figure 6.2).

In response to concerns about potential moral hazard problems, credit-guarantee coverage was reduced from 100 percent to 80 percent in October 2007, placing the remaining 20 percent of the risk of default in the hands of the lending institutions. The number of guaranteed loans that went into default increased immediately after the 2008 Lehman Crisis, but by 2010, the number of defaults returned to the 2006 pre-crisis level. In 2008, newly guaranteed loans also increased in number by about 20 percent, but by 2011 that number had hit an all-time low. At the time of this writing, it is still too early to know if lenders have improved their ability to assess risk, and if the rates of default have declined as a result of changes in the coverage of credit guarantees. Nonetheless, such regulatory changes may also have contributed to the decline in the use of credit guarantees.

Labor Regulation Also Moving Away from Favoring SMEs

The move away from compensatory and protective policies extended beyond SME financing and into areas such as labor and tax policies. For example, in recent years there has been growing concern about the rise in the number and proportion of non-regular workers in the workforce, especially among younger workers. Historically, most non-regular workers were primarily housewives and older workers who explicitly sought flexible, non-regular work. In 1990, 37.9 percent of female workers were non-regular workers, the vast majority of whom were housewives working part-time; in contrast, only 8.7 percent of male workers were non-regular workers.

More recently, younger workers who would prefer to have regular employment have taken on non-regular work out of necessity. In 2011, 17.2 million workers (35.4 percent of all workers) were non-regular workers, of whom 9.1 million (54.6 percent of all female workers) were part-time female workers and as many as 2.7 million (20.1 percent of all male workers) were part-time male workers.[55] These trends led to the bifurcation of the labor force between regular and non-regular workers, creating greater disparities

54 During this period, the number of SMEs declined from 4.84 million in 1999 (available data closest to 1998) to 4.20 million in 2009 (the most recent data available), or a decline of 13.2 percent, a much smaller decline than the decline in guaranteed loans.

55 Ministry of Internal Affairs and Communications, Statistics Bureau, *Rōdōryoku chōsa*, various years.

in income levels, benefits coverage, and long-term earning potential among workers of the same generation. In an effort to mitigate this growing divide between regular and non-regular workers, benefits have been extended to non-regular workers who work over a certain number of hours. Such new regulations, which were passed despite resistance from SMEs eager to keep labor costs low and their labor force flexible, attest to the declining influence of SMEs. The more recent passage of an increase in the consumption tax is yet another example of new legislation that disadvantages SMEs.[56] Because SMEs are often responsible for purchasing the materials that go into the parts they supply, due to the increase in the consumption tax, they have to shoulder a hike in input prices that they cannot pass on to their purchasers due to an imbalance in bargaining power that favors buyers at larger firms. Although the government is considering legal stipulations banning this practice,[57] the stiff competition among SME suppliers renders it virtually impossible to pass up these costs.

SME Policies Going Forward

Overall, the current state of SME policies, especially as they pertain to SME financing, is a mixed bag. Dominance in numbers and deft organization have not spared SMEs from the economic hardships experienced by the rest of Japan. The economic slowdown since the early 1990s has taken a toll on SME profitability. The effectiveness of using public funds to support weaker SMEs remains questionable in light of the fact that total labor productivity for SMEs and total factor productivity have not improved much since the mid-1990s.[58] After 2008, many SMEs faced increased difficulties accessing capital and many more declared bankruptcy. What has not happened in this sector, however, is exposure to foreign competition, which forced many of the larger corporations to alter their business practices. The same can be said of the regional banks. In their heyday, regional banks had branch offices that extended well beyond their local base areas, with some banks even opening offices overseas. But unlike their mega-bank counterparts, few

56 The increase in the consumption tax was approved by the Upper House in August 2012.

57 Sankei News Online, October 26, 2012, accessed June 23, 2013, http://sankei.jp.msn .com/economy/news/121026/fnc12102620110011-n1.htm. Specific data available from Zenkoku Shōkōkai Rengōkai [Central Federation of Societies of Commerce and Industry].

58 "Graph 2-1-23 Total Labor Productivity," in *Chūshō kigyō hakusho 2011*; H. Maeda, "Chūshō kigyō wa tsuyoku nareru ka? (2) Hirogaru oote to no kakusa" [Can SMEs become strong? (2) Growing disparities with larger firms], *Nihon Keizai Shimbun*, August 7, 2012.

regional banks were forced to merge in order to remain competitive and even fewer were directly exposed to foreign competition.

Although policies to support weaker SMEs continued to decline in the 2000s, the 2008 Lehman crisis and the 2011 Tohoku earthquake reversed some of these trends, leading to the reemergence of a wide range of support measures. In particular, there has been a resurgence of efforts to facilitate SME financing. After the 2011 Tohoku earthquake, Japan was reawakened to the existence of numerous SMEs that had carved out niche positions in the global economy. As Schaede has shown, many of these SMEs serve as critical links in global supply chains, producing high value-added components and holding large market shares in a wide range of products.[59] Numerous emergency measures were put in place after the earthquake to ensure the survival of these firms. But even these SMEs have been threatened by rising energy prices and the overall slowdown in both the domestic and global economies. Additionally, there has also been a renewed effort to stimulate the growth of profitable healthy firms and to encourage the birth of new firms. These include SMEs with ambitions to develop overseas operations, those attempting to develop new businesses or to change their main line of business, and new start-ups.

More traditional forms of support for SMEs have also regained traction. For example, there have been renewed efforts to revitalize shopping districts (*shōtengai*), which are typically filled with small, independent retail shops instead of franchises or chain stores. City centers in locations outside of the major metropolitan areas have also received additional funding to support struggling SMEs.

Conclusion: The Fate of Regional Banks

SMEs remain at the heart of the Japanese economy and are the primary employers for the majority of workers in Japan. It is not an exaggeration to state that the future of the Japanese economy depends in large part on the future of SMEs and how they are influenced by the policies that govern them. In particular, the fate of the regional banks has been, and continues to be, closely linked to the fate of SMEs. As such, the ups and downs in SME policy directly influence the performance of regional banks.

59 Ulrike Schaede, "Phoenix Rising from the Ashes: Japan's Business Response After the Tohoku Disaster." Paper presented at the annual meeting of the Association for Asian Studies, Toronto, March 15–18, 2012.

Since their establishment, regional banks have served their local SMEs and regional governments, nurturing long-term relationships with both. These relationships have given the regional banks a significant advantage over their larger domestic and foreign competitors by providing them with critical information about profitability and business forecasts for local SMEs. Lenders have long had a difficult time amassing this type of information from SMEs, building a "conventional wisdom" about the compatibility of smaller banks and SME lending through relationship lending.

This conventional wisdom held true to some extent prior to the age of information technology. Regular visits from loan officers served as the primary source of information about borrowers. Torre et al. have shown, however, that there is now a significant gap between this conventional wisdom and what banks armed with vast amounts of information and technology can actually provide.[60] Larger city banks with better funding and more staff have a clear advantage in terms of consolidating and analyzing the information necessary to make SME lending profitable. Additionally, as the economy slows and profits shrink, competition for the SME market has increased, with both larger city banks and smaller credit cooperatives competing with the regional banks for a share of the profits. For ambitious and profitable SMEs looking to expand or to go overseas, the larger banks provide services beyond banking, such as broader networks of business contacts, thereby making them more attractive than the regional banks that are limited in what they can provide. It has even been suggested that the regional banks have a limited future because their original roles are no longer relevant.[61]

The regional banks face a number of possible future scenarios, ranging from rapid consolidation via large-scale mergers, as was the case for the city banks, to overseas expansion similar to the trajectory of some of Japan's most active SMEs. Whatever the case, it is certain that those regional banks that are continuing the old retail banking model will have a limited lifespan. As public support for weaker SMEs continues to diminish, the regional banks that have also depended on this support will need to find new sources of profit.

60 Augusto de la Torre, María Soledad Martínez Pería, and Sergio L. Schmukler, "Bank Involvement with SMEs: Beyond Relationship Lending," Policy Research Working Paper 4649, World Bank Development Economics Research Group, June 2008.
    61 Author's interview with a former Ministry of Finance official.

References

Agency for Small and Medium Enterprises. *Waga kuni kigyō keiei jittai chōsa* [A survey of Japan's firm performance]. Tokyo, December 2009.

Bank of Japan. *Keizai tōkei nenpō* [Annual statistics on the economy]. Tokyo, 1999.

Caballero, Ricardo J., Takeo Hoshi, and Anil K. Kashyap. "Zombie Lending and Depressed Restructuring in Japan." *American Economic Review* 98, no. 5 (2008): 1943–77.

Calder, Kent E. *Crisis and Compensation: Public Policy and Political Stability in Japan, 1949–1986.* Princeton: Princeton University Press, 1988.

Central Federation of Societies of Commerce and Industry. *Zenkoku Shōkōkai Rengōkai.*

Chūshō kigyō hakusho [Small and medium enterprise white paper]. Tokyo: Okurasho Isatsukyoku Kyoku, various years 1986–2011), accessed June 15, 2013, http://www.chusho.meti.go.jp/sme_english/whitepaper/whitepaper.html.

Chūshō Kigyō Sōgō Jigyōdan [Organization for Small and Medium Enterprises and Regional Innovation], *Shinyō hoken geppō* [Monthly report on credit guarantees], accessed June 15, 2013, http://www.smrj.go.jp/fsw/cgi-bin/fsclient.cgi?andor1=o&category1=1&dispnum=2o&matchlv=o.8&keyword1=monthly+report+of+credit+guarantees&x=o&y=o.

Estévez-Abe, Margarita. *Welfare and Capitalism in Postwar Japan.* New York: Cambridge University Press, 2008.

Maeda, H. "Chūshō kigyō wa tsuyoku nareru ka? (2) Hirogaru oote to no kakusa" [Can SMEs become strong? (2) Growing disparities with larger firms]. *Nihon Keizai Shimbun*, August 7, 2012.

Ministry of Finance. *Financial Statements Statistics of Corporations by Industry.* Annual, accessed June 15, 2013, http://www.mof.go.jp/english/pri/reference/ssc/.

Ministry of Health. *Annual Health, Labour and Welfare Report, 2010–2011,* accessed April 24, 2013, http://www.mhlw.go.jp/english/wp/.

Ministry of Internal Affairs and Communications. Statistics Bureau. *Rōdōryoku chōsa* [Labor force survey]. Various years.

Ministry of Internal Affairs and Communications. Statistics Bureau. *Rōdōryoku chōsa tokubetsu chōsa* [The special survey of the labour force survey]. Tokyo, 2001, accessed June 15, 2013, http://www.stat.go.jp/english/.

National Conference of Association of Small Business Entrepreneurs. "Survey of 1005 Firms." 2005, http://www.doyu.jp/research/theme/data/option2005 05.html.

Okimoto, Daniel I. *Japan's Economy: Coping with Change in the International Environment*. Boulder, CO: Westview Press, 1982.

Olson, Mancur. *The Logic of Collective Action: Public Goods and the Theory of Groups*. Cambridge: Harvard University Press, 1971.

Rosenbluth, Frances McCall. *Financial Politics in Contemporary Japan*. Ithaca, NY: Cornell University Press, 1989.

Schaede, Ulrike. "The 'Middle Risk Gap' and Financial System Reform: Small Firm Financing in Japan." Institute for Monetary and Economic Studies, Bank of Japan. 2004, accessed April 24, 2013, http://www.imes.boj.or.jp.

Schaede, Ulrike. "Phoenix Rising from the Ashes: Japan's Business Response After the Tohoku Disaster." Paper presented at the annual meeting of the Association for Asian Studies, Toronto, March 15–18, 2012.

Small and Medium Enterprise Agency. *Statistics on Small and Medium Enterprises in Japan 2012*, accessed June 15, 2013, http://www.chusho.meti.go.jp/pamflet/hakusyo/H24/download/2012hakusho_eng.pdf.

Tokyo Shōkō Research. Various years, accessed July 1, 2012, http://www.tsr-net.co.jp/english/.

Torre, Augusto de la, María Soledad Martínez Pería, and Sergio L. Schmukler. "Bank Involvement with SMEs: Beyond Relationship Lending," Policy Research Working Paper 4649, World Bank Development Economics Research Group, June 2008.

United States Census Bureau. *Statistics About Business Size (Including Small Business) from the U.S. Census Bureau*. 2012, accessed June 28, 2013, http://www.census.gov/econ/smallbus.html.

Vogel, Steven K. "When Interests Are Not Preferences: The Cautionary Tale of Japanese Consumers." *Comparative Politics* 31, no. 2 (1999): 187–207.

Yamori, Nobuyoshi. *Chiiki kinyu sisutemu no kiki to chushō kigyō kinyū* [The crisis of the regional financial system and small and medium enterprise finance]. Tokyo: Chikura Shobō, 2004.

Zenkoku Seikatsu Eisei Eigyō Shidō Sentaa [National Environmental Health Business Guidance Center]. "Number of Enterprises and Workers (Private Sector) in Life Sanitation Industries (by Industry), 1996 and 2001," http://seiei.or.jp.

7 Converging to a Market-based Type of Human Resource Management?

COMPENSATION SYSTEM REFORMS IN JAPAN SINCE THE 1990S

Harald Conrad

The academic literature makes frequent references to the so-called "three pillars of the traditional Japanese employment system," namely "seniority-based pay," "lifetime employment," and "enterprise labor unions."[1] The former two practices in particular have attracted considerable academic attention. Although several authors argue that these practices are reflective of Confucian values, such as care and concern for other human beings and the significance of seniority and hierarchy in society,[2] a larger body of literature stresses the economic dimensions and institutional complementarities as explanatory factors.[3]

Against the background of broad transformations in Japan's political economy in areas such main-bank–centered financing, foreign direct investment, and corporate governance since the 1990s, it is important to question to what extent the traditional Japanese employment system has been reshaped in the last two decades and whether such changes are indicative of a convergence toward more market-based practices.

---

1 For example, Organisation for Economic Co-operation and Development (OECD), *The Development of Industrial Systems: Some Implications of the Japanese Experience* (Paris, 1977); Philippe Debroux, *Human Resource Management in Japan: Changes and Uncertainties* (Brookfield, VT: Ashgate, 2003).

2 For example, Ying Zhu, Malcolm Warner, and Chris Rowley, "Human Resource Management with 'Asian' Characteristics: A Hybrid People-Management System in East Asia," *International Journal of Human Resource Management* 18, no. 5 (2007): 745–68.

3 For example, Masahiko Aoki, *Information, Incentives and Bargaining in the Japanese Economy* (New York: Cambridge University Press, 1988); Harald Conrad, "From Seniority to Performance Principle: The Evolution of Pay Practices in Japanese Firms since the 1990s," *Social Science Japan Journal* 13, no. 1 (2010): 115–35.

The issue of convergence or diversity of business and management practices across countries dominates one of the central debates in the management literature.[4] Whereas one school of thought suggests a cross-national convergence of practices, an erosion of institutional differences among different national economies, and a trend toward more market-oriented institutions,[5] the nonconvergence school of thought stresses the embeddedness of national management practices in their cultural and institutional contexts.[6]

This chapter will address these issues, focusing primarily on changes to the traditional pay systems as one of the "three pillars." Rather than merely focusing on changes to seniority-based base pay as the most significant part of a typical compensation package, the chapter will also address changes in occupational pensions and other company welfare benefits to provide a holistic picture of the newly evolving compensation schemes.[7]

The key argument developed in this chapter is that seniority-oriented wages for long-term employees in larger firms have lost some of their former significance, but they continue to play an important role for blue-collar workers and white-collar employees up to a certain managerial level. Performance factors are gaining in importance, but are by no means the sole determinants of pay. Wage systems remain highly complex, with wage components reflecting traditional factors such as age and skills, as well as new factors such as individual and group performance. A similar complexity can be found in the newly evolving multilayered occupational pension systems, which frequently combine defined-benefit and defined-contribution schemes. Other types of welfare benefits have proven to be relatively resilient

4 Richard Deeg and Gregory Jackson, "Towards a More Dynamic Theory of Capitalist Variety," *Socio-Economic Review* 5, no. 2 (2007): 149–79.

5 For example, Christel Lane, *Industry and Society in Europe: Stability and Change in Britain, Germany and France* (Brookfield, VT: Edward Elgar, 1995); Clark Kerr et al., *Industrialism and Industrial Man: The Problems of Labor and Management in Economic Growth*, 2nd ed. (New York: Oxford University Press, 1964).

6 For example, Deeg and Jackson, "Towards a More Dynamic Theory of Capitalist Variety"; Peter A. Hall and David Soskice, eds., *Varieties of Capitalism: The Institutional Foundations of Comparative Advantage* (New York: Oxford University Press, 2001); Richard Whitley, *Divergent Capitalisms: The Social Structuring and Change of Business Systems* (New York: Oxford University Press, 1999).

7 For more details, see Harald Conrad, "Change and Continuity in Japanese Employment Practices: The Case of Occupational Pensions since the Early 2000s," *International Journal of Human Resource Management* 22, no. 15 (2011): 3051–67 and Harald Conrad, "National System of Production and Welfare Regime Dynamics in Japan since the Early 2000s: The Case of Occupational Pensions," *Journal of Social Policy* 41, no. 1 (2012): 119–40.

to change. Overall, we find a growing diversity of wage and benefit systems, highlighting a growing heterogeneity across firms within the economy.

The analysis is based on secondary and primary research data. Although the overall assessment of trends in Japanese compensation system reforms relates primarily to Japanese secondary statistical and academic sources, the sections on occupational pension and welfare benefit program reforms are to a large extent based on semi-structured interviews with labor union officials, human resource managers, experts in governmental institutions, as well as research experts at academic institutions. To avoid a sectoral bias, specialists were chosen from manufacturing (automobiles, electronics, food, and heavy machinery) and the services industries (retail, finance, transport, and utilities). Whenever possible, statements and assessments were cross-checked against those of other informants and secondary sources. The one-to-two hour-long interviews, conducted in Japanese with sixty informants, were carried out between April 2009 and November 2011.

The chapter proceeds as follows: In order to set the stage for an analysis of recent changes in compensation systems, the following section takes a brief look at the historical development of modern pay systems and introduces some of the key explanatory factors. This is followed by an overview of traditional pay practices and a discussion of the factors driving reform. The next section describes and analyzes the recent changes in more detail and the final section assesses the results against the convergence/diversity debate.

Historical Developments and Interdependencies

The Japanese labor market and employment practices historically have been characterized by a pronounced dual structure between larger and smaller firms. Today, almost 50 percent of Japanese workers are employed in establishments with fewer than 100 employees.[8] It is therefore important to note that the "traditional" pay practices discussed in this chapter are mainly to be found in larger establishments, although certain aspects have gained a normative character to which small and medium-sized enterprises (SMEs) aspire.[9] Moreover, it is important to note that the vast majority of workers who are hired on career tracks with pay linked to seniority are hired upon college graduation.

Seniority-based wage structures first gained importance during Japan's wartime economy in the 1930s and 1940s, when the authorities aimed to

8 Ministry of Internal Affairs and Communications, *Japan Statistical Yearbook 2012*, accessed April 24, 2013, http://www.stat.go.jp/english/data/nenkan/index.htm.

9 Conrad, "From Seniority to Performance Principle."

restrict labor movement and improve industrial productivity through job security and wages that met livelihood or life-cycle needs, with age the best single proxy for need.[10] After World War II, employers hoped to move away from such livelihood wages. The emerging management-labor compromise saw the establishment of wage systems that consisted of several components reflecting primarily livelihood factors, for instance, age, educational background, and gender, but also production quotas and incentive pay factors.[11] Following the slowdown of the economy at the end of the catch-up period and as a result of mounting employer pressures in the late 1960s, the weight of living costs and seniority elements was gradually reduced, whereas that of work-related elements was increased. At the center of these changes was the so-called skill-grading system (*shokunō shikaku seido*) that aimed to link employee skills to pay levels, a system that was actively promoted by Nikkeiren beginning in the mid-1960s.[12] Thus, wages, for the most part, were no longer formally directly linked to age or tenure, but because employee skills were judged to increase with longer tenure, the new systems were still very much seniority-oriented. The fact that seniority-oriented wages became widely accepted in the postwar period can be attributed not only to a political compromise or ideological factors. These practices also satisfied perceived societal needs and fit well with the emerging production system.

Aoki[13] has demonstrated that particular features of the postwar Japanese production system, such as frequent job rotations, mutual coordination of operating tasks among workers, team work, and feedback loops, require an incentive system such as seniority-based pay in which remuneration is not tightly linked to a specific job category and which motivates wide-ranging job experience among employees. Therefore, Japanese companies have designed incentives that are not tightly related to a specific job category but that motivate wide-ranging job experience among employees. At the center of their incentive schemes have been rank hierarchies, with separate rank hierarchies for blue-collar workers, white-collar workers, and engineers as well as for supervisory and managerial employees. Each rank is usually associated with

10 Andrew Gordon, *The Evolution of Labor Relations in Japan: Heavy Industry, 1853–1955* (Cambridge: Council on East Asian Studies, Harvard University, 1985).

11 Ibid.

12 Nikkeiren Nōryōkushugi Kanri Kenkyūkai (NNKK), *Nōryōku shugi kanri: Sono riron to jissen* [Administration of skill-based pay: Theory and practice] (Tokyo: Nihon Keieisha Dantei Renmei Kōhōbu, 1969); Marcus Rebick, *The Japanese Employment System: Adapting to a New Economic Environment* (New York: Oxford University Press, 2005).

13 Aoki, *Information, Incentives and Bargaining in the Japanese Economy;* Masahiko Aoki, "The Japanese Firm as a System of Attributes: A Survey and Research Agenda," in *The Japanese Firm: The Sources of Competitive Strength,* ed. Masahiko Aoki and Ronald Dore, 11–40 (New York: Oxford University Press, 1994).

a certain range of pay, which consists of, as will be discussed in more detail later, several pay elements. Employees with the same educational backgrounds start their company careers with identical pay and for some years (until they are in their 30s), they are promoted at an equal pace. When they are in about their mid-30s they start to compete for promotions. The central criteria for promotions are the number of years of continuous employment and merit. According to the underlying skill-grading system, merit depends not so much on a particular job or output, but is broadly based on problem-solving and communication skills as well as other qualifications. Thus, employees are neither rewarded for achieving a given well-defined objective nor with respect to a subjective evaluation of their performance. Rather, frequent appraisals assess potential ability based on adaptability to technical changes as well as soft skills, such as loyalty and the ability to cooperate well with other workers. It is also important to note that the pace of promotion does vary during an employee's later years, with some reaching higher ranks only shortly before the mandatory company retirement age, and others proceeding to supervisory ranks during mid-career. Those who do not show continuous progress might be posted to minor subsidiaries or affiliated companies.

Overview of Traditional Compensation Components

The previous section has outlined the important relationship between the rank-hierarchy system and compensation practices. However, pay in Japan has never been merely a function of rank. In fact, compensation systems have been, and for the most part remain, highly complex, taking into account numerous other factors. Table 7.1 provides an overview of the various compensation components and their relative weights: monthly salary, bonuses, social security contributions, company welfare benefits, occupation pension contributions, and others.

The largest proportion of the monthly salary is made up of "base pay." Base pay closely reflects the position of the employee in the rank-hierarchy

TABLE 7.1

Components of compensation for Japanese employees, 2002 and 2010 (%)

Total compensation	Monthly salary	Bonus	Social security contribution	Company welfare benefits	Occupational pension contribution	Training costs	Recruitment costs	Other
(2002) 100	65.4	16.4	9.3	2.3	5.8	0.3	0.2	0.2
(2010) 100	67.2	14.3	10.8	2.0	5.0	0.3	0.1	0.1

Source: Kōseirōdōshō, *Heisei 22-nen shūrōjōken sōgō chōsa* [2010 general survey on working conditions], accessed July 22, 2013, http://www.mhlw.go.jp/toukei/itiran/roudou/jikan/syurou/10/index.html, and Kōseirōdōshō, *Heisei 14-nen shūrōjōken sōgō chōsa* [2002 general survey on working conditions], accessed July 22, 2013, http://www.mhlw.go.jp/toukei/itiran/roudou/jikan/syurou/02/index.html.

and is a function of ability/skills, age, and performance. However, the latter formerly played only a marginal role, whereas ability/skills and age were the most important determinants. Most companies used to have a pay component that was explicitly and directly linked to age, but, in principle, ability/skills as criteria for evaluation in the skill-grading system have been the most important factors for base pay.

Bonuses have traditionally been paid biannually. Although they might appear to have been a kind of profit-sharing scheme, academic opinion on this issue is divided, with some stressing the profit-sharing aspect,[14] but most others downplaying it.[15] Bonus payments are usually negotiated twice a year between employers and labor unions, and the latter have, at least until recently, considered bonuses as part of regular pay, and that they should not be linked to company profits.

Given that monthly salaries and bonuses make up over 80 percent of the compensation packages, most observers have tended to focus primarily on changes in these components of the Japanese compensation system. However, there are two other important pay components: occupational pensions and many employee welfare benefit schemes. In terms of occupational pensions, most large, but also many medium-sized, Japanese companies traditionally offered a defined-benefit (DB) occupational pension and/or final lump-sum retirement payments that mirrored the seniority-oriented pay structure of the base pay. The strong link between pension benefits and seniority meant that voluntary leave was associated with high opportunity costs, since pension benefits would increase disproportionately during the later part of one's career. In DB plans employees are promised an eventual pension benefit that is determined by a prespecified pension formula, typically reflecting a worker's age, pay, and/or service level. The major advantage of DB plans from the employee's perspective is that they provide a stable replacement rate of final income. As real wages change, employers have to adjust their funding rates and thus bear the investment risks in these plans.[16]

14 For example, Richard B. Freeman and Martin L. Weitzman, "Bonuses and Employment in Japan," *Journal of the Japanese and International Economies* 1, no. 2 (1987): 168–94.

15 For example, Isao Ohashi, "On the Determinants of Bonuses and Basic Wages in Large Japanese Firms," *Journal of the Japanese and International Economy* 3, no. 4 (1989): 451–79; Giorgio Brunello, "Bonuses, Wages and Performances in Japan: Evidence from Micro Data," *Ricerche Economiche* 45, no. 2–3 (1991): 377–96; Motohiro Morishima, "Pay Practices in Japanese Organizations: Changes and Non-changes," *Japan Labour Bulletin* 41, no. 4 (2002): 8–13.

16 Dennis E. Logue and Jack S. Rader, *Managing Pension Plans: A Comprehensive Guide to Improving Plan Performance* (Boston: Harvard Business School Press, 1998).

In addition to DB pensions, most companies also paid many of the welfare benefits listed in table 7.2. They can be categorized in groups, including housing support, medical support, child-care support, financial assistance, pension benefits, long-term care support, recreational benefits, and education support.

TABLE 7.2

Traditional employee benefit schemes in Japanese firms

Housing support
- Housing allowance and rent aid
- Company housing (for families; company-owned or contracted out)
- Company housing (for bachelors; company-owned or contracted out)
- Loans and/or a financial support scheme for the acquisition of employee-owned housing

Medical support
- Yearly medical examinations (in addition to statutory requirements)
- Medical examinations for life-style related illnesses
- Monetary aid for out-of-pocket medical expenses
- Mental health consultations
- Income compensation system for nonworking employees with long-term disabilities
- Monetary assistance for fertility-related medical expenses

Child-care support
- Child-care and babysitter support
- Nursery (company-owned or contracted out)
- System of child-care leave and/or shorter working hours during child care
- Information system to keep employees on child-care leave updated about work
- Web-based bulletin board for employees on child-care leave
- Income support for employees on child-care leave

Financial assistance
- Monetary gifts for celebrations (e.g., marriage, childbirth, school entry)
- Monetary gifts for condolence and hospital visits
- Informational support for private insurance
- Workers' asset accumulation or internal financial deposit system
- Employee stock-ownership plans
- Employee stock options
- Mutual aid insurance
- Financial assistance for employees' cafeteria food consumption
- Support system to pay private insurance contributions directly out of the employees' monthly pay

Pension benefits
- Lump-sum retirement payments for dependents of a deceased employee
- Survivors' pensions, orphans' pensions, and orphans' education grants
- Defined-contribution pension plan (401K-plan)
- Defined-benefit pension plan
- Lump-sum retirement benefits

TABLE 7.2 (continued)

Long-term care support
- Dispatch of long-term care helper (including financial assistance)
- Income support for employees on long-term care leave

Recreational benefits
- Workplace cafeteria
- Leisure facilities (company-owned or contracted out: resorts and sports facilities)
- Financial support for club activities
- System to facilitate taking a longer vacation once a year (longer than one week)
- Organization or support for workplace vacations
- Organization or support for company sports days
- Organization or support for meetings to acknowledge employee achievements (e.g., group drinking events)
- Organization or support for company competitions

Education support
- Life planning courses/seminars
- Financial planning courses/seminars
- Preparatory education for soon-to-be retired employees
- System to facilitate external studies (at foreign or domestic colleges or companies)
- Support for acquisition of official qualifications and participation in correspondence courses
- Long-term leave system for personal development/refreshments

Note: Since the 1980s some companies have introduced so-called "cafeteria plans" that offer a wide variety of the benefits listed in this table and allow employees to choose freely among the benefits up to a designated point value.

Source: Based on Meiji Yasuda Seikatsu Fukushi Kenkyūjo, *Fukuri kōsei shisaku no aratana hōkōsei* [Toward a new plan for employee welfare benefit systems] (Tokyo: Meiji Yasuda Seimei, 2008).

In summary, traditional Japanese compensation practices have been part of a human resource management system that one might characterize as paternalistic: seniority-based pay with comprehensive benefit packages, high employment security, extensive on- and off-job training and comparatively little employee influence. The issues to be addressed in the remainder of this chapter are the kinds of pressures the traditional compensation systems have faced since the 1990s and whether the resultant changes have led to a reorientation that might be characterized as convergence toward a more market-based model of human resource management.

Pressures for Change

During the latter half of the 1990s the pay practices described above came under increasing criticism. Underlying this criticism were various challenges that I will briefly review in this section.

Probably the single most important challenge is the aging of Japanese society and the resultant increase in the number of older employees. The ratio of persons 55 and older in the total Japanese labor force increased from 18 percent in 1985 to 26.8 percent in 2006.[17] Given the age-related compensation and promotion practices, this has led to a quasi-automatic increase in labor costs and a need to create more managerial positions. However, the deteriorating business climate and the general trend toward organizational structures with fewer managerial layers and flatter hierarchies demanded steps in the opposite direction.[18] Therefore, since the mid-1990s companies attempted to reduce overall personnel expenditures and to turn fixed expenditures into variable costs.[19]

However, as Abe points out, the rising labor management costs alone cannot explain the shift to the new salary systems.[20] There were periods in the past, especially in the 1970s and early 1980s, when labor costs surpassed company income, but this did not lead to any fundamental changes. Technological innovations seem to be the important driver of the recent reforms. Innovation in information and communications technology (ICT) has led to a mismatch between the skills of many older white-collar workers and the types of skills that are actually needed. The pay systems attempt to address this problem by introducing a new incentive structure.[21]

Overall, the fast-changing business environment and the increased use of ICT have made it more difficult to rely on continuous long-term technological progress and generalist skills, which until now have been the comparative strengths of Japanese companies.[22] A key problem with the skill-grading system is that it assumes a constant accumulation of skills and, in principle,

17 Sōmuchō Tōkeikyoku/Tōkei Kenkyūjo, *Heisei 20-nen Nihon tōkei nenpō* [Japan statistical yearbook 2008] (Tokyo: Sōmushō Tōkeikyoku, 2008).

18 Note that the prevailing implicit long-term employment guarantee for regular workers in large firms, together with the strong legal employment protection, by and large did not result in the shedding of older employees. In reaction to the burst of the bubble economy at the beginning of the 1990s, companies resorted instead to hiring freezes for new graduates.

19 Yonosuke Ogoshi, "Current Japanese Employment Practices and Industrial Relations: The Transformation of Permanent Employment and the Seniority-Based Wage System," *Asian Business and Management* 5, no. 4 (2006): 469–85.

20 Masahiro Abe, "Why Companies in Japan are Introducing Performance-based Treatment and Reward Systems: The Background, Merits and Demerits," *Japan Labor Review* 4, no. 2 (2007): 7–36.

21 Ibid.

22 Dai Miyamoto and Junpe Higuchi, "Paying for Success: Performance-Related Pay Systems and its Effects on Firm Performance in Japan," *Asian Business and Management* 6, S1 (2007): S9–S31.

it does not take into account whether certain skills may have become obsolete due to technological changes.

In 2000, the Japan Productivity Center for Socio-Economic Development conducted a survey among 2,398 stock-listed companies (with a response rate of 13.2 percent) in which human resource managers were asked to indicate three major problems with the skill-grading systems. Over 70 percent of the companies complained that these systems in fact had become seniority-based systems. Over 50 percent stated that they did not allow demotions according to actual performance, and almost 40 percent noted that the concentration of workers in the higher ranks had caused problems by increasing labor costs.[23] Let us now turn to the evolution of the compensation systems that were created by these pressures.

Adjustments to the Compensation Systems since the 1990s

Seniority-oriented Pay

Seniority-oriented pay practices have undergone considerable changes since the 1990s. Most importantly, we find a growing diversity of pay systems across and within companies. Compared to the past when companies often followed similar models, this growing diversity makes it much more difficult to discern common features. Nevertheless, we can summarize the general trend in the pay system reforms as far as they relate to the core long-term labor force (excluding the growing ranks of non-regular workers) as follows:[24] the pay systems for managers (section or department managers and above) underwent the greatest changes, whereas the changes for rank-and-file employees remained limited but were also significant.

In general, the number of pay components is decreasing. More and more companies are eliminating, or at least reducing, age-based pay (*nenreikyū*) as well as the varying allowances. For management positions, ability/skill pay (*shokunōkyū*) is often abolished, whereas for rank-and-file employees it continues to play an important but diminishing role. Accordingly, the surveys

23 Shakai Keizai Seisansei Honbu, *Nihonteki jinji seido no genjō to kadai* [The actual state of and problems in the Japanese human resource management system] (Tokyo: Shakai Keizai Seisansei Honbu Seisansei Rōdō Jōhō Sentâ, 2006).

24 Based on Mitsuo Ishida, "Chingin Seido Kaikaku to Rōshi Kankei" [Wage system reform and industrial relations]. In *Chingin seido to rōdō kumiai no torikumi ni kan suru chōsa kenkyū hōkokusho*, 11–49 (Tokyo: Rengō Sōgō Seikatsu Kaihatsu Kenkyūjo, 2006); Keisuke Nakamura, *Seika shugi no jijitsu* [The truth about performance-based pay] (Tokyo: Tōyō Keizai Shinpōsha, 2006); Nihon Rōdō Seisaku Kenkyū Kenshū Kikō, "Gendai Nihon Kigyō no Jinzai Manējimento" [Contemporary management of Japanese companies], *Rōdō seisaku kenkyū hōkokusho*, no. 61 (2006).

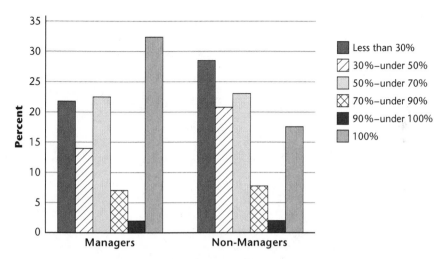

FIGURE 7.1 Weight of the role/job pay component (*yakuwarikyū*) in the base pay
Source: Shakai Keizai Seisansei Honbu, *Nihonteki jinji seido no genjō to kadai*
[The actual state of and problems in the Japanese human resource management system
(Tokyo: Shakai Keizai Seisansei Honbu Seisansei Rōdō Jōhō Sentâ, 2006).

of the Japan Productivity Center for Socio-Economic Development indicate that between 2000 and 2005, the percentage of companies that claimed to have ability/skill pay systems declined from 82.4 percent to 57.5 percent for managers, and from 87 percent to 70.1 percent for non-managers.[25]

For workers in managerial positions, regular pay rises, which formed the core of the seniority-based wage system, have been more or less abolished. The ability/skill pay for managerial workers has been replaced by a pay component that reflects a particular job class or the hierarchical role that the employee fulfils in the organization (*yakuwarikyū*). There are, however, companies like Mitsubishi Motors that have introduced *yakuwarikyū* for their manufacturing workers.[26] As can be seen in figure 7.1, in over 30 percent of companies, role/job pay for managerial-class workers constitutes 100 percent of base pay. Frequently, this job or role pay component consists of a fixed amount and a performance-related amount. Thus, managers within each class receive different and fluctuating salaries, depending on their performance assessments.

25 Shakai Keizai Seisansei Honbu, *Nihonteki jinji seido no genjō to kadai* [The actual state of and issues in the Japanese human resource management system] (Tokyo: Shakai Keizai Seisansei Honbu Seisansei Rōdō Jōhō Sentâ, 2002).

26 Mitsubishi Motors, *Kumiaiin shain no jinji seido kaisei keikaku ni tsuite* [Reform of the human resource management system for union members] (Tokyo, 2003).

TABLE 7.3

*Relative importance of different wage components
over an employee's career course*

	Non-managerial worker	Lower manager	Section chief	Department chief
	Age: 20s	Age: 30s	Age: 40s	Age: 50s
Age pay (*nenreikyū*)	OO	O	–	–
Ability/skill pay (*shokunōkyū*)	O	OO	OO	O
Role/job pay (*yakuwarikyū*)	–	–	O	OO

Note: The number of circles indicates the relative importance of the respective wage component in a worker's salary depending on the career level.

Source: Shakai Keizai Seisansei Honbu, *Nihonteki jinji seido no genjō to kadai* [The actual state of and problems in the Japanese human resource management system] (Tokyo: Shakai Keizai Seisansei Honbu Seisansei Rōdō Jōhō Sentâ, 2002).

Although role/job pay also plays an increasingly important role for non-managerial workers, the overall weight of this component—consequently the significance of performance for pay determination—remains limited. Table 7.3 indicates how the weight of the different pay components might change over an employee's career course.

What is being evaluated as "performance" varies among companies, and is commonly a combination of individual and/or team performance. With regard to the performance appraisals, it is important to note that performance is rarely assessed in terms of simple quantitative results, such as sales, profits, or cost reductions. The new performance systems generally focus on what Nakamura calls "process-oriented performance-based salary systems" (*purosesu jūshigata seika shugi*).[27] Here performance is evaluated not only in terms of the degree of success in achieving quantitative goals, but also in terms of the process of achieving those goals.

Although performance has gained in importance as a determining variable for pay, skill factors have not been abolished and skill-grading systems still play a large role, at least for rank-and-file employees. This is confirmed by a survey of the 199 largest employers on the Tokyo Stock Exchange

27 Nakamura, *Seika shugi no jijitsu*.

that found that only 23.9 percent of employers that use performance to determine employee wages plan to discontinue the skill-grading system.[28] However, whereas companies used to operate with an all-embracing concept of skills, which included personal attributes such as educational background and age (with a focus on "capable of doing"), the evolving systems focus more on work-related usable skills and performance (with a focus on "doing"), and with much less emphasis on the age factor. In line with this transformation, the rather vague assessment of skills in the past has been replaced by a "management by objectives" appraisal system. Despite the continuation of skill-based pay systems for rank-and-file employees, this change in skill assessments in principle has capped the past age-related wage increases.

Occupational Pensions

Prior to new legislation that was enacted in 2001–2, Japanese occupational retirement benefit systems were largely of the DB type: internally managed lump-sum payments through book-reserve plans (BRPs) and externally managed annuities or lump-sum payments from tax-qualified pension plans (TQPPs) or employee pension funds (EPFs). Defined-contribution (DC) plans were not tax-advantaged and companies frequently split their retirement benefits between BRPs (which were an attractive source of internal capital for reinvestments) and TQPPs or EPFs (which were comparatively more attractive in terms of the tax treatment).[29] The EPFs have a semi-public character as they are closely linked with the public employees' pension system by substituting a part of the public pension in return for lower social security contributions with a rebate rate.

The depressed stock market and declining interest rates following the burst of the bubble economy in the early 1990s contributed to a rapid increase in underfunding of the prevailing DB plans. Data from the Pension Fund Association show that during the 1989–2003 period, the average return on assets managetd by the EPFs was just 2 percent in nominal terms, whereas the government-set guaranteed rate was 5.5 percent.[30] Furthermore, the new accounting standards that were introduced in April 2000 for the

28 Morishima, "Pay Practices in Japanese Organizations."

29 Margarita Estévez-Abe, *Welfare and Capitalism in Postwar Japan* (New York: Cambridge University Press, 2008).

30 Kigyō Nenkin Rengōkai, *Kigyō nenkin ni kan suru kiso shiryō* [Basic data regarding corporate pensions] (Tokyo: Kigyō Nenkin Rengōkai, 2003).

first time made these unfunded pension liabilities visible on the companies' balance sheets.[31]

In response to these problems, firms lobbied for new benefit options and options to leave the EPFs, which were finally granted by the 2001–2 pension reform laws that introduced the following options:[32] (a) return of assets of the EPFs related to the contracted-out portion of the public Employees' Pension Insurance back to the government (put-back); (b) establishment and benefit transfers to new types of DC, cash-balance (CB), and DB plans that are not intertwined with the public pension system; (c) scheduled elimination of the TQPPs by 2012.

The mix of retirement benefits offered by companies has changed significantly since the 2001–2 reforms, while overall employee coverage has declined. In 1997, 99.5 percent of firms with more than 1,000 employees paid retirement benefits, but by 2008 this percentage had decreased slightly to 95.2 percent. Today, 84 percent of Japanese companies with more than thirty employees pay retirement benefits,[33] constituting 6.8 percent of the total labor costs in manufacturing.[34] The number of active participants has declined from 20.1 million in 2001 to 17 million in 2007. See figure 7.2 for the changes over time. Note the substantial decline in the EPF and TQPP, which were, to a large extent, compensated for by the newly introduced DB and DC plans. Table 7.4 shows the number of plans, number of members, and amount of assets in each type of occupational pension plan since the late 1990s.

Of the 1,737 EPFs with 10.87 million participants in 2001, only 620 plans with 4.8 million members remained in 2008. About 50 percent of the former EPFs were converted into new DB plans, a process during which the companies returned their obligations for the contracted-out portion of the public Employees' Pension Insurance to the government.[35] This has had the effect

31 Kigyō Nenkin Kenkyūkai, *Kigyō nenkin seido no shikō jōkyō no kenshō kekka— an—shiryō 1* [Results from a review of the enforcement of the corporate pension system—Proposal—material no.1] (Tokyo: Kōseirōdōshō, July 10, 2007); Shiniapuran Kaihatsu Kiko, *Taishokukin–kigyō nenkin seido kaikaku no shinchoku jōkyō to kongo no hōkō ni kan suru chōsa kenkyū* [Research report on the progress and future direction of retirement benefits and occupational pensions] (Tokyo: Shinapuran Kaihatsu Kiko, 2004).

32 Kigyō Nenkin Kenkyūkai, *Kigyō nenkin seido no shikō jōkyō no kenshō kekka— an—shiryō 1*.

33 Kōseirōdōshō, *Jurō jōken sōgō chōsa* [General survey of employment conditions] (Tokyo, 2008).

34 Japan Institute of Labour, *Japanese Working Life Profile 2008/2009* (Tokyo, 2008)

35 Kōseirōdōshō Nenkinkyoku, *Kigyō nenkin seido–Heisei 21-nen 4-gatsu, 13-nichi* [The occupational pension system, 13 April 2009] (Tokyo: Internal Ministerial Document, 2009).

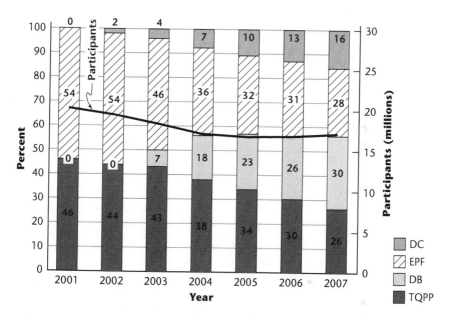

FIGURE 7.2 Occupational pension plan participants (relative and absolute numbers)

Source: Kigyō Nenkin Kenkyūkai, Tekikaku taishoku nenkin no ikō no genjō oyobi
torikumi - shiryō 2 [The current situation regarding the transfer of the Tax-Qualified
Pension Plans: material no. 2) (Tokyo: Kōseirōdōshō, October 21, 2008).

Note: TQPP = Tax-qualified pension plan; DB= Defined benefit;
EPF= Employee pension fund plan; DC= Defined contribution

TABLE 7.4

Indicators of major Japanese occupational pension plans, 1998–2008

Name of Plan	Nature of Plan	Year	Number of Plans	Number of Members (million)	Amount of Assets (trillion Yen)
Employee Pension Fund Plan (EPF)	DB	1998	1,858	12.00	53.3
		1999	1,832	11.69	62.2
		2000	1,801	11.39	58.0
		2001	1,737	10.87	57.0
		2002	1,656	10.38	51.2
		2003	1,357	8.35	48.6
		2004	838	6.15	26.9
		2005	687	5.31	24.7
		2006	658	5.25	23.9
		2007	626	5.25	20.6
		2008	620	4.80	...

TABLE 7.4 (continued)

Name of Plan	Nature of Plan	Year	Number of Plans	Number of Members (million)	Amount of Assets (trillion Yen)
Tax Qualified Pension Plan (TQPP)	DB	1998	88,312	10.29	20.0
		1999	85,047	10.01	21.2
		2000	81,533	9.68	22.4
		2001	78,148	9.16	22.6
		2002	73,582	8.58	21.4
		2003	66,741	7.77	20.7
		2004	59,162	6.54	17.1
		2005	52,761	5.68	17.2
		2006	45,090	5.06	15.6
		2007	38,885	4.43	11.7
Contract-Type DB Plan*	DB	2001	X	X	X
		2002	15	0.003	...
		2003	164	1.35	...
		2004	478	3.14	8.1
		2005	833	3.84	21.7
		2006	1,335	4.30	33.0
		2007	2,480	5.06	36.9
Fund-Type DB Plan*	DB	2001	X	X	X
		2002	0	0.003	...
		2003	152	1.35	...
		2004	514	3.14	8.1
		2005	597	3.84	21.7
		2006	605	4.30	33.0
		2007	619	5.06	36.9
Corporate DC Plan	DC	2001	70	0.088	...
		2002	361	0.325	1.4
		2003	845	0.708	5.6
		2004	1,402	1.255	12.0
		2005	1,866	1.733	22.8
		2006	2,313	2.187	31.1
		2007	2,710	2.711	36.5
		2008	2,566	...	...

Notes: X = not applicable; ... = not available; *numbers of members and amount of assets do not distinguish between contract-type and fund-type plans.

Sources: Life Design Kenkyūjo, Heisei 12-nenban kigyō nenkin hakusho [Occupational pension white paper 2000) (Tokyo: Life Design Kenkyūjo, 2000); Nomura Research Institute, "Japan's Asset Management Business (Summary)," Lakyara 28 (2007), accessed April 24, 2013, http://www.nri.com/sites/default/files/reports/lakyara%20vol.28.pdf; Kigyō Nenkin Kenkyūkai, Tekikaku taishoku nenkin no ikō no genjō oyobi torikumi—shiryō 2 [The current situation regarding the transfer of the Tax-Qualified Pension Plans: material no. 2] (Tokyo: Kōseirōdōshō, October 21, 2008); Kigyō Nenkin Rengōkai, Kigyō nenkin ni kan suru kiso shiryō [Basic data regarding corporate pensions] (Tokyo: Kigyō Nenkin Rengōkai, 2008).

of removing large pension liabilities from corporate balance sheets,[36] fundamentally altering the state-enterprise welfare mix because almost all large companies have now left the semi-public EPFs and only smaller companies remain. Given the scheduled elimination of the TQPPs by 2012, it is not surprising that these plans, which are most dominant among smaller firms, have also experienced a significant decline since the 2001–2 reforms. Both in terms of the number of plans and participants, the TQPPs have declined by over 50 percent. However, just as in the case of the EPFs, many of these schemes were transferred to the newly available types of DB or DC plans.

The most significant development with regard to medium and large-sized companies, which are the focus of this chapter, is that they have largely left the semi-public EPFs and have replaced those plans with innovative multilayered retirement benefit systems that offer a combination of DB (usually 75–90 percent of total benefits) and DC benefits (usually 10–25 percent of total benefits). In contrast, over 50 percent of companies with fewer than 300 employees now offer only DC plans.

Other Company Welfare Benefits

Let us also assess changes in other company welfare benefit plans. As can be seen in figure 7.3, legally required welfare benefits, i.e., social security contributions to the public health, pension, and unemployment insurance systems, have risen more or less consistently since the 1980s. Occupational pension contributions rose until the mid-2000s but thereafter declined, whereas voluntary welfare benefits have remained more or less stable since the 1990s.

How can we explain the relative stability of voluntary welfare expenditures despite the worsening economic climate since the 1990s? Although companies can hardly escape increasing public social security contributions, it is reasonable to assume that they try to drive down voluntary welfare benefits as part of their cost-cutting initiatives.

Analysis of interview data collected in 2010 and 2011 suggests that cuts to voluntary welfare benefits did not occur for a number of reasons. First, about 50 percent of voluntary welfare expenditures are related to housing benefits. Although some companies sold off employee dormitories, many still regard such facilities as indispensable for the socialization of new staff members and for the nurturing of strong employee ties. Moreover, many companies stress the important role of dormitories to facilitate smooth job rotations in manufacturing facilities across the country. Thus, even though some companies outsourced the maintenance of dormitories to specialized

36 Michio Sato, "2007 Problems Loom Large," *Daily Yomiuri*, July 30, 2005.

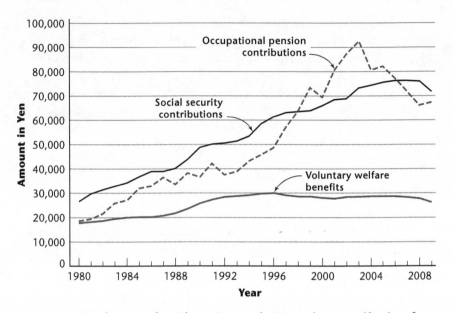

FIGURE 7.3 Development of social security contributions, voluntary welfare benefits, and occupational pension contributions, 1980–2008

Source: Nihon Keizai Dantai Rengōkai, *Fukuri kōseihi chōsa kekka hokoku 2008-nendo* [Report on the survey on company welfare benefits in fiscal year 2008] (Tokyo: Nihon Keizai Dantai Rengōkai, 2010).

providers, the associated monthly costs have remained virtually unchanged since the 1990s.

Another reason for the relative stability of the voluntary welfare benefit expenditures might be the way these benefits are negotiated between employers and labor unions. Interview responses show that changes to welfare benefits commonly are not strictly part of the yearly wage negotiation cycle *(shuntō)*, but instead are often discussed over longer periods in special expert committees *(senmon iinkai)* in which union officials and relevant members of the human resource departments are represented. Changes to welfare benefit systems require careful consideration because of the potential negative repercussions on employee morale. In the interviews, not a few labor union representatives responded that keeping welfare benefit and wage negotiations separate was beneficial because unified treatment would ultimately result in a focus on costs and thus would weaken the unions' negotiating position.

Finally, the overall stability of voluntary welfare benefit expenditures masks some noteworthy compositional changes. Whereas benefits like additional insurance or shopping benefits have been reduced since the 1990s, child care, long-term care, and mental health benefits increased over the same period. Child-care benefits are increasingly regarded as important to attract and retain qualified female workers, and mental-health problems have increased due to work-related stress.

In sum, compared to changes in seniority-based wages and occupational pension systems, since the 1990s welfare benefit schemes have proven to be relatively resilient to the increasing cost pressures.

We end this section with a stylized overview in table 7.5 of the key changes to the compensation systems over the last two decades.

TABLE 7.5

Changes in pay systems since the 1990s

	Past	Present/Future	Type of Workers Affected
Base pay	A function of age pay (*nenreikyū*), ability/skill pay (*shokunōkyū*), and performance pay (*seisekikyū*), with different weightings depending on the career stage	Greater weight attached to the performance pay component, whereas the ability/skill pay and age pay components have been reduced or eliminated In some cases base pay is transferred to annualized pay schemes where the part of the annual salary that is comparable to the former base pay remains more or less unchanged, whereas the part comparable to the semi-annual bonus depends on individual and/or firm performance	All types of regular workers, but the performance-orientation is strongest for managerial workers Annualized schemes are usually limited to managerial and specialist workers
Allowances	Various livelihood allowances reflecting the idea of a "living wage" based on the different life stages	Livelihood allowances are often transferred to the base pay	All types of regular workers, especially workers in upper-management positions and specialists who are paid according to an annual salary scheme
Bonuses	Usually paid semi-annually as a defined number of months' worth of the base pay, with little consideration of firm or employee performance	More and more companies split their bonuses into various components, including a fixed amount and a flexible amount linked to firm, individual, and/or group performance	All types of regular workers, although bonuses for managerial workers tend to have a larger performance-based component
Retirement lump-sum payments	Benefits depending on age, tenure, and final salary, with progressively rising benefits	Lump-sum payments reflect changes in the base pay through the benefit formula Some companies have introduced options for pre-payment as part of the regular salary Some companies link benefits to employee performance through merit point systems	All types of regular workers (non-regular workers typically are not eligible for these benefits)

TABLE 7.5 (continued)

	Past	Present/Future	Type of Workers Affected
Occupational pensions	Predominantly defined-benefit plans tied to seniority	Many companies have introduced multi-layered systems that combine defined-benefit and defined-contribution schemes Some companies link benefits to employee performance through merit point systems	All types of regular workers (non-regular workers typically are not eligible for these benefits)
Other welfare benefits	A large number of welfare benefits, as shown in table 7.2	Although some companies have reduced the number of benefits, there have been no radical overall changes Long-term care, child care, and mental health benefits have increased in importance	All types of regular workers (non-regular workers typically are not eligible for these benefits)
Employee appraisals	Focusing on latent skills with strong seniority orientation	Stronger focus on proven and relevant skills, with less focus on seniority Many companies have introduced management-by-objective schemes and the concept of competency (behavioral assessments)	All types of regular workers

Notes: This table highlights some stylized facts about those companies that have introduced performance-based pay. It should be kept in mind that we are witnessing a growing diversity of wage and benefit systems and major differences exist in the way companies introduce and mix the different measures.

Sources: Based on Yoshio Sasajima and Shakai Keizai Seisansei Honbu, *Seika shugi jinji · chingin IV, V, VI, VII, IX* [Performance-based pay: Examples from various companies] (Tokyo: Shakai Keizai Seisansei Honbu Seisansei Rōdō Jōhō Sentā, 2000, 2002, 2003, 2004, and 2007); Marcus Rebick, *The Japanese Employment System: Adapting to a New Economic Environment* (New York: Oxford University Press, 2005); Japan Institute for Labor Policy and Training, *Labor Situation in Japan and Analysis: Detailed Exposition 2009/2010* (Tokyo, 2009); anonymous informants.

Convergence or Diversity

This chapter has demonstrated that compensation systems in Japan have undergone considerable change since the 1990s. In particular, the former significance of seniority-oriented wage systems has decreased. Overall, the discussion of the changes has highlighted the fact that compensation systems appear to have moved away from paternalistic-type practices toward more market-type practices, with a stronger emphasis on performance factors. Thus, some authors explicitly subscribe to the convergence thesis. For example, Suda concludes that Japanese pay systems have converged with UK market-based practices.[37] Suda's conclusions about convergent development based on her theoretical framework about fundamental differences between pay systems are credible. However, the limitations to her approach and her conclusions highlight some important theoretical aspects of the convergence

37 Toshika Suda, "Converging or Still Diverging? A Comparison of Pay Systems in the UK and Japan," *International Journal of Human Resource Management* 18, no. 4 (2007): 586–601.

debate that are easily overlooked. First, similar trends are not identical with convergence. Convergence in the strictest sense requires that the development of a variable in various countries points toward a common end-point so that we witness a consistent diminution of variance over time.[38] Second, determination of whether a development is convergent depends considerably on the choice, definition, and degree of aggregation of the researched variables. For example, Jacoby argues that even though employment and pay policies in Japan and the United States are moving toward a market-oriented model,[39] their differences are actually widening since the United States is transforming more rapidly than Japan. Furthermore, there is substantial evidence that within-country variations in employment practices are growing in many of the industrialized countries, including Japan, the United States, and the UK.[40] These issues highlight some inherent difficulties in the convergence/divergence debate.

Although we can conclude that certain aspects of Japanese human resource practices are becoming more market-based, at the same time there is evidence of increasing within-country variations and country-specific adjustments. Moreover, several of our findings highlight a pattern of change that the editors of this volume describe as *syncretism*. For example, the same companies that have introduced new performance factors to their wage systems often continue to use a wide range of traditional welfare benefits. At the same time, the newly evolving compensation systems often combine existing practices with new practices to create *syncretic* systems that do not exist in other countries. For example, even though we have witnessed a rapid decline of defined-benefit–type pensions in the United States and the UK over the last two decades, Japanese companies appear to have bucked this trend. Instead of simply replacing defined benefits with defined-contribution occupational pensions, as has occurred in the United States and the UK, Japanese companies have created unique multilayered retirement benefit systems that combine the benefits of both schemes and also increasingly reflect employee performance indicators.[41]

38 Geoffrey Wood et al., "The Antecedents of Comparative Differences in Collective Bargaining," Working Paper, School of Management, University of Sheffield, 2009; Wolfgang Mayrhofer and Chris Brewster, "European Human Resource Management: Researching Developments over Time," *Management Revue* 16, no. 1 (2005): 36–62.

39 Sanford M. Jacoby, *The Embedded Corporation: Corporate Governance and Employment Relations in Japan and the United States* (Princeton: Princeton University Press, 2005).

40 Ibid. Harry C. Katz and Owen Darbishire, *Converging Divergencies: Worldwide Changes in Employment Systems* (Ithaca, NY: ILR Press, 2000).

41 For more details, see Conrad, "Change and Continuity in Japanese Employment Practices"; Conrad, "National System of Production and Welfare Regime Dynamics."

References

Abe, Masahiro. "Why Companies in Japan are Introducing Performance-based Treatment and Reward Systems: The Background, Merits and Demerits." *Japan Labor Review* 4, no. 2 (2007): 7–36.

Aoki, Masahiko. *Information, Incentives and Bargaining in the Japanese Economy*. New York: Cambridge University Press, 1988.

———. "The Japanese Firm as a System of Attributes: A Survey and Research Agenda." In *The Japanese Firm: The Sources of Competitive Strength*, edited by Masahiko Aoki and Ronald Dore, 11-40. New York: Oxford University Press, 1994.

Brunello, Giorgio. "Bonuses, Wages and Performances in Japan: Evidence from Micro Data." *Ricerche Economiche* 45, no. 2–3 (April 1991): 377–96.

Conrad, Harald. "From Seniority to Performance Principle: The Evolution of Pay Practices in Japanese Firms since the 1990s." *Social Science Japan Journal* 13, no. 1 (2010): 115–35.

———. "Change and Continuity in Japanese Employment Practices: The Case of Occupational Pensions since the Early 2000s." *International Journal of Human Resource Management* 22, no. 15 (2011): 3051–67.

———. "National System of Production and Welfare Regime Dynamics in Japan Since the Early 2000s: The Case of Occupational Pensions." *Journal of Social Policy* 41, no. 1 (2012): 119–40.

Debroux, Philippe. *Human Resource Management in Japan: Changes and Uncertainties*. Burlington, VT: Ashgate, 2003.

Degg, Richard, and Gregory Jackson. "Towards a More Dynamic Theory of Capitalist Variety." *Socio-Economic Review* 5, no. 1 (2007): 149–79.

Estévez-Abe, Margarita. *Welfare and Capitalism in Postwar Japan*. New York: Cambridge University Press, 2008.

Freeman, Richard B., and Martin L. Weitzman. "Bonuses and Employment in Japan." *Journal of the Japanese and International Economies* 1, no. 2 (1987): 168–94.

Gordon, Andrew. *The Evolution of Labor Relations in Japan: Heavy Industry, 1853–1955*. Cambridge: Council of East Asian Studies, Harvard University, 1985.

Hall, Peter. A., and David Soskice, "An Introduction to Varieties of Capitalism." In *Varieties of Capitalism: The Institutional Foundations of Comparative Advantage*, edited by Peter A. Hall and David Soskice, 1–68. New York: Oxford University Press, 2001.

Ishida, Mitsuo. "Chingin seido kaikaku to rōshi kankei" [Wage system reform and industrial relations]. In *Chingin seido to rōdō kumiai no torikumi ni kan suru chōsa kenkyū hōkokusho*, 11–49. Tokyo: Rengō Sōgō Seikatsu Kaihatsu Kenkyūjo, 2006.

Jacoby, Sanford, M. *The Embedded Corporation: Corporate Governance and Employment Relations in Japan and the United States.* Princeton: Princeton University Press, 2005.

Japan Institute for Labour Policy and Training (JILPT). *Labor Situation in Japan and Analysis: Detailed Exposition 2009/2010.* Tokyo, 2009.

Japan Institute of Labour. *Japanese Working Life Profile 2008/2009.* Tokyo, 2008.

Katz, Harry C., and Owen Darbishire. *Converging Divergencies: Worldwide Changes in Employment Systems.* Ithaca, NY: ILR Press, 2000.

Kerr, Clark, John T. Dunlop, Frederick Harbison, and Charles A. Myers. *Industrialism and Industrial Man: The Problems of Labor and Management in Economic Growth*, 2nd. ed. New York: Oxford University Press, 1964.

Kigyō Nenkin Rengōkai. *Kigyō nenkin ni kan suru kiso shiryō* [Basic data regarding corporate pensions]. Tokyo: Kigyō Nenkin Rengōkai, 2003.

———. *Kigyō nenkin ni kan suru kiso shiryō* [Basic data regarding corporate pensions]. Tokyo: Kigyō Nenkin Rengōkai, 2008.

Kigyō Nenkin Kenkyūkai. *Kigyō nenkin seido no shikō jōkyō no kenshō kekka—an—shiryō 1* [Results from a review of the enforcement of the corporate pension system—Proposal—material no.1]. Tokyo: Kōseirōdōshō, July 10, 2007.

———. *Tekikaku taishoku nenkin no ikō no genjō oyobi torikumi—shiryō 2* [The current situation regarding the transfer of the Tax-Qualified Pension Plans–material no. 2]. Tokyo: Kōseirōdōshō, October 21, 2008.

Kōseirōdōshō. *Heisei 14-nen shūrōjōken sōgō chōsa* [2002 general survey on working conditions], accessed July 22, 2013, http://www.mhlw.go.jp/toukei/itiran/roudou/jikan/syurou/02/index.html.

———. *Jurō jōken sōgō chōsa* [General survey of employment conditions]. Tokyo, 2008.

———. *Heisei 22-nen shūrōjōken sōgō chōsa* [2010 general survey on working conditions], accessed July 22, 2013, http://www.mhlw.go.jp/toukei/itiran/roudou/jikan/syurou/10/index.html.

Kōseirōdōshō Nenkinkyoku. *Kigyō nenkin seido—Heisei 21-nen 4-gatsu, 13-nichi* [The occupational pension system, 13 April 2009]. Tokyo: Internal ministerial document, 2009.

Lane, Christel. *Industry and Society in Europe: Stability and Change in Britain, Germany and France.* Brookfield, VT: Edward Elgar, 1995.

Life Design Kenkyūjo. *Heisei 12-nenban kigyō nenkin hakusho* [Occupational pension white paper 2000]. Tokyo: Life Design Kenkyūjo, 2000.

Logue, Dennis E., and Jack S. Rader. *Managing Pension Plans: A Comprehensive Guide to Improving Plan Performance.* Boston: Harvard Business School Press, 1998.

Mayrhofer, Wolfgang, and Chris Brewster. "European Human Resource Management: Researching Developments over Time." *Management Revue* 16, no. 1 (2005): 36–62.

Meiji Yasuda Seikatsu Fukushi Kenkyūjo. *Fukuri kōsei shisaku no aratana hōkōsei* [Toward a new plan for employee welfare benefit systems].Tokyo: Meiji Yasuda Seimei, 2008.

Ministry of Internal Affairs and Communications. *Japan Statistical Yearbook 2012*, accessed April 24, 2013, http://www.stat.go.jp/english/data/nenkan/index.htm.

Mitsubishi Motors. *Kumiaiin shain no jinji seido kaisei keikaku ni tsuite* [Reform of the human resource management system for union members]. Tokyo, 2003.

Miyamoto, Dai, and Junpe Higuchi. "Paying for Success: Performance-Related Pay Systems and its Effects on Firm Performance in Japan." *Asian Business and Management* 6, no. S1 (2007): S9–S31.

Morishima, Motohiro. "Pay Practices in Japanese Organizations: Changes and Non-changes." *Japan Labour Bulletin* 41, no. 4 (2002): 8–13.

Nakamura, Keisuke. *Seika shugi no jijitsu* [The truth about performance-based pay]. Tokyo: Tōyō Keizai Shinpōsha, 2006.

Nihon Keizai Dantai Rengōkai. *Fukuri kōseihi chōsa kekka hokoku 2008-nendo* [Report on the survey on company welfare benefits in fiscal year 2008]. Tokyo: Nihon Keizai Dantai Rengōkai, 2010.

Nihon Rōdō Seisaku Kenkyū Kenshū Kikō. "Gendai Nihon kigyō no jinzai manējimento." [Contemporary management of Japanese companies]. *Rōdō seisaku kenkyū hōkokusho*, no. 61 (2006).

Nikkeiren Nōryokushugi Kanri Kenkyūkai (NNKK). *Nōryōku shugi kanri: Sono riron to jissen* [Administration of skill-based pay: Theory and practice]. Tokyo: Nihon Keieisha Dantei Renmei Kōhōbu, 1969.

Nomura Research Institute. "Japan's Asset Management Business (Summary)." *Lakyara* 28 (2007), accessed April 24, 2013, http://www.nri.com/sites/default/fieles/reports/lakyara%20vol.28.pdf.

Ogoshi, Yonosuke. "Current Japanese Employment Practices and Industrial Relations: The Transformation of Permanent Employment and the Seniority-Based Wage System." *Asian Business and Management* 5, no. 4 (2006): 469–85.

Ohashi, Isao. "On the Determinants of Bonuses and Basic Wages in Large Japanese Firms." *Journal of the Japanese and International Economy* 3, no. 4 (1989): 451–79.

Organisation for Economic Co-operation and Development. *The Development of Industrial Systems: Some Implications of the Japanese Experience.* Paris, 1977.

Rebick, Marcus. *The Japanese Employment System: Adapting to a New Economic Environment*. New York: Oxford University Press, 2005.

Sasajima, Yoshio, and Shakai Keizai Seisansei Honbu. *Seika shugi jinji · chingin IV, V, VI, VII, IX* [Performance-based pay: Examples from various companies]. Tokyo: Shakai Keizai Seisansei Honbu Seisansei Rōdō Jōhō Sentā, various years, 2000, 2002, 2003, 2004, 2007.

Sato, Michio. "2007 Problems Loom Large." *Daily Yomiuri*, July 30, 2005.

Shakai Keizai Seisansei Honbu. *Nihonteki jinji seido no genjō to kadai* [The actual state of and problems in the Japanese human resource management system]. Tokyo: Shakai Keizai Seisansei Honbu Seisansei Rōdō Jōhō Sentâ, 2000.

————. *Nihonteki jinji seido no genjō to kadai* [The actual state of and problems in the Japanese human resource management system]. Tokyo: Shakai Keizai Seisansei Honbu Seisansei Rōdō Jōhō Sentâ, 2002.

————. *Nihonteki jinji seido no genjō to kadai* [The actual state of and problems in the Japanese human resource management system]. Tokyo: Shakai Keizai Seisansei Honbu Seisansei Rōdō Jōhō Sentâ, 2006.

Shiniapuran Kaihatsu Kikō. *Taishokukin—kigyō nenkin seido kaikaku no shinchoku jōkyō to kongo no hōkō ni kan suru chōsa kenkyū* [Research report on the progress and future direction of retirement benefits and occupational pensions]. Tokyo: Shinapuran Kaihatsu Kikō, 2004.

Sōmuchō Tōkeikyoku/Tōkei Kenkyūjo. *Heisei 20-nen Nihon tōkei nenpō* [Japan statistical yearbook 2008]. Tokyo: Sōmushō Tōkeikyoku, 2008.

Suda, Toshika. "Converging or Still Diverging? A Comparison of Pay Systems in the UK and Japan." *International Journal of Human Resource Management* 18, no. 4 (2007): 586–601.

Whitley, Richard. *Divergent Capitalisms: The Social Structuring and Change of Business Systems*. New York: Oxford University Press, 1999.

Wood, Geoffrey, Chris Brewster, P. Johnson, and Mick Brookes. "The Antecedents of Comparative Differences in Collective Bargaining." Working Paper, School of Management, University of Sheffield, 2009.

Zhu, Ying, Malcolm Warner, and Chris Rowley. "Human Resource Management with 'Asian' Characteristics: A Hybrid People-Management System in East Asia." *International Journal of Human Resource Management* 18, no. 5 (2007): 745–68.

8 Foreign Multinational Corporations and Japan's Evolving Syncretic Model of Capitalism

Kenji E. Kushida

This chapter examines the relationship between foreign multinational corporations (MNCs) and Japan's evolving model of capitalism. Japan's postwar political economy developed with a markedly smaller presence of MNCs than almost all other developed and developing countries. Inward foreign direct investment (FDI) to sectors deemed strategic, such as finance, automobiles, and telecommunications, was strictly limited.

However, beginning in the mid-1990s, Japan experienced the largest surge of inward FDI in its entire history. Figure 8.1 shows how inward FDI stocks as a proportion of GDP grew from less than 0.5 percent—a level it had maintained for decades—to just over 4 percent in 2008 before dipping slightly in 2010.[1]

Many of the inward FDI flows were concentrated in the very sectors that had been relatively closed. These included pharmaceuticals, automobiles, telecommunications, and the financial sectors of banking, insurance, and securities (see table 8.1).[2]

---

1 We should note that inward FDI is not a perfect proxy for the presence of foreign MNCs. For a fuller discussion, see Kenji E. Kushida, "Inside the Castle Gates: How Foreign Multinational Firms Navigate Japan's Policymaking Processes," Ph.D. diss., University of California, Berkeley, 2010.

2 The Ministry of Finance (MOF) sector labels are chemicals, machinery, telecommunications, finance and insurance, and services.

An earlier version of this chapter was prepared for the conference, "The Varieties-of-Capitalism Revisited: Japan and the United Kingdom since the 1990s," University of Sheffield, 2011. The author wishes to thank Harald Conrad for organizing the conference, and conference participants who provided valuable and insightful feedback. This research was also partly supported by the Ford Foundation through the project on Financial Institutions for Innovation and Development, led by William Lazonick.

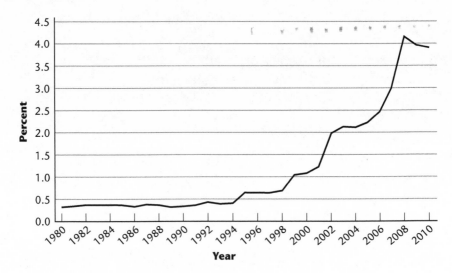

FIGURE 8.1 Japan's inward FDI stock as a percentage of GDP, 1980–2010
Source: UNCTAD.

The degree to which foreign MNCs became prominent players in these sectors since the late 1990s had been unthinkable a decade earlier. In the 1980s, access of foreign MNCs to Japanese markets was a major issue in the trade wars between Japan and its trading partners. By the early 2000s, however, Nissan and Mitsubishi were foreign-managed, the venerable Long-Term Credit Bank had been bought out by an American investment fund, foreign insurers were insurance market leaders, Vodafone was one of the three nationwide cellular carriers, and Pfizer was soon to overtake Japanese firms as the largest domestic pharmaceuticals employer. Foreign MNCs in the financial sectors were by far the strongest financial performers throughout the 2000s, and in all industries, MNCs influenced the competitive dynamics by introducing new business models.[3]

Not only did foreign MNCs become prominent players in their respective industries, but many were notable in overtly departing from Japanese traditional corporate organization, norms, and strategies. Many paid higher wages (some extremely so), but with less job security (far less, for most) than Japanese employers. Some aggressively departed from traditional *keiretsu* supplier arrangements. Others shaped business models that flew in the face of prevailing Japanese conventions, for example by taking advantage of regulatory loopholes. Yet the new practices introduced by foreign firms did not entirely replace those of their Japanese competitors.

3 Kushida, "Inside the Castle Gates."

TABLE 8.1

Inward direct investments (100 million yen), 1989–2004

FY	1989	1990	1991	1992	1993	1994	1995	1996	1997	1998	1999	2000	2001	2002	2003	2004
Food	4	3	77	0	0	–	–	–	–	–	0	–	0	69	–	–
Textiles	–	2	–	–	–	1	22	–	–	–	–	–	–	–	–	0
Rubber & Leather	–	1	0	–	–	–	1	–	–	8	–	–	–	–	–	–
Chemicals	9	52	203	64	37	42	61	23	91	22	472	361	317	2,560	46	30
Metal	3	30	1	1	5	0	0	229	3	–	10	–	–	91	3	–
Machinery	103	116	63	107	69	45	12	1	356	369	109	353	66	435	494	28
Petroleum	7	45	29	51	52	139	10	24	26	4	4	2	9	15	101	38
Glass & Ceramics	1	7	1	–	–	–	0	–	–	–	–	–	–	–	–	–
Other	7	19	81	33	2	9	0	3	8	29	6	10	44	22	21	0
Manufacturing Total	134	275	455	256	165	236	107	280	483	431	601	726	436	3,192	666	96
Telecommunications	3	1	4	0	2	3	4	4	–	32	61	7,025	11	523	374	2,208
Construction	1	8	18	–	1	–	–	–	–	–	–	0	–	0	5	5
Trading	157	73	93	116	189	43	105	508	86	65	77	753	78	632	65	31
Finance & Insurance	12	19	1	25	–	10	0	40	102	870	614	2,356	1,371	254	2,216	2,018
Services	32	122	290	28	27	26	16	81	78	318	226	541	631	837	152	198
Transportation	2	9	0	3	0	0	0	0	–	0	–	7	–	2	–	2
Real Estate	31	2	2	1	5	0	0	86	6	1	35	3	108	0	117	35
Other	8	7	4	0	4	1	1	0	86	12	0	0	2	–	0	3
Non-manufacturing Total	246	241	411	173	228	83	126	720	360	1,298	1,013	10,687	2,202	2,248	2,929	4,501
Total	380	515	865	429	393	320	233	1,000	843	1,729	1,615	11,413	2,638	5,439	3,596	4,597

Source: Ministry of Finance.

Nor did all foreign firms depart dramatically from Japanese practices in all respects. In short, foreign MNCs were drivers of syncretism in Japan's political economy. Many introduced new norms, practices, and organizational forms into a variety of sectors that became bifurcated between the traditional and the new.

In the broader theoretical context, these developments can be viewed as an interaction between multiple capitalist systems. In the comparative capitalisms literature, Japan is almost always categorized, along with Germany, as a non-liberal or coordinated market economy. Japan and Germany occupy the opposite end of the spectrum from the United States and Great Britain, labeled Anglo-American, or liberal market economies.[4] Japan's experience provides conditions akin to a natural experiment: What happens when Anglo-American firms enter coordinated market economies? This gets us to the heart of the debates over comparative capitalisms and institutional change. What drives institutional change and how does globalization unfold for diverse forms of political economies?

The critical question when considering how MNCs can drive globalization, using Japan's experience, is to what degree did foreign MNCs in Japan drive institutional change? Or, conversely, to what degree was MNC entry a *result* of institutional change? This can be determined by a historical analysis of how institutions changed in relation to the influx of MNCs and their adoption of new practices.

Which Institutions? National and Firm-Level

To answer questions of institutional change, we must begin by determining which institutions we are analyzing, and what we mean by institutions.[5] Here, the comparative capitalisms literature usefully provides two levels of analysis: national and firm.

At the national level, the "Japanese model" of political economy is associated with several distinctive features, such as enterprise-based unions, long-term employment with seniority wages, the main-bank system, *keiretsu*

4 Suzanne Berger and Ronald Dore, eds., *National Diversity and Global Capitalism* (Ithaca, NY: Cornell University Press, 1996); Kozo Yamamura and Wolfgang Streeck, *The End of Diversity? Prospects for German and Japanese Capitalism* (Ithaca, NY: Cornell University Press, 2003); Peter A. Hall and David Soskice, eds., *Varieties of Capitalism: The Institutional Foundations of Comparative Advantage* (New York: Oxford University Press, 2001). For an overview of this literature, see Gregory Jackson and Richard Deeg, "From Comparing Capitalisms to the Politics of Institutional Change," *Review of International Political Economy* 15, no. 4 (2008): 680–709.

5 See, for example, John L. Campbell, *Institutional Change and Globalization* (Princeton: Princeton University Press, 2004).

business networks, and "corporatism without labor" in which peak associations confer with one another, but without organized labor.[6] These features can be considered institutions if we follow North in considering institutions to be "rules of the game" established by formal and informal rules that pattern the strategic interactions among actors.[7] The "Japanese model" is therefore a constellation of institutions.[8]

Conceptions of national models are derived from observations at the firm level, usually in key sectors within finance and manufacturing. The varieties of capitalism (VoC) framework articulated by Hall and Soskice is most explicit in building national-level typologies from firm-level activities. In their conception, distinct solutions to a series of firm-level coordination problems drive the diversity of capitalist systems. The areas include: (1) industrial relations—how firms coordinate with labor as a class or interest group over issues such as wages and working conditions; (2) vocational training and education—how firms obtain appropriate skilled workers; (3) corporate governance—how firms finance their activities; (4) interfirm relationships—coordination among firms and their suppliers, clients, and others; and (5) employees—the means by which firms coordinate with their employees to mitigate problems such as adverse selection and moral hazard.[9] In their conception, the role of institutions is to support particular means of coordination; institutions are the "rules of the game" that support particular solutions to coordination problems.

However, critically, Hall and Soskice posit that firms drive institutional change, i.e., if firms alter their means of coordination, institutional change will follow. This is a clear proposition that can be tested using the Japanese case because foreign MNCs clearly introduced a new set of practices. The

---

6 T.J. Pempel and K. Tsunekawa, "Corporatism without Labor? The Japanese Anomaly," in *Trends Toward Corporatist Intermediation*, ed. Philippe C. Schmitter and Gerhard Lehmbruch, 231–70 (London: Sage, 1979).

7 Douglas North, *Institutions, Institutional Change and Economic Performance* (New York: Cambridge University Press, 1990).

8 Steven K. Vogel, *Japan Remodeled: How Government and Industry are Reforming Japanese Capitalism* (Ithaca, NY: Cornell University Press, 2006).

9 The VoC framework differentiates between two types of economies based on the patterns of firm-level coordination. In "liberal market economies" (LMEs) coordination occurs through hierarchies and competitive market arrangements. In "coordinated market economies" (CMEs), nonmarket relationships are the primary means of coordination. Hall and Soskice contend that firms tend to gravitate toward the means of coordination supported by the institutions in the country. These institutions are complementary in that each depends on the existence of others to function. The CME typology is based closely on an ideal-type of postwar Germany, but Hall and Soskice note that Japan also fits the typology, with some differences in industrial relations and the corporate network.

findings also contribute to a stream of inquiry regarding institutional change.[10] Did the new practices introduced by foreign MNCs drive changes in the institutions to support new mechanisms of coordination?

A related point is the motivations of foreign MNCs that entered Japan beginning in the mid-1990s. Hall and Soskice hypothesize that MNCs move across national borders to take advantage of "comparative institutional advantages."[11] The question is whether this was the case for foreign MNCs that entered Japan in the late 1990s to the early 2000s, and if not, what were their motivations? This can be determined by examining the conditions of their initial entry and the business models of foreign MNCs in Japan as they changed over time.

Findings

The main findings of this chapter are as follows. The influx of foreign MNCs into the sectors receiving the most inward FDI resulted largely from regulatory shifts that (1) facilitated MNC entry; and (2) reorganized the dynamics of competition that advantaged the introduction of new practices, often the MNCs' global business models and products. Numerous MNCs took advantage of the new opportunities, and many pushed the envelope to introduce new possibilities enabled by the new regulatory frameworks. The regulatory changes themselves were driven primarily by political dynamics stemming from the aftermath of Japan's asset-price bubble bursting in 1990.

On balance, domestic political dynamics, rather than actions of MNCs or the adoption of new practices by domestic firms, drove the institutional changes enabling the MNCs to enter and introduce new practices. Regulatory changes created opportunities for the MNCs, which then took advantage of them. By doing so, the MNCs expanded the normative range of acceptable (and potentially successful) practices.

The motivations of MNCs entering Japan were not necessarily to take advantage of "comparative institutional advantages" distinct to Japan. If anything, they were interested in new market conditions and opportunities created by the regulatory shifts. They were taking advantage of regulatory shifts that enabled them to introduce business models from their global operations.

10 Wolfgang Streeck and Kathleen Ann Thelen, eds., *Beyond Continuity: Institutional Change in Advanced Political Economies* (New York: Oxford University Press, 2005); Robert Boyer, "The Diversity of Institutions Governing the 'New Economy': Against Technological Determinism," Seminar on Institutional Complementarity, Paris, 2002.

11 Hall and Soskice, eds., *Varieties of Capitalism*, 36–44.

The pattern of syncretism, sparked by regulatory reform driven by domestic politics, is most dramatic in finance, where foreign firms departed farthest from traditional Japanese firms in terms of organization, business models, and coordination with other actors. This is also clear in other sectors that experienced a major influx of foreign MNCs beginning in the late 1990s. These sectors include telecommunications, pharmaceuticals, and automobiles, which will be briefly reviewed later in this chapter.

Roadmap

The chapter first revisits the strengths and weaknesses of the VoC framework, applying it to Japan in order to identify relevant institutions to be traced over time. The chapter then briefly establishes the context for Japan's FDI inflows. It traces in some detail the banking and securities sectors with respect to foreign firms and institutional change. It then provides shorter overviews of telecommunications, pharmaceuticals, and automobiles based on a similar analytical perspective.

Comparative Capitalisms and the VoC Framework Revisited

A longstanding thrust of scholarship best characterized as "comparative capitalisms" seeks to understand the sources of diversity in how advanced industrial economies organize their capitalist systems and the drivers of change.[12] MNCs are often cited as one of the many drivers of economic globalization, dominated by trade and investment flows, but there are few analyses that take MNCs as the central focus.

VoC Reconsidered

Hall and Soskice's 2001 *Varieties of Capitalism* has been one of the most influential frameworks of the decade. Its strengths are many, including, in addition to its clear hypotheses, a focus on the micro-foundations of firm-level activities to create macro-level typologies.

The VoC framework spawned a healthy debate, in which several critiques and alternatives to the approach were raised. Some disagreed with the analytical foundations of placing firm-level coordination as the lynchpin for how political economies are organized, contending that a different set of variables best captures the relevant diversity of capitalist systems.[13]

---

12 For an excellent overview of the literature, see Jackson and Deeg, "From Comparing Capitalisms to the Politics of Institutional Change."

13 Bruno Amable, *The Diversity of Modern Capitalism* (New York: Oxford University Press, 2003).

Others disagreed with the relatively static view presented in the initial VoC formulation.[14] Some political scientists argued that the role of the state as a potentially autonomous actor is missing and that interest-group politics are ignored.[15] Another view was that political bargains establish the institutions that shape firm-level coordination in the first place.[16] Finally, the degree to which institutions are actually complementary to one another has been called into question.[17]

A critical advantage of the VoC framework, however, is that it provides two simple, testable hypotheses, the answers to which transcend the framework itself. First, if a group of MNCs brings new forms of coordination to a particular country and becomes prominent market actors, we should expect institutional adjustments, particularly if the firms are moving from LMEs to CMEs. Second, if MNCs enter a CME to take advantage of the host country's comparative institutional advantage, upon entry this should be observable in their business models.

VoC Applied to Japan's Traditional Model:
Adding Government as an Actor

In applying the VoC framework to Japan, it immediately becomes clear that the role of the government was highly significant in establishing and sustaining the key national-level institutions. The institutions themselves were not the direct results of corporate political lobbying or policy infiltration, although in many cases business interests were served.

First, taking the variables from the VoC framework, we see that: (1) "Industrial relations" maps onto Japan's structure of enterprise-based unions: (2) "Worker skills" applies to Japan's meritocratic education system focusing on raising the mean achievement of students based on effort-based testing; (3) "Corporate governance" was historically based on the main-bank–centered governance system in which bank loan–centered

---

14 Colin Crouch, *Capitalist Diversity and Change: Recombinant Governance and Institutional Entrepreneurs* (New York: Oxford University Press, 2005).

15 Jackson and Deeg, "From Comparing Capitalisms to the Politics of Institutional Change."

16 Dan Breznitz and John Zysman "Introduction: Facing the Double Bind: Maintaining a Healthy and Wealthy Economy in the Twenty-First Century," in *The Third Globalization: Can Wealthy Nations Stay Rich in the Twenty-First Century?*, ed. Dan Breznitz and John Zysman (New York: Oxford University Press, 2013).

17 Robert Boyer, "Coherence, Diversity, and the Evolution of Capitalisms: The Institutional Complementarity Hypothesis," *Evolutionary and Institutional Economics Review* 2, no. 1 (2005): 43–80; Colin Crouch et al., "Dialogue on 'Institutional Complementarity and Political Economy,'" *Socio-Economic Review* 3, no. 2 (2005): 359–82.

financing was coupled with the banks' implicit guarantee against failure in exchange for exercising management control in times of duress ("contingent governance," as articulated by Aoki);[18] (4) "Interfirm relations" map onto *keiretsu* business structures; and (5) "Employees" refers to long-term employment and seniority wages.

The early origins of these institutions date from Japan's initial industrialization in the late 1800s. In the mobilization for war from about 1940 and in the early postwar period, specific political bargains established and sustained the institutions in the form described as the "Japanese model" of capitalism.

(1) Enterprise unions were initially formed by government initiatives that dissolved industry-based unions during mobilization for war.[19] They were further entrenched by the Allied Occupation government that reversed its initial support for labor unions as a force for democratization: unions were purged of suspected Communist sympathizers, preventing the development of broad interfirm unions.[20] Large firms, backed by the Ministry of Labor, limited union development before trans-industry ties were forged;[21] (2) The education system was reshaped by the Occupation government, which shifted the system away from training a small number of elite toward compulsory education through middle school, with a meritocratic, multi-tracked system in which students were differentiated by ability;[22] (3) The main-bank system grew out of the government's wartime mobilization effort that consolidated the number of commercial banks from over 1,400 in 1926 to 61 in 1945, assigned particular banks to industrial groups, and promoted bank consortia for long-term investment loans. In the early postwar period, the government promoted a bank-centered financial system that provided support for long-term credit banks and targeted investment projects;[23] (4) The cross-shareholdings underlying the *keiretsu* structures were the result of industrial policy by the Ministry of International Trade and Industry (MITI)

18 Masahiko Aoki and Hugh T. Patrick, eds., *The Japanese Main Bank System: Its Relevance for Developing and Transforming Economies* (New York: Oxford University Press, 1994).

19 Yukio Noguchi, "The 1940 System: Japan under the Wartime Economy," *American Economic Review* 88, no. 2 (1998): 404–7.

20 Peter Duus, *Modern Japan*, 2nd ed. (Boston: Houghton Mifflin, 1998).

21 Gregory Jackson, "The Origins of Nonliberal Corporate Governance in Germany and Japan," in *The Origins of Nonliberal Capitalism: Germany and Japan in Comparison,* edited by Kozo Yamamura and Wolfgang Streeck, 121–70 (Ithaca, NY: Cornell University Press, 2001).

22 Duus, *Modern Japan*, 266.

23 Noguchi, "The 1940 System"; Aoki and Patrick, *The Japanese Main Bank System.*

TABLE 8.2
Political origins of Japan's VoC characteristics

VoC Variables	Traditional Japanese Model	Political Origins of J-Model Characteristics
Industrial relations	Enterprise unions	Gov't support of enterprise-based unions
Worker skills	New hire generalists	Education system set up by gov't
Corporate governance	Main Banks	Gov't's strategic resource allocations, "convoy system"
Interfirm relations	*Keiretsu*	Gov't encouraged cross-shareholding for protection from foreign takeover
Employment system	Long-term employment, seniority wages	Pension and social security systems focused on employers to lower direct government costs

Source: Author.

in the 1960s. MITI revised the commercial code and provided strong administrative guidance for corporate groups to engage in cross-shareholdings for protection against potential foreign takeovers as Japan acceded to international organizations such as the OECD; (5) Long-term employment was strongly supported by the government in a social bargain to keep welfare costs low by focusing on stable employment in large enterprises. Long-term employment was also sustained by a series of judicial rulings that made it difficult for firms to fire employees (see table 8.2).[24]

There is a clear hand of government, particularly in the overall strategic focus, in the "developmental" model of capitalism centered on the financial system. The main-bank system was a central part of Japan's postwar growth strategy, with the government shaping the allocation of resources in the economy. Banks were shielded from bankruptcy through the "convoy" system of implicit government bailouts and government-orchestrated mergers for troubled banks. Coordination with the government was therefore one of the critical elements in firm-level coordination. The government itself was also an actor, in many cases acting with relative autonomy from the firm-level interests rather than simply reflecting corporate preferences. Therefore, in a variety of sectors strong government-industry coordination was critical to firm business, particularly in highly regulated sectors. For example, banks hired Ministry of Finance (MOF) "MOF-*tan*," that is, MOF handlers. Administrative guidance was delivered through interpersonal networks, and

24 Curtis J. Milhaupt, J. Mark Ramseyer, and Michael K. Young, *Japanese Law in Context: Readings in Society, the Economy, and Politics* (Cambridge: Asia Center, Harvard University, 2001): 384–98.

information exchanges went both ways through dense webs of interpersonal networks. We therefore need to add "government-industry coordination" to the set of VoC variables.[25]

Japanese firm coordination patterns are the basis of this model. The characteristics are stronger in some sectors than others and in some firms than others.

Japan's Emerging New Model and the "F Firm" Model

Recent scholarship has shown how these traditional institutions began to change substantially from the mid- to late 1990s. (1) Enterprise unions declined as union membership in general fell, partly fueled by the firms' increasing reliance on contract and temporary workers; (2) Labor markets shifted as the fluidity in mid-career hiring increased, spawning growing markets for headhunters and temporary agencies. In particular, sectors such as securities-related finance, information technology, and foreign firms in general were among the major employers of mid-career hires; (3) The main-bank system weakened as the importance of bank lending decreased for large healthy firms while it increased for less competitive and small and medium firms. Regulatory changes facilitated a greater diversity of corporate governance structures, such as the introduction of outside directors, executive board systems, and stock options; (4) The nature of the *keiretsu* changed as stable cross-shareholdings eroded, large firms reduced their levels of diversification, major mergers occurred between previously distinct groups, and firms adopted a greater openness toward business partners; and (5) Long-term employment was eroded as a series of court cases and changes to the Labor Standards Law removed much of the legal and doctrinal underpinnings of corporate obligations to maintain employment. Seniority wages shrank as firms increased their use of temporary and contract workers, and many firms incorporated some form of performance-based component to their wage structure (see table 8.3).[26]

25 Daniel I. Okimoto, *Between MITI and the Market: Japanese Industrial Policy for High Technology* (Stanford: Stanford University Press, 1989); Richard J. Samuels, *The Business of the Japanese State: Energy Markets in Comparative and Historical Perspective* (Ithaca, NY: Cornell University Press, 1987).

26 Vogel, *Japan Remodeled*; Ulrike Schaede, *Choose and Focus: Japanese Business Strategies for the 21st Century* (Ithaca, NY: Cornell University Press, 2008); Masahiko Aoki, Gregory Jackson, and Hideaki Miyajima, eds., *Corporate Governance in Japan: Institutional Change and Organizational Diversity* (Oxford: Oxford University Press, 2007); Harald Conrad, "From Seniority to Performance Principle: The Evolution of Pay Practices in Japanese Firms since the 1990s," *Social Science Japan Journal* 13, no. 1 (2010): 115–35.

TABLE 8.3

Japan's emerging new model, tracing VoC characteristics

VoC Variables	Traditional Japanese Model	Emerging New Japan Model
Industrial relations	Enterprise unions	Overall union decline
Worker skills	New hire generalists	Growing mid-career labor market
Corporate governance	Main Banks	Less bank dependence by large firms, greater diversity of governance structures
Inter-firm relations	*Keiretsu*	Traditional *keiretsu* weakened, cross-shareholding declined
Employment system	Long-term employment, seniority wages	Increased temporary and contract workers, performance component to wages
Government-industry relations	Dense formal and informal interpersonal networks	Greater formalization of interactions, decreasing importance of informal interpersonal networks

Source: Author.

Foreign firms are mostly at the forefront of this new emerging model, adopting practices that depart most clearly from Japan's traditional postwar model. In particular, firms in securities finance, such as the U.S. Wall Street firms Goldman Sachs, Merrill Lynch, and the now-defunct Lehman Brothers, along with European investment banks such as Deutsche Bank, BNP Paribas, and UBS Warburg, departed most dramatically from traditional Japanese corporate organizations and practices.[27] Since they are the most extreme cases, the VoC hypothesis would expect that they are also the most responsible for driving institutional changes supporting their mechanisms of coordination.

There is, of course, considerable heterogeneity among the practices of foreign firms. Some adopt structures and strategies closer those of their Japanese competitors, whereas others find that defying traditional organizations are their strategic strength. IBM Japan, for example, famously adopted a very Japanese corporate organization and succeeded. Nissan, on the other hand, actively reduced cross-shareholding and *keiretsu* ties once bought out by Renault, contributing to its dramatic recovery, but it did not engage in mass layoffs.

27 Mari Yamauchi, "Kinyū kikan ni okeru koyōseido no tayōsei" [Employment systems of financial institutions in Japan: Their varieties by capital, products, and individual strategies], *Japan Journal of Human Resource Management* 12, no. 1 (2010); Mari Yamauchi, " Tayōsei to shūren: Rīman shokku ikō no shōken gaisha ni okeru koyō seido no henka" [Convergence and divergence: Employment systems at Tokyo-based investment banks after the Lehman shock], *Mita Business Review* 54, no. 2 (2011).

TABLE 8.4

The "F Firm" model compared to the traditional "J Firm" model, VoC variables

VoC Variables	Traditional Japanese Model (Large J firm)	Stereotypical Foreign MNC in Japan
Industrial relations	Enterprise unions	No unions
Worker skills	Generalist new hires	Mid-career hires
Corporate governance	Main Banks	Shareholder, home headquarters
Interfirm relations	*Keiretsu*	Fluid relations
Employment system	Long-term employment, seniority wages	Short-term, performance- based wages
Government-industry relations	Informal interpersonal networks cultivated with government officials	Little reliance on ex-bureaucrats, willing to defy government

Source: Author.

It is worth specifying a stylized "F firm" model to clarify how it departs from the traditional stylized Japanese firm ("J firm") model. The F firm is characterized by: (1) no unions; (2) heavy reliance on mid-career hires; (3) rarely established or utilized main-bank relationships; (4) less reliance upon *keiretsu*, with little if any cross-shareholding, and; (5) no guarantee of long-term employment and performance-oriented pay. Moreover, the F firm is far more willing to defy the government's informal administrative guidance and is less interested in cultivating dense interpersonal networks (see table 8.4).

Let us now turn to the various sectors. Securities and banking, in which F firms depart most dramatically from traditional Japanese firms, will be examined in the greatest detail.

Banking and Securities

In the banking and securities sector, regulatory changes, driven by domestic politics, drove syncretism by enabling the introduction of new actors, new business models, and new patterns of coordination. Foreign MNCs took the most advantage of the new opportunities and profited greatly, but they were not the primary drivers of the regulatory change.

The traditional model entailed domination by large Japanese financial firms, with MOF compartmentalizing and strongly managing the sector. Japanese financial firms were the archetype for Japan's J firm organization and mechanisms of coordination. MOF shaped firm business models through formal and informal policy tools as part of the "developmental" state that limited foreign firms to a particular market segment.

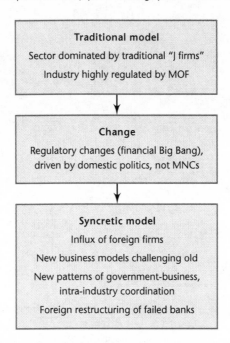

FIGURE 8.2 Syncretism in Japan's banking and securities sector
Source: Author.

The most dramatic change was the result of the regulatory shifts in the late 1990s—Japan's financial "Big Bang" policies promulgated under Prime Minister Hashimoto. The reforms were driven by domestic politics stemming from a series of scandals that seriously eroded the reputation and power of both MOF and domestic financial institutions. Reform occurred in the context of a banking crisis, and the perceived need among the political elite to make Japan's financial system more open, internationally relevant, and competitive.

In the new syncretic model, an influx of foreign MNCs introduced new business models and new patterns of interfirm and government-business coordination. Foreign actors were also responsible for the dramatic restructuring and turnarounds of several Japanese financial institutions. Domestic firms adjusted, but slowly, resulting in the simultaneous coexistence of the new, old, and hybrid in Japan's financial sector (see figure 8.2).

The Traditional Model: Foreign Firms Limited During the Heyday of the "Developmental State" (1950 to the late 1960s)

During most of Japan's high-growth era from the 1950s to the late 1960s, MOF compartmentalized the financial sector and exercised strong strategic control over the allocation of funding in the economy. Foreign banks were confined to a particular market segment, but they enjoyed a cartel-like status and did not push hard for change. During this period, the banking sector as a whole was essentially closed to new entrants and new business models.

In the early 1950s, foreign banks were limited to certain areas, including trade financing and foreign currency–related activities, but this was later expanded to a particular type of loan known as "impact loans"—medium-term foreign currency loans to Japanese firms. MOF used administrative guidance to protect these foreign market segments from entry attempts by Japanese firms. The number of foreign banks in Japan only increased from twelve to fifteen between 1951 and 1967. Though largely excluded from domestic policy processes, the foreign banks enjoyed profitable market niches and did not actively press for change.[28]

External Pressure for Foreign Entry, But Not From Foreign Firms Already in Japan (mid-1970s to the 1980s)

In the 1970s and 1980s, foreign financial institutions drawn to Japan's rapidly growing economy mobilized their home governments to pressure MOF to allow their entry.[29] This pressure was relatively successful, and the number of foreign banks grew from fifteen in 1967 to thirty-three in 1974. The increased level of competition, however, eroded the foreign firms' previous cartel-like profitability, driving them to enter new market segments such as securities and trust banking. Foreign pressures, both from foreign governments and from foreign firms partnering with Japanese firms to take advantage of regulatory loopholes, led to the Tokyo Stock Exchange (TSE) accepting foreign members.[30]

The MNCs already in Japan, however, did not strongly advocate deregulation. For example, early foreign TSE members, each having paid over one billion yen in direct fees and indirect costs to enjoy fixed commission rates, were opposed to new entries.[31]

The impact of foreign financial institutions was limited. There were eighty-two foreign banks in Japan by 1990, but almost none of them had widespread retail or business operations. Until 1999, foreign banks were

28 Louis W. Pauly, *Regulatory Politics in Japan: The Case of Foreign Banking* (Ithaca, NY: China-Japan Program, Cornell University, 1987): 17–19, 67–68; Kazuo Tatewaki, *Gaikoku ginko to Nihon: Zainichi gaigin hyaku-yonjunen no kobo* [Foreign banks and Japan: 140 years of battles by foreign banks in Japan] (Tokyo: Sotensha Shuppan, 2004).

29 For details, see Pauly, *Regulatory Politics in Japan*.

30 Henry Laurence, *Money Rules: The New Politics of Finance in Britain and Japan* (Ithaca, NY: Cornell University Press, 2001): 129–30.

31 Ibid., 132.

unable to join the industry association as full members. The number of foreign securities firms grew from one in 1972 to fifty-two in 1990, but they accounted for less than 10 percent of Japan's share trading volume. In trust banking, foreign firms were excluded from the positions of executive director and ordinary committee member in the Trust Company Association of Japan, and even with full membership they were not allowed to vote.[32]

Change: Financial Big Bang Reforms Enabling a Foreign Influx, New Market Dynamics (mid-1990s to the present)

The financial Big Bang reforms dramatically altered Japan's financial industry. They enabled new entries, deregulated business models by abolishing fixed commission rates, and removed the segmentation between market areas. Combined with the government move to abandon the "convoy" system as the non-performing loans crisis hit banks, foreign financial firms were major beneficiaries of the reforms.

The financial Big Bang reforms consisted of a variety of measures to deregulate and de-compartmentalize Japan's financial sector over a period of several years. It was essentially an omnibus bill, consisting of almost 1,000 pages, that revised twenty-four financial and tax laws. Passed in March 1998, it took effect in December of that year. (For details, see chapter 3 in this volume.)[33]

In contrast to Great Britain's financial Big Bang reforms in the 1980s, Japan's Big Bang reforms were not pushed by incumbent firms, either domestic or foreign. Whereas it was British brokerages lobbying the government to deregulate financial markets so they could compete against U.S. firms, Japan's reforms were not the direct results of lobbying by Japanese banks, securities firms, insurers, or foreign financial institutions.[34]

Lower entry barriers, such as registration rather than licensing for securities firms, and the de-compartmentalization of industry segments enabled a surge of new foreign entrants. For example, brokerages such as Charles Schwab, Signa International, American Express, Bank One, and others rushed into the market immediately following the 1998 deregulation.[35]

32 Kushida, "Inside the Castle Gates," 67.

33 For a comprehensive political analysis, see Tetsuro Toya, *The Political Economy of the Japanese Financial Big Bang: Institutional Change in Finance and Public Policymaking* (New York: Oxford University Press, 2006).

34 Laurence, *Money Rules.*

35 TDB, *TDB Report: Gyoukai doukou 1999-II* [TDB report: Industry developments 1999-II] (Tokyo: Teikoku Databank, 1999): 19.

The government's abandonment of the convoy system also facilitated foreign expansion. In 1997, MOF allowed Yamaichi Securities, one of Japan's "big four" brokerages, to collapse. Targeting Japanese household assets, Merrill Lynch purchased thirty-three retail branches and hired about 2,000 of the approximately 7,500 former Yamaichi employees.[36] In 1999, Salomon SmithBarney created a joint venture with troubled Nikko Securities, creating Nikko Salomon Smith Barney, which became quite successful, and captured 59 percent of the equity underwriting market by 2000.[37]

Syncretism: New, Old, and Hybrid Business Models and Organizations

In the securities sector, the deregulation of brokerage commission fees advantaged foreign firms; they could deploy their global business models, whereas Japanese firms were forced to rework their core business models. Japanese securities brokerages had been focused on attaining volume, since brokerage commission-fee rates were fixed by regulatory statute. U.S. and European firms had developed new products and services following the U.S. and UK deregulations of the 1980s.

Brokerage commission fees in Japan were deregulated gradually beginning in 1994, culminating in a complete deregulation by 1998 as part of the Big Bang reforms. Within three months of the 1994 deregulation of trades larger than 1 billion yen, commission fees dropped by one-half as brokerages competed over price.[38] A month after the 1996 deregulation on trades exceeding 50 million yen, Daiwa Securities, the second-largest Japanese firm, saw commission revenue drop by one-fourth. A 2001 poll of the 200 largest brokerages found an average decline in commission-fee revenue of 20 percent since 1999, and over 70 percent since 1994.[39]

Foreign financial firms excelled in introducing products and expertise to Japan's new securities markets. For example, in convertible bonds, foreign firms quickly topped the list of trades and issuances. Their program trading algorithms were widely deemed superior, offering far greater

36 In 2002, however, unable to make the enterprise profitable, Merrill closed all but two branches, losing an estimated US$900 million over four years. Lawrence White, "Asia: Is Japan Still a Tough Nut to Crack?" *Euromoney* 38, no. 453 (2007): 134–37.

37 Thomson Financial Securities Data, cited in Ani Hadjian Laura, "Nikko Salomon Logs a Stellar First Half In Japan, Which Leaves Rivals Frothing," *Investment Dealers' Digest* 66, no. 26 (2000): 3–4.

38 Shinhua Liu, "Commission Deregulation and Performance of Securities Firms: Further Evidence from Japan," *Journal of Economics and Business* 60, no. 4 (2008): 355–68.

39 "Brokerage Commissions Still Declining," *The Nikkei Weekly*, March 26, 2001.

flexibility and speed. Their advanced computer systems were capable of conducting large basket trades (trades involving a portfolio of multiple shares and bonds), leading even Japanese brokerages to place orders with the foreign firms.[40] Foreign research analysts also offered data and evaluations to institutional investors, services not traditionally provided by Japanese brokerages.[41]

Foreign financial firms leveraged their global footprints to aid Japanese firms raise equity finance abroad. Critically, they also had longstanding relationships with foreign institutional investors that flowed into Japanese equity markets. In March 1997, 11.9 percent of the total shares (by market value) of all listed companies in Japan were held by foreigners, but by 2005, this number had climbed to 23.3 percent. In terms of volume traded, foreigners accounted for 19.9 percent of stock transactions in 1996 and 39.3 percent in 2005.[42]

As the profits of foreign financial firms soared, Japanese brokerages struggled. In 1996, the operating profits of the Japanese members of the Japan Securities Dealers Association (JSDA) dropped 40 percent from the previous year, while those of foreign securities firms grew a whopping 21-fold.[43] In 2000, the total operating income for the 238 domestic firms dropped 23 percent, reflecting a 45 percent drop in commission revenues, whereas the total operating income of the fifty foreign firms rose 33 percent, with revenue increasing by 44 percent.[44] (Despite the subprime bubble that led to the 2008 full-scale crisis among global firms, the Japanese market had limited exposure to these products. Foreign financial firms do not disclose their revenue breakdown, but employees contend that most revenue of the Japanese branches of foreign financial firms was from operations within the Japanese market.)

40 Basket trades were often used in the late 1990s to quietly unwind cross-shareholdings. If it became clear that a major shareholder was unwinding, speculation could drive down share prices, reducing the value of the shares that the firm was attempting to unwind.

41 Interview with investment banker who wished to remain anonymous. Tokyo, Japan.

42 TSE, *TSE Factbook 2008* (Tokyo Stock Exchange, 2008), accessed April 25, 2013, http://www.tse.or.jp/english/market/data/factbook/index.html.

43 TDB, *TDB Report: Gyōkai dōkō 1998-I* [TDB report: Industry developments 1998-I] (Tokyo: Teikoku Databank, 1998): 370.

44 TDB, *TDB Report: Gyōkai dōkō 2002-I* [TDB report: Industry developments 2002-I] (Tokyo: Teikoku Databank, 2002): 22. In 1999, small and medium firms, of which an estimated 80 percent relied primarily on commission revenues, began going out of business. TDB, *TDB Report: Gyōkai dōkō 1999-II*, 18.

Foreign trust banks, which had struggled after Japan's asset bubble burst in 1990, experienced a major surge.[45] After 1998, Japan's financial Big Bang reforms enabled foreign trust banks to offer dollar-denominated overseas investment trusts. Combined with Japan's low interest rates and banking crisis, this led to an inflow of Japanese savings; between 1998 and 1999, despite an overall shrinkage of Japanese corporate pension funds entrusted to major Japanese trust banks, the nine foreign trust banks recorded a combined 30 percent increase in corporate pension fund assets.[46] In the first half of fiscal year 1998, total assets held by foreign trusts increased by approximately 40 percent.[47] A particularly successful dollar-denominated investment trust developed by LTCB Warburg took in 50 billion yen in its first week.[48] By late 2004, a survey revealed that foreign institutions took 26.5 percent of all shares of funds managed by investment trusts, investment advisers, and pension funds, totaling 147 trillion yen, an increase of 80 percent since 1997.[49]

New Interfirm Coordination: The Rise of Foreign Firms as "Suppliers." Deregulation also fueled new relationships between foreign and major Japanese financial firms. In 1999, the Ministry of Health and Welfare removed most restrictions on asset mobilization for welfare pension funds. Each fund could select its own investment advisory firm, and the range of investment products and destinations was considerably broadened. Funds seeking higher returns rushed to find higher yielding investments overseas, fueling demand by Japanese financial institutions for the expertise of foreign trust banks and investment advisers.

Japanese banks, trust banks, insurers, and even securities firms were among those that sought partnerships with foreign firms. For example, Sumitomo Bank and Daiichi Kangyo Bank created tie-ups with Templeton and JP Morgan, respectively. Sumitomo Trust Bank partnered with Chase Manhattan. Japan's largest life insurer, Japan Life, entered a tie-up with Deutsche Bank, Yasuda Life with PaineWebber, and Yasuda Fire and Marine with Signa International. New joint ventures were created as well,

---

45 For details, see Kushida, "Inside the Castle Gates," 94–95.

46 Makoto Satō, "Realignments Sweep Trust-bank Sector: Government Push to Speed Disposal of Bad Loans Adds to Impetus for Change," *The Nikkei Weekly*, January 25, 1999.

47 TDB, *TDB Report: Gyōkai dōkō 1999-II*, 31.

48 "Foreign Innovations Lure Investors: Financial Institutions Tailor Higher Yielding Instruments to Japanese Individuals' Aversion to High Risk," *The Nikkei Weekly*, August 31, 1998.

49 Cerulli Associates calculations based on data from the Investment Trusts Association, the JSDA, the Japan Securities Investment Advisers Association, and other sources.

including Prudential-Mitsui Trust Investments, Nomura BlackRock Asset Management, Meiji Dresdner Asset Management, and others.

New Patterns of Government-Business Relations: Foreign Firms Driving Disruptive Challenges. Foreign financial firms, particularly in the fast-moving securities sector, spearheaded new patterns of government-business relations by challenging the government in new ways.

One pattern was to defy informal political pressures. In the summer of 2000, Goldman Sachs was summoned to the National Diet to testify about an issue surrounding the bankruptcy of Sogo, a major department store chain. As adviser to the government in selling Sogo's main bank to an American investment fund, Goldman allegedly had not advised the government of the risk of the foreign-managed bank to returning soured debt to the government, though Goldman contended that the Financial Services Agency (FSA) had asked to insert a clause allowing this. The issue was politically sensitive since the government appeared to have subsidized a foreign investment bank to profit by allowing a major employer to fail. Upon consulting its lawyers, Goldman found that the Diet had no authority to compel testimony, so it refused.[50]

Another pattern was to take advantage of areas of regulatory ambiguity. In 2005, Lehman Brothers enabled Livedoor, an aggressive Japanese Internet start-up firm, to engage in a hostile M&A of a venerable broadcasting corporation by utilizing after-hours acquisitions on an off-exchange system operated by the TSE.[51] Although Livedoor's bid eventually failed, Lehman's controversial role became a topic of political discussion regarding how far Japan's economic system should be reformed using "Anglo-American" elements.

A third pattern was to defy informal bureaucratic guidance. When MOF attempted to create a strengthened securities investor protection fund in 1998 to protect investors against bankruptcies such as that of Yamaichi, foreign firms refused to join. They discovered that although fund membership was mandatory, nowhere in the regulatory structure did it stipulate that only one fund could exist. Foreign firms therefore went ahead and created their own parallel fund. This left Japan with two parallel securities investor protection funds—the Japan Investor Protection Fund with 241 members

---

50 Gillian Tett, *Saving the Sun: A Wall Street Gamble to Rescue Japan from its Trillion-dollar Meltdown* (New York: HarperBusiness, 2003): 212–16.

51 This theoretically circumvented the securities-rules requirement that an acquisition of greater than one-third of a public company be conducted through tender offers open to all shareholders. Curtis J. Milhaupt, "In the Shadow of Delaware? The Rise of Hostile Takeovers in Japan," *Columbia Law Review* 105 (2005): 2179.

comprised of Japanese financial institutions, and the Securities Investor Protection Fund with 51 foreign member institutions—until 2002 when the two were merged.[52]

Finally, foreign firms precipitated the collapse of a longstanding Japanese industry organization simply by exiting. The TSE Participants' Association, essentially a political donation fund, had once been a significant link between the securities industry and politicians.[53] As their market presence grew, foreign firms were required to pay a greater proportion of the association's fees, but they were dissatisfied with their low level of voice in the organization. In late 2003, Morgan Stanley, discovering that membership was not mandatory, withdrew, followed by other major foreign brokerages. This created an exodus of Japanese firms as well, plunging the association into financial distress and eventually, in the following summer, it was dissolved.[54] A coordinated withdrawal from a voluntary organization, although always a possibility, had never been acted upon in this way or in this magnitude.

Bank Restructuring and Reform by Foreign Investment Funds

As Japan's banking crisis hit in the late 1990s and the government abandoned the convoy system, several ailing or failed Japanese banks were sold to foreign investment funds. Under new management, these banks substantially transformed their business models and organizational structures. Two former long-term credit banks and two regional banks were sold, and although the foreign investment funds initially raised some political and societal concern, they were later largely regarded as saviors, injecting capital and management expertise to spark reform.

The Long-Term Credit Bank (LTCB), which had supported Japan's postwar recovery and growth, became insolvent in 1998 despite restructuring, downsizing, an attempted tie-up and buyout deal with Swiss Bank Corporation and Sumitomo Bank, and a government injection of 170 billion yen earlier that year.[55] By October 1998 it was nationalized.

52 For details, see Kushida, "Inside the Castle Gates."

53 In 2000, it contributed 100 million yen, in 2001 95 million yen, and in 2002 and 2003 75 million yen each, in addition to 10 million yen worth of party ticket purchases. These amounts ranked just below the contribution levels by major industry associations—the Japan Automobile Manufacturers' Association and the Japan Iron and Steel Federation. Kushida, "Inside the Castle Gates."

54 "Seijikenkin, kakusha goto ni, madoguchi ipponka wo shōkenkai minaoshi— Gaku wo kaiji no kaishamo" [Political donations reported on individual company basis: Securities industry association to revise consolidated donation window, considering reporting amounts], *Nihon Keizai Shimbun*, March 20, 2004.

55 Vogel, *Japan Remodeled*, 179–81.

The government, keen to avoid the traditional convoy approach (which would have entailed a takeover by the historically close Dai-Ichi Kangyo Bank or the Industrial Bank of Japan) sold LTBC to Ripplewood Holdings in March 2000 for approximately 121 billion yen.

The new bank that began operations in June 2000, renamed Shinsei, departed sharply from prevailing banking practices. Under a new president whose previous career had included work in a foreign oil company and at Citibank, Shinsei moved away from traditional retail banking. The traditional centralized, hierarchical corporate structure was flattened and decentralized. New employees and teams were hired from outside, many of them from foreign financial institutions operating in Japan, such as Citigroup, Lehman Brothers, and Bear Stearns. The Fujitsu IT system was overhauled by a team of Indian IT experts brought in from the outside who created a new modular server architecture. The new president demanded better quantitative risk assessments and monthly revenue data, which the LTCB previously had neither quantified rigorously nor collected frequently.[56] It also implemented a two-tiered compensation scheme. "Permanent staff" enjoyed higher job security but lower pay, whereas "market staff," mostly mid-career hires and foreigners, received higher pay in return for lower job security. Women were allowed to apply for and were given managerial posts, a departure from previous norms.[57]

Nippon Credit Bank (NCB) was also nationalized in 1998 following scandals and a failed government bailout.[58] Initially sold to a consortium of Japanese firms in 2000 and renamed Aozora Bank, it was resold in 2002 to Cerberus, a politically well-connected U.S. investment fund. The sale to Cerberus had political support, as Prime Minister Koizumi's trusted economic reformer Heizō Takenaka, who was in charge of financial, economic, and fiscal policy, actively encouraged foreign participation in Japan's banking-sector reforms; in his view, foreign firms were valuable allies in reforming Japan's financial system.[59]

Reforms at Aozora, mostly enacted before Cerberus took over, were less dramatic than those undertaken by Shinsei or Tokyo Star. Aozora's restructuring relied on ties with its owners and established partnerst. For example, in overhauling and operating its IT system, Aozora contracted Hitachi, with which it had a longstanding relationship; Aozora launched an online

56 Tett, *Saving the Sun*, 197–204.
57 Vogel, *Japan Remodeled*, 182–83. For more, see Kushida, "Inside the Castle Gates."
58 For details, see Kushida, "Inside the Castle Gates."
59 Personal interview, June 2011.

consultancy on an M&A run jointly by Softbank Orix and Tokio Marine & Fire. Aozora also formed ties with California-based Silicon Valley Bank, which specialized in start-up firms.

Two failed regional banks, Tokyo Sowa Bank and Kofuku Bank, were sold to U.S. private equity fund Lone Star and a partnership led by WL Ross & Co., respectively. In January 2001, Lone Star won the bid against Shinsei Bank, Orix, and the Cerberus Group, renaming the bank Tokyo Star Bank and restructuring it extensively. Installing a young American as president, it jettisoned previous operating manuals, replaced the IT system by using primarily Indian engineers located in Tokyo and Bangalore, and shifted workflows. Branches were reorganized to provide a consumer-friendly space, and some new products, such as deposit-linked mortgages, were introduced.[60] Tokyo Star Bank took mid-career hires for foreign currency deposits and investment trust operations, in which it lacked expertise, and introduced outside personnel in its marketing and public relations departments. It also introduced performance-based salaries.[61]

Kofuku Bank, a second-tier Osaka-based regional bank, which became insolvent in 1999, subsequently came under government management. A partnership led by WL Ross & Co. purchased the bank in 2000, renaming it Kansai Sawayaka Bank and transitioning it away from traditional relational banking practices. With the help of the Boston Consulting Group, Kansai Sawayaka focused on retail loans to small and medium businesses in the Kansai area. It partnered with a consumer loan company and became the first mainstream bank in the region to offer unsecured loans at higher interest rates (5–14 percent), a niche previously reserved for the consumer finance–market segment.[62] It reduced the number of branches and implemented new employee incentives, such as stock ownership and stock options.[63]

The turnaround in performance of these banks was significant during most of the 2000s until the onset of the 2007–8 global financial crisis. In most cases, the foreign owners exited with substantial profits. Shinsei went public, Tokyo Star was acquired by a Japanese investment fund, Kansai Sawayaka Bank was sold to a larger regional bank, and Aozora became profitable.

60 Tim Clark and Carl Kay, *Saying Yes to Japan: How Outsiders are Reviving a Trillion Dollar Services Market* (New York: Vertical, 2005): 44–46.

61 "Foreign Funds Changing Regional Banks," *The Nikkei Weekly*, September 2, 2002.

62 "Kansai Sawayaka Bank Focused on Unsecured Loan Business," *The Nikkei Weekly*, April 15, 2002.

63 American Chamber of Commerce in Japan, "Kansai Sawayaka Bank (KS Bank): FDI to the Rescue."

Summary

In sum, foreign firms in Japan's banking and securities sectors did not drive the regulatory changes that reshaped the dynamics of competition. They introduced new products, services, practices, organizational structures, and mechanisms of coordination with the government, but they did so as a result of regulatory changes that enabled them to do so. They entered Japan not to take advantage of Japan's pre-existing comparative institutional advantage, but to take advantage of potential new advantages enabled by the reforms, to which Japanese competitors were slow to adjust. The most significant regulatory changes were driven by domestic politics.

Telecommunications

In telecommunications, the pattern of syncretism and change was similar to that in finance, though somewhat less dramatic. Regulatory changes, driven by domestic factors, drove syncretism by enabling new actors to introduce new business models and mechanisms for coordination.

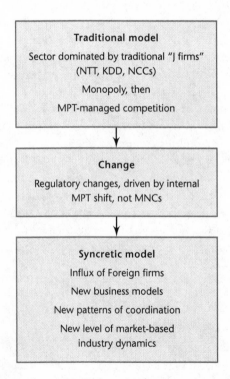

FIGURE 8.3 Syncretism in Japan's telecommunications sector
Source: Author.

The traditional model through much of the postwar era had entailed government-owned monopoly carriers with a closed set of Japanese equipment suppliers. After liberalization in the mid-1980s, foreign MNCs were limited to specific, relatively peripheral, sectors.

Change came in the form of regulatory changes during the mid- to late 1990s that essentially enabled foreign firms to enter all areas of the sector and to introduce new business models. This was driven primarily by a shift in the regulatory priorities of the Ministry of Posts and Telecommunications (MPT) as Japan's telecommunications sector was falling behind in international competition.

The new syncretic model (see figure 8.3) entailed a dramatically higher foreign presence in core areas of the sector, new business models, and new government-business coordination. Foreign firms were not the most significant drivers of change, however, as new Japanese entrants also took advantage of the new regulatory possibilities, and the change came *after* regulatory shifts enabled new entry.

The Traditional: Foreign Firms Limited Before and After Liberalization (1985–mid-1990s)

The telecommunications infrastructure and services in Japan were in the hands of a state-owned monopoly, similar to the situation in most other countries, until liberalization in 1985. Nippon Telegraph and Telephone (NTT) operated domestic telephony while Kokusai Denshin Denwa (KDD) monopolized international telephony. They procured equipment from a stable set of suppliers known as the "NTT family," consisting of NEC, Hitachi, Fujitsu, and Oki, along with numerous smaller firms, all of which competed for procurement orders. As a key part of Japan's developmental strategy, the focus of telecommunications was to build the technological competency of Japanese electronics firms, with NTT subsidizing R&D efforts by manufacturers.[64] The market was essentially closed to outsiders, both domestic and foreign.

In the late 1970s, the U.S. firm Motorola mobilized the U.S. government to sell pagers to NTT. Its strategy, which succeeded by the early 1980s, was to join the closed group of "NTT family" firms rather than to push for open procurement procedures.[65]

64 See Marie Anchordoguy, "Nippon Telegraph and Telephone Company (NTT) and the Building of a Telecommunications Industry in Japan," *Business History Review* 75, no. 3 (Autumn 2001): 507–41.

65 Laura D'Andrea Tyson, *Who's Bashing Whom? Trade Conflicts in High-Technology Industries* (Washington, DC: Institute for International Economics, 1992): 66–67.

In 1985, a complex domestic political process resulted in ending the NTT and KDD monopolies, along with a regulatory structure that compartmentalized and limited competition. Foreign firms were limited to specific industry segments and prohibited from owning extensive infrastructure. The first global carriers in Japan, such as AT&T, British Cable & Wireless, and France Telecom, served foreign MNCs operating in Japan to provide international and data services. In the areas of satellite and cellular services, after political battles involving home-country diplomatic pressures, foreign participation was allowed, but it was limited to minority stakes in operators and providing equipment.[66]

Change: Telecommunications "Regime Shift" Reforms— Enabling a Foreign Influx and Reorganizing Market Structures

Japan's telecommunications regulatory structure underwent a major shift in the mid- to late 1990s. MPT was de-compartmentalized, largely deregulating pricing and enabling foreign investment in infrastructure.[67] The shift mainly reflected changing views within the ministry regarding the merits of freer competition, in part a reaction to the advent of the Internet and the rapid decline of Japanese firms in international equipment markets. Neither external pressures nor corporate lobbying were the main drivers.

Japan's deregulation of foreign network ownership occurred in 1998 after Japan entered the World Trade Organization (WTO) Telecommunications Agreement. This, too, was driven primarily by domestic factors rather than lobbying by foreign firms. MPT officials, concerned that NTT, though privatized, dominated the sector and stifled competition, welcomed foreign entrants to facilitate competition. Moreover, MPT wanted Japanese firms to have access to overseas markets, since foreign governments, for instance the United States, insisted on reciprocal access.[68]

Foreign MNCs immediately rushed into Japan in a variety of areas. Some focused on international services; in 1998 U.S. carrier Worldcom was awarded a class one telecoms operating license, and Global One and Pacific

---

66 For details, see Kushida, "Inside the Castle Gates."

67 For details, see Kenji E. Kushida, "Japan's Telecommunications Regime Shift: Understanding Japan's Potential Resurgence," in *How Revolutionary was the Digital Revolution? National Responses, Market Transitions, and Global Technology in the Digital Era*, ed. John Zysman and Abraham Newman (Stanford: Stanford Business Books, 2006): 125–47.

68 Yuko Suda, *Tsūshin gurobaru ka no seijigaku: "Gaiatsu" to Nihon no denki tsūshin seisaku*, Shohan ed. [The politics of globalization in telecommunications: "External pressure" on Japanese policies] (Tokyo: Yūshindō Kōbunsha, 2005).

Gateway Exchange entered to lay trans-Pacific fiber optic networks. In 1999, British Cable & Wireless won an unprecedented bidding war over IDC, a Japanese international carrier, against NTT. Other foreign firms became Internet Service Providers (ISPs). The American firm PSINet purchased Japanese ISPs Rimnet and Tokyo Internet, becoming the second largest competitor to NTT for business users. Foreign firms also invested in domestic telecommunications services; in 1999 British Telecom and AT&T purchased shares of Japan Telecom, one of NTT's largest competitors. By mid-2002, twenty-five foreign carriers had registered as infrastructure-owning carriers.

In a related area, the deregulation of foreign ownership of cable television in 1995 enabled J:Com, a foreign-managed cable company, to expand its business, becoming the largest cable company in Japan. In 1997 and 1999, it expanded to telephony and Internet services, respectively.[69]

In communications equipment, Silicon Valley–based Cisco Systems, which dominated global Internet infrastructure markets, captured 70 to 80 percent of Japan's market for Internet routers as the market grew from 55 billion yen in 1995 to 202 billion yen in 2002.[70]

New Business Models, New Mechanisms of Coordination, and New Market Dynamism

Vodaphone's Japan Adventure.   The entry of British carrier Vodafone into Japan spearheaded a major industry shift. Vodafone entered in 2001 through the largest M&A deal in Japan's history at that time by purchasing Japan Telecom, which owned J-Phone, one of Japan's three nationwide cellular carriers. Unlike the troubled banks discussed above, J-Phone was enjoying several years of rapid growth, having pioneered color displays and camera-embedded handsets that could email pictures. Therefore, Vodafone's strategy was not to bring about a turnaround, but rather to take advantage of the know-how in J-Phone's mobile Internet platform and to introduce something similar in its European markets. It did so with its VodafoneLive! offering to become the largest European cellular Internet service provider at the time.

Vodafone attempted to orchestrate a major change in Japan's mobile handset industry structure by linking Japan's domestic manufacturers with global markets. Domestic manufacturers had been stuck in the domestic

69 Kushida, "Inside the Castle Gates."

70 Tatsuo Tanaka and Reiko Murakami, "Network Externalities in the Japanese Market of Routers," Competition Policy Research Center Discussion Paper, Fair Trade Commission of Japan, no. 1-E (2003), accessed April 25, 2013, http://www.jftc.go.jp/en/cprc/discussionpapers/1-e_abstract.html.

market competing against one another for procurement orders from Japanese carriers, but their handsets were incompatible with global markets. Vodafone offered its Japanese manufacturers access to all of Vodafone's global markets by producing global model handsets for Vodafone. However, unfortunately for Vodafone, in Japan's advanced but proprietary domestic market the global model handsets were actually a step backwards in performance and features. Consumers fled from Vodafone, and the company ended up exiting Japan in 2006.

Dynamism in Japan's Telecommunications Industry. In entering and exiting, however, Vodafone provided an unprecedented opportunity for the Japanese telecommunications market by facilitating dynamic ownership changes. First, after initially purchasing Japan Telecom, Vodafone reorganized the company under a holding company and sold off the landline business to the U.S. investment fund Ripplewood. Ripplewood then sold Japan Telecom to Softbank, an aggressive upstart firm that had brought Nasdaq to Japan as a joint venture, and purchased the failed Nippon Credit Bank (renamed Aozora). Ripplewood's profits from the transaction were estimated at about 90 billion yen, and Japan Telecom's original long-term shareholders are unlikely to have sold their shares directly to Softbank, often viewed by large established firms with suspicion.[71] When Vodafone exited Japan, Softbank purchased its cellular operations through Japan's largest leveraged buyout at that time. Softbank therefore became one of the three major Japanese cellular carriers through market mechanisms that had been unavailable only a few years earlier.[72]

In a similar move on a smaller scale, investment fund Carlyle purchased 60 percent of another Japanese wireless carrier, DDI Pocket, in mid-2004.[73] After initial growth based on data services, the company, renamed Willcom, was out-competed by other wireless carriers and ended up in bankruptcy in early 2010. Carlyle lost approximately US$330 million,[74] but Softbank pur-

71   For further details, see Kenji E. Kushida, "Leading Without Followers: How Politics and Market Dynamics Trapped Innovations in Japan's Domestic 'Galapagos' Telecommunications Sector," *Journal of Industry, Competition and Trade* 11, no. 3 (2011): 279–307.

72   Ibid. Vodafone's exit was not entirely a failure since it raised an amount similar to what it had paid to enter and invest in its Japanese operations.

73   For details, see Kenji E. Kushida, "Wireless Bound and Unbound: The Politics Shaping Cellular Markets in Japan and South Korea," *Journal of Information Technology and Politics* 5, no. 2 (2008): 231–54.

74   Alison Tudor, "Bankruptcy by Willcom Stings Carlyle," *Wall Street Journal*, February 19, 2010, 1, accessed April 25, 2013, http://online.wsj.com/article/SB200014240527 48703315004575072830634735458.html.

chased the bankrupt company and refocused it on low-cost voice communications, leading to another increase in subscribers. Softbank also gained access to a precious wireless spectrum, which it can potentially use for other services.

New Patterns of Government-Business Coordination: Suing the Government, but Not Driven by Foreign Firms. Spearheading new patterns of government-business coordination, NTT's competitors and some foreign firms banded together to sue the ministry in charge of telecommunications—the first such lawsuit in the industry. Spearheaded by KDDI, the major competitor to NTT, the 2003 lawsuit was a signal designed to show the government the industry's willingness to use the judicial branch as an arena for policymaking.

Five telecommunications carriers, including KDDI, Japan Telecom, Poweredcom, Cable & Wireless IDC, and Fusion Communications (Japan Telecom and Cable and Wireless IDC each had foreign presidents), sued the minister of the Ministry of Internal Affairs and Communications (MIC) over the issue of interconnection fees charged by NTT for access to its network. MIC's approval of increased interconnection rates, the first time such an increase had been approved, triggered the lawsuit. Although the lawsuit was dismissed two years later, the firms considered it a success, since the possibility of such lawsuits deterred MIC from discretionary policymaking. More importantly, both the industry and MIC could avoid political intervention in network policy on behalf of NTT.[75]

Summary

Thus, in telecommunications the traditional model of Japanese carriers and a closed set of equipment manufacturers shifted dramatically after the regulatory changes of the mid-1990s. These regulatory changes were driven primarily by changes in domestic regulatory preferences. Foreign firms, previously kept out of the infrastructure business, became major players. They contributed to new competitive dynamics whereby firms could be bought and sold, with Vodafone's entry and exit resulting in a new Japanese entrant becoming the third largest telecommunications firm. Syncretism resulted, in which NTT retained a dominant market presence with a traditional organization, whereas its competitors, both domestic and foreign, engaged in a variety of strategies through varying organizational structures, forging new patterns of government-industry coordination.

75 Personal Interviews, former MIC officials, KDDI executive, Tokyo and Stanford, 2008, 2011.

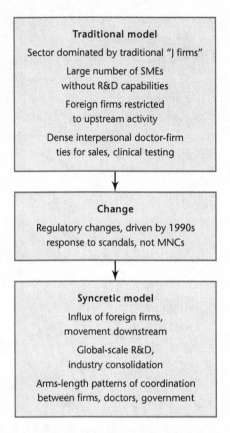

FIGURE 8.4 Syncretism in Japan's pharmaceuticals sector
Source: Author.

Pharmaceuticals

In the pharmaceutical sector as well, regulatory changes, driven by domestic politics, drove syncretism by shifting business models, government-industry coordination, intra-industry coordination, and allowing foreign MNCs, which had had a long historical presence in upstream activities, a full range of activities in the industry.

The traditional model for most of the postwar period had limited foreign firms to upstream activities, providing raw materials and licensing compounds.

Change was driven by regulatory shifts—shifts that were incremental in the 1980s but far more pronounced during the 1990s. The regulatory shifts during the 1990s were a response to political dynamics created by a series of scandals involving government ties to pharmaceutical firms and industry practices.[76] The regulatory shifts changed the dynamics of competition in the domestic market to the benefit of foreign firms.

The syncretic model became clear as foreign firms moved into the downstream activities of sales, marketing, distribution, and manufacturing. They brought globally developed products and employed professional workforces, many of which were mid-career hires, thereby becoming the largest pharmaceutical firms operating in Japan. They displaced major and medium-sized Japanese firms, most of which had depended on licenses or off-patent products and had to reconfigure their sales forces to comply with the new regulations. Thus, after the regulatory changes, new, old, and hybrid models coexisted (see figure 8.4).

Foreign firms were interested in the Japanese market primarily because of its size, second only to that in the United States. But market size was even larger than simple population or economic proportions vis-à-vis the United States since the regulatory structure created strong incentives for doctors to prescribe relatively large quantities of pharmaceutical products. Direct institutional features and industry-level coordination were not the primary considerations.

Historical Restrictions Limiting Foreign Participation to Upstream Activities

From the inception of Japan's modern pharmaceutical sector, foreign firms were limited to upstream activities, providing new materials and licensing products to Japanese manufacturers.

In both the prewar and immediate postwar periods, acute shortages of foreign products upon which the nation depended led the government to orchestrate the entry of a large number of small and medium firms that first imported bulk ingredients from foreign producers, then combined them locally, and finally sold the resultant products in the domestic market. By the 1950s, such firms numbered over one thousand, and few possessed their own R&D capabilities.[77]

Japan's pharmaceutical market was attractive to MNCs as it grew rapidly from half a trillion yen in sales in 1965 to one trillion yen in sales in 1970 and then quadrupled by 1980.[78] However, a variety of regulatory restrictions

76 This section draws heavily from Kushida, "Inside the Castle Gates."

77 Makoto Noguchi, *Yoku wakaru iyakuhin gyōkai* [Understanding the pharmaceutical industry] (Tokyo: Nihon Jitsugyo Shuppansha, 2003): 14–15.

78 Robert Neimeth, "Japan's Pharmaceutical Industry Postwar Evolution," in *The Changing Economics of Medical Technology*, ed. Annetine C. Gelijns and Ethan Halm (Washington, DC: National Academy Press, 1991): 161.

limited MNCs to upstream activities. From the 1950s through most of the 1960s, the Japanese government strategically leveraged regulations, such as the Foreign Exchange Control Law, to force MNCs to form (often multiple) joint ventures or licensing agreements for distribution and sales.[79] Foreign investments in Japanese pharmaceutical firms were prohibited until a 50 percent limit was set in 1967. This was raised to 100 percent in 1975. Before the 1980s, foreign MNCs were restricted from critical activities, such as applying for clinical testing and manufacturing.

The industry dynamics also hindered foreign MNC operations in Japan. First, sales activities were highly labor intensive and time consuming. The health-care delivery system, consisting of hospitals and clinics, was highly fragmented, and pharmaceutical firms competed for procurement orders from doctors, who both prescribed and dispensed pharmaceuticals. Second, wholesale distribution networks were complex and fragmented. This mattered in terms of providing volume discounts, since Japan's National Health Insurance (NHI) system set the prices for doctors' fees and the retail prices of pharmaceuticals; therefore wholesalers sold discounted products to doctors, who could then earn a "doctors' margin." Third, and arguably most critically, Japan's pre-clinical and clinical trials required proprietary procedures and data generated in Japan, the result of the Ministry of Health and Welfare (MHW) reacting to a major worldwide scandal in the 1960s (birth defects from thalidomide) due to insufficient testing. MHW allocated clinical trials to prominent university professors, with whom applicant firms had no direct formal contact. For further explanation or information concerning rejected applications, informal interpersonal networks were critical, prompting MNCs to form partnerships with Japanese firms.[80]

Regulatory Changes Enabling the Surge of Foreign MNCs, Shifting Industry Dynamics

Regulatory shifts in the 1990s and the reactions to scandals and some foreign pressures led to greater formalization in the coordination among actors.

---

79 Pfizer entered by creating a joint venture with Tanabe in 1953 and with Daito in 1955. Ciba (now part of Novartis), which had been exporting to Japan from 1870 to the early 1900s through Takeda, entered in 1952. Other entrants in the 1950s included Schering, Lederle, and Roussel, followed in the 1960s by Sandoz, Bristol Myers, Hoechst, and Merck.

80 Nagami Kishi, *Gaishi kei seiyaku kigyō gekidō no jidai* [The era of upheaval, foreign pharmaceutical firms] (Tokyo: Nihon Noritsu Kyōkai Manejimento Sentā, 1996): 136–41.

In the early 1990s, partly resulting from the U.S.-Japan bilateral Structural Impediments Initiative talks, and directly following a Japan Fair Trade Commission ruling in 1992, pharmaceutical firms were prohibited from negotiating prices with doctors. Instead, wholesalers became the exclusive price negotiators with doctors, dramatically reducing the intensity of labor in pharmaceutical firms' sales practices.[81] From about 1999, wholesaler networks became far simpler due to a major consolidation as they faced increased price pressures, both as the negotiators of prices with doctors and hospitals and after MHW's reimbursement price reductions in the 1990s.[82]

A major scandal in 1996 due to informal government-business ties decreased the legitimacy of informal interpersonal networks. The scandal involved pharmaceutical firms, employing retired MHW bureaucrats in upper management, using HIV-tainted blood for transfusions. This was despite the availability of treatment processes and in disregard of internal MHW study group warnings.

Informal doctor-pharmaceutical firm ties were also professionalized. In 1997 the Japan Pharmaceutical Manufacturers' Industry Association (JPMA) implemented a standardized testing and accreditation system for sales forces, known as medical representatives (MRs). Thereafter, many university and general hospitals prohibited non-accredited salespeople from soliciting staff doctors. This benefited the MNCs in that they did not have to invest in large general sales forces but could provide rapid specialist responses to doctors' queries.

Japan's procedures for clinical trials shifted toward international standards beginning in the 1980s and accelerating in the 1990s. A 1983 revision of the Pharmaceutical Affairs Law allowed foreign firms to apply for clinical testing directly. The "market-oriented sector-selective" (MOSS) talks resulted in allowing foreign pharmaceutical firms to exit from existing partnerships with Japanese firms, thereby facilitating their moves downstream.[83]

Japan's involvement in the International Conference on Harmonization (ICH), founded in 1990 to standardize clinical testing, led to considerably

81 Noguchi, *Yoku wakaru iyakuhin gyōkai*, 84–88.

82 By 2007, membership of the Japan Pharmaceutical Wholesalers Association had declined to 129, from 486 in 1985, and the 129 members were largely comprised of four major wholesalers and their subsidiaries. Ralph Paprzycki and Kyoji Fukao, *Foreign Direct Investment in Japan: Multinationals' Role in Growth and Globalization* (New York: Cambridge University Press, 2008): 181.

83 Aki Yoshikawa, "The Other Drug War: U.S.–Japan Trade in Pharmaceuticals," *California Management Review* 31, no. 2 (1989): 83.

relaxed local data requirements.[84] Most notably, a 1998 reform enabled limited use of overseas clinical test results, spawning a market for outsourced overseas clinical testing.[85] The 2005 revision of the Pharmaceutical Affairs Law simplified clinical approval processes, further relaxing data requirements. Global-scale pharmaceutical MNCs were the main beneficiaries.

From the 1980s, MHW aggressively began cutting pharmaceutical reimbursement prices, a result of Japan's broader health-care politics. Put simply, the government wanted to cut health-care expenditures but the doctors' association was too powerful to cut doctors' fees, leading the government to reduce reimbursement prices for pharmaceuticals.[86] With base prices at 100 in 1980, they fell to 53 by 1989.[87] MHW continued to lower prices, with decreases of 10 percent every year in 1996, 1997, and 1998, and another 7 percent in 1999, 6 percent in 2002, and 4 percent in 2004.[88] Beginning in 1996, as MHW reduced prices it also began to significantly shift the relative weight, more rapidly reducing the prices of older products and "knock-offs." This favored MNCs that tended to have newer products, and it hurt small and medium Japanese pharmaceutical firms, with few R&D resources, that had been protected by high reimbursement prices even after their patents

84 ICH brought together the industry associations and regulatory agencies of pharmaceutical manufacturers in Europe, the United States, and Japan. Members include the European Federation of Pharmaceutical Industries and Associations (EFPIA), the U.S. Food and Drug Administration (FDA), Pharmaceutical Research and Manufacturers of America (PhRMA), Japan's Ministry of Health, Labor, and Welfare (MHLW), and the Japan Pharmaceutical Manufacturers Association (JPMA).

85 This occurred through contract research organizations (CROs) after the 2005 revision of the Pharmaceutical Affairs Law. Sales totaled 15.6 billion yen in 2000, employing approximately 1,700 people, grew fourfold to 61 billion yen sales in 2004 with almost 5,700 employees, and reached 113 billion yen by 2009 with almost ten thousand employees. With the proportion of foreign firms employing CROs at approximately 30 percent, the rapid growth of this industry represents a major reduction in the internal organizational investments necessary for foreign firms to engage in clinical testing procedures.

86 For details, see Kushida, "Inside the Castle Gates"; John Creighton Campbell and Naoki Ikegami, *The Art of Balance in Health Policy: Maintaining Japan's Low-cost, Egalitarian System* (New York: Cambridge University Press, 1998): 108–11.

87 Neimeth, "Japan's Pharmaceutical Industry: Postwar Evolution," 161.

88 TDB, *TDB Report: Gyōkai dōkō 2000-II* [TDB report: Industry developments 2000-II] (Tokyo: Teikoku Databank, 2000): 209; TDB, *TDB Report: Gyōkai dōkō 2003-I* [TDB report: Industry developments 2003-I] (Tokyo: Teikoku Databank, 2003): 223; TDB, *TDB Report: Gyōkai dōkō 2005-I* [TDB report: Industry developments 2005-I] (Tokyo: Teikoku Databank, 2005): 225.

had expired.[89] Although foreign MNCs had been advocating such regulatory changes for decades, the timing was determined by domestic politics.

The Surge of Foreign MNCs: Moving Downstream. By the late 1990s, the dynamics of competition within Japan's domestic pharmaceutical sector—pricing, sales and distribution, and clinical testing—had shifted significantly, facilitating the expansion of MNCs into the downstream activities of sales and distribution.

Global mergers occurred throughout the 1990s, widening the gap in scale between Japanese firms and global MNCs. By 2001, global sales and R&D capabilities of the largest multinationals, such as Pfizer, Glaxo SmithKline, and Merck, dwarfed those of the major Japanese firms, to say nothing of the medium-sized Japanese firms.

Foreign MNCs surged into the Japanese market by several means. First, they exited historical partnerships, a movement that accelerated in the late 1990s. For example, in 1985 Ciba-Geigy, which had been contracting sales to Takeda and Fujisawa, began selling independently. Also in the 1980s, Bayer separated from Takeda, Sund from Sankyo, and SmithKline Beecham from Fujisawa. By the early 2000s, most foreign firms had shifted to selling their own products on their own.[90] The dissolution of partnerships was highly detrimental to medium-sized Japanese firms. For example, in 1998, after Pharmacia dissolved its partnership with Sumitomo Seiyaku, the latter's sales dropped by one-quarter within one year.[91]

Second, MNCs expanded their sales forces through new graduate and mid-career hires. For example, between 2000 and 2001 Pfizer hired over 600 people, followed by another 600 in 2002. Many of these new employees were mid-career hires from Japanese pharmaceutical firms.[92] In stark contrast to the entire history of the industry until the late 1990s, by 2000 foreign firms sported the largest presence of salespeople in the industry. In 2000 the size of the sales forces representing Pfizer, Merck, Glaxo SmithKline, Novartis,

89 For example, Eizai and Daiichi Tanabe relied on older products for almost 40 percent of their sales, and Chugai for 30 percent of sales. For mid-sized firms Mochida, Kyorin, and Kissei, reliance on older products was above 70 percent. By the mid-2000s, the prices for generics and other knock-offs were reduced to 15 to 70 percent of the original product, averaging about 50 percent. Paprzycki and Fukao, *Foreign Direct Investment in Japan,* 177.

90 Noguchi, *Yoku wakaru iyakuhin gyōkai,* 46–47.

91 "Gaishikei ga tainichi kōsei wo kakeru iyakuhin bijinesu gekihen no shōgeki" [The shock to pharmaceutical businesses caused by foreign firms on the offensive in Japan], *Shukan Daiamondo* (2002): 52–54.

92 "Nippon kōryaku Faizā hahiru: MR tsugitsugi hikinuki, uriagedaka mokuhyō kokunai toppu" [Pfizer rushes to capture Japan, hires away MRs, aims for top sales in the domestic market], *Nikkei Sangyo Shimbun,* June 11, 2002.

TABLE 8.5

*Number of salespeople ("MR"s) in the top
foreign and Japanese pharmaceutical firms*

Top Foreign Firms	MRs	Top Japanese Firms	MRs
Pfizer	1,700	Takeda	1,350
Banyu (Merck)	1,476	Sankyo	1,240
Glaxo SmithKline	1,300	Yamanouchi	1,300
Novartis	1,300	–	–
Astra Zeneca	1,300	–	–
Boehringer Ingelheim	600	–	–
Pharmacia	700	–	–

Source: Adapted from "Gaishikei ga tainichi kōsei wo kakeru iyakuhin bijinesu
gekihen no shōgeki" [The shock to pharmaceutical businesses caused by foreign
firms on the offensive in Japan], *Shukan Daiamondo* (2002): 52–54. Citing Japan
Pharmaceuticals Manufacturing Association.

TABLE 8.6

M&A activity in pharmaceuticals

	Multinational Firm	Japanese M&A Target
1983	Merck	Banyu
1998	BASF (Germany)	Hokuriku Seiyaku
	AkzoNobel (Netherlands)	Kanebo's Pharma Divison
2000	UCB (Belgium)	Fujirebio
	Boehringer Ingelheim (Germany)	SS Pharmaceutical
2001	Schering (Germany)	Mitsui Pharmaceutical
	Abbott Laboratories (US)	BASF/Hokuriku Seiyaku
2002	Roche	Chugai

Source: Author.

and Astra Zenaka equaled or exceeded that of the largest Japanese firms,
Takeda, Sankyo, and Yamanouchi (see table 8.5).

Third, foreign MNCs acquired numerous medium-sized firms to increase their domestic sales forces and wholesale distributions networks. The
earliest such move was Merck's purchase of Banyu in 1983, but the wave of
major buyouts began in earnest in 1998, with Boehringer Ingelheim's purchase of SS Pharmaceutical and Roche's purchase of Chugai. These were
not bailouts, since although the Japanese firms sported reasonably strong
sales and wholesale networks, they were relatively weak in R&D. In several
cases, such as the relatively strong Banyu and Chugai, MNCs did not replace top management, instead granting relative autonomy (see table 8.6).

Summary

In pharmaceuticals, the traditional model of limiting foreign MNCs to upstream activities had been eroding over time, but this erosion drastically accelerated in the 1990s, driven by domestic political and bureaucratic scandals. Many of the regulatory shifts, such as globalizing clinical testing procedures, had been advocated by foreign MNCs for years, but the timing was due to domestic political factors.

The new, syncretic model was shaped by foreign MNCs expanding their operations in Japan through various means to become among Japan's largest players, coexisting with the traditional large-, small-, and medium-sized Japanese pharmaceutical firms that still depended on traditional business models and that lacked R&D capabilities.

Automobiles

In the automobile sector, regulatory changes enabled foreign entry beginning in the 1980s, but it was not until the market crises among Japanese manufacturers in the late 1990s that there was a major influx of foreign MNCs.

The traditional model consisted of MITI's infant industry protection measures that restricted inward FDI and imports, thereby promoting domestic firms. Subsequent regulatory changes reduced formal barriers to entry for foreign firms, leading to some early tie-ups.

The syncretic model developed as troubled Japanese firms entered into major tie-ups with foreign firms, receiving capital infusions and ceding management control. Some of the foreign firms significantly restructured their existing organizations and business models.

The Traditional Model: A Strategically Closed Industry

The heyday of MITI's industrial policy toward the Japanese automobile industry began in the late 1940s and lasted until about 1970. Japan's prewar automobile industry had been dominated by Ford and GM, but in the immediate postwar period, the Japanese government rescued domestic firms teetering on collapse.[93]

---

93 Despite some internal disputes, MITI carried the day, and the government offered direct support through the Bank of Japan (BOJ) and bank loans from the Japan Development Bank (JDB) and the Industrial Bank of Japan (IBJ). It was only with this support that Nissan, Toyota, and Isuzu were able to survive. Michael A. Cusumano, *The Japanese Automobile Industry: Technology and Management at Nissan and Toyota* (Cambridge: Council on East Asian Studies, Harvard University, 1985): 19.

MITI segmented the market, protected it from foreign imports and FDI, and nurtured Japanese firms.[94] MITI did, however, facilitate some tie-ups between Japanese and foreign firms for technology transfers.[95]

Regulatory Reforms Enabling Foreign Entry, but J Firms Outcompeting

Trade pressures from the U.S. government in the 1960s, mobilized by the U.S. "Big Three" auto firms, reduced the Japanese government's explicit protection of the domestic market. In 1970, foreign equity investment ceilings were lifted and foreign firms rushed to form capital tie-ups with Japanese firms. Also in 1970, Chrysler, contributing 15 percent, was involved in creating Mitsubishi Motors as a joint venture with Mitsubishi Heavy Industries. In 1971, GM purchased 34.1 percent of Isuzu, which had faced financial collapse. In 1979, Ford acquired 24.5 percent of Mazda after the latter was rescued by its main bank, Sumitomo Bank, and had returned to profitability in 1976.

However, the Big Three failed to gain substantial market shares in Japan. They pointed to non-tariff barriers, which still existed to some degree. At the same time, however, Japanese pointed out that although large American cars were popular as status symbols, many of the small and medium American cars suffered quality problems throughout the 1980s and lacked many of the mass-market features optimized for Japanese parking and driving conditions (folding side mirrors, for example).

94 MITI segmented the market through automobile manufacturing licenses, foreign exchange allocations, and by setting import taxes to restrict imports. It privileged the "Big 5" domestic auto companies, including Nissan, Toyota, and Isuzu, Hino Motors, and Mitsubishi Heavy Industries. A second set of manufacturers specializing in small cars and three-wheeled vehicles—Toyo Kogyo (later to become Mazda), Daihatsu, Fuji Heavy Industries (later to become Subaru), Suzuki, and Mitsubishi—received less support. Akira Kawahara, *The Origin of Competitive Strength: Fifty Years of the Auto Industry in Japan and the U.S.* (New York: Springer, 1998): 9–10.

95 The tie-ups included: In 1952, Nissan with the British firm Austin, and in 1953, Isuzu with Rootes (another British firm), Hino with Renault, and Mitsubishi with Willy-Overland (an American firm). All four tie-up contracts prohibited the Japanese partner from exporting their cars. Three of the four contracts ended in 1960 (Mitsubishi's ended in 1958), though some were extended. For Nissan, the tie-up lasted seven years, for Isuzu, twelve years after an extension, for Hino, eleven years after an extension, and for Mitsubishi, ten years after an extension. Toyota was the only Big 5 manufacturer that chose to avoid a partnership.

The Syncretic Model: J Firm Management Crises Drive
Foreign Entry Opportunities and Restructuring

Market developments took a dramatic turn in the mid- to late 1990s, leading to a major foreign influx. As economic stagnation slowed growth of the automobile market and the high yen hurt the profitability of exports, several firms faced financial crises. Foreign auto firms entered Japan to an extent that had been unthinkable in the previous decades to turn around the major auto firms. Three major tie-ups, between Renault and Nissan, Ford and Mazda, and DaimlerChrysler and Mitsubishi Motors, led to different degrees of restructuring and new business practices.

Renault and Nissan: The Paradigmatic Revival.   Following Renault's 1999 purchase of a 37 percent stake in Nissan for approximately US$5.4 billion, Nissan's turnaround under management control by Renault was dramatic.

By the late 1990s, Nissan was teetering on the edge of bankruptcy due to factors such as aggressive product and dealer expansion in the United States, miscalculations regarding dealer valuations in the United States, poor differentiation among its products, high debt, and damage inflicted by depreciation of the yen. It incurred losses for six of the seven years until 1998.[96] Its main banks, Fuji Bank and the Industrial Bank of Japan, also facing extensive non-performing loans, rejected potential bailouts. Following unsuccessful talks with DaimlerChrysler and Ford, Nissan negotiated with Renault, which was willing to inject massive capital in return for complete management control. Renault sent Carlos Ghosn, a Brazilian-born Frenchman of Lebanese descent, to become Nissan's president in 2000 and CEO in 2001.

Ghosn restructured Nissan extensively. Supplier chains were reorganized and the number of suppliers was reduced from 1,145 in 2000 to 595 in 2002. Nissan closed a major manufacturing plant and worked with unions to offer early retirement or transfers to other plants. The workforce in the entire group was reduced by approximately 15,000 people, and the company also poached a chief designer from Isuzu, an unprecedented move in the Japanese auto industry. Nissan sold many of its assets, including real estate, to repay its debts. By sharing product development elements, for instance vehicle platforms, with Renault and by combining purchasing operations, Nissan reduced its procurement costs by 20 percent. In overseas operations, Renault

---

96 Daniel Arturo Heller, "An Inquiry into the Role of Interfirm Relationships in Recent Organizational Change Initiatives in Japanese Automobile Firms," *Shinshū Daigaku Keizaigaku Ronshū* [Shinshū University Economic Review], no. 49 (2003): 45–88.

and Nissan shared plants. By 2002 Nissan had reached its performance targets one year ahead of schedule, becoming profitable and eliminating its interest-bearing debts. Overall, Ghosn implemented dramatic but successful reforms without resorting to massive layoffs.

Ford and Mazda: A Major Turnaround Under the Radar. In 1996 Ford expanded its tie-up with Mazda and strengthened its management control. By the mid-1990s, Mazda was facing a crisis due to factors such as dealer overexpansion and a lack of hit products. Mazda logged operating losses for three consecutive years from 1993 to 1996. Its main bank, Sumitomo, which had brought Mazda and Ford together in the past, in late 1993 once again called upon Ford and invited it to examine Mazda's books.[97] In 1996 Ford doubled its executives on Mazda's board, increased its stake to 33 percent (for an estimated US$ 480 million), and appointed a Ford executive as CEO of Mazda. Mazda became the first Japanese auto firm to have a foreign CEO. Several other Ford executives and groups of mid-level engineers and managers were also dispatched to Mazda.

Restructuring at Mazda, although extensive, was less dramatic than that at Nissan. Mazda's production plans were frozen and were examined by Ford-dispatched management, subsidiaries were reduced by one-half between 1999 and 2000 (34 to 17), and cost-cutting measures, such as expense reductions and exchange-rate exposure hedges, were pursued. Mazda rebranded itself, internal divisions were reorganized, and a major voluntary retirement program led to a reduction of over 2,000 personnel. The reform had the dramatic slogan "change or die," and English was adopted as the primary internal language for top-level meetings. In 2002, numerous new products were released, returning the firm to profitability.[98] In the meantime, Ford learned from Mazda some aspects of supplier management, particularly in terms of quality and delivery.[99]

DaimlerChrysler and Mitsubishi Motors: Difficulties and Failure. Not all foreign management takeovers of Japanese auto firms were successful, however. In 2000 DaimlerChrysler (the result of a de facto acquisition of Chrysler by

97 Daniel Arturo Heller, "The Rebirth of Mazda Under Ford's Shadow," in *The Second Automobile Revolution: Trajectories of the World Carmakers in the 21st Century*, edited by Michel Freyssenet, 129–40 (Basingstoke: Palgrave Macmillan, 2009).

98 Heller, "An Inquiry into the Role of Interfirm Relationships in Recent Organizational Change Initiatives in Japanese Automobile Firms"; Heller, "The Rebirth of Mazda Under Ford's Shadow."

99 James R. Lincoln and Michael L. Gerlach, *Japan's Network Economy: Structure, Persistence, and Change* (New York: Cambridge University Press, 2004): 337.

Daimler in 1998) purchased a controlling 33.4 percent stake of Mitsubishi Motors, which was also facing a crisis.

In stark contrast to Renault's management team, the DaimlerChrysler executives failed to stage a dramatic turnaround of Mitsubishi Motors. In 2003 it incurred losses and in the following year a major scandal erupted when it was revealed that the management of Mitsubishi Motors had been covering up serious defects for over a decade. Refusing Mitsubishi's request for a new injection of capital, DaimlerChrysler divested in 2005. As part of the exit deal, it acquired 85 percent of Mitsubishi's truck division, spinning it off as Mitsubishi Fuso Truck and Bus.[100]

New Patterns of Interfirm Coordination: A Market for Japanese Auto Firms. The entry of MNCs facilitated the reorganization of the automobile sector, entailing an unprecedented marketization of firms in the sense that they could be bought, split apart, and sold. As Nissan divested its *keiretsu* relationships, it sold Nissan Diesel, a trucking company, to Volvo. In 2007, the latter made the trucking company into a wholly owned subsidiary, paying just over US$1 billion.

The sudden exit of GM from its investments in Japanese firms created shockwaves in the sector, especially among firms in which the company had invested. GM's exit demonstrated how factors relatively unrelated to the Japanese market could precipitate major exogenous shifts in MNC strategies in Japan. In the mid- to late 2000s, facing higher gas prices and a collapse in demand for its core revenue-producing large vehicles, GM confronted a financial crisis. As its need to raise operating capital became acute in 2005, GM sold its entire 49 percent stake in Isuzu in 2006, a stake it had held since 1999 when it had raised its level of ownership. By 2008 it had sold its remaining shares.

GM's sudden exit from its Japanese investments and partnerships in 2005 and 2006, as it faced its own crisis, led to a realignment of capital holdings and relationships among Japanese auto firms. Toyota purchased a large proportion of GM's stake in Fuji Heavy Industries, and GM suddenly sold off all of its shares of Fuji Heavy Industries (Subaru), much to the surprise and shock of the latter. Toyota then cultivated deep production ties with Subaru and also became a major shareholder of Isuzu, after GM sold its 49 percent stake, and integrated many of its operations with Toyota's Hino truck division. After GM lowered its 20 percent stake in Suzuki to 3 percent

100 Holm-Detlev Köhler, "From the Marriage in Heaven to the Divorce on Earth: The DaimlerChrysler Trajectory since the Merger," in *The Second Automobile Revolution*, ed. Freyssenet, 309–31.

in 2006 (selling off the rest in 2008), Suzuki entered into a partnership with Volkswagen, receiving a 20 percent investment in early 2010.

Summary

In automobiles, unlike in other sectors, regulatory shifts alone did not precipitate an immediate influx of foreign firms. It was only in the 1990s, when Japanese firms faced serious financial crises, did foreign firms enter in dramatic fashion. Strong firms, mainly Toyota, retained their traditional J-firm organization as a competitive strength, but those taken over by foreign firms, particularly Nissan, restructured extensively and introduced new practices and organizational structures, thereby taking on a syncretic form.

Conclusion

Analysis of the sectors that received the largest influxes of foreign direct investment clearly shows that foreign MNCs were the drivers of syncretism in Japan's political economy. Although this chapter is necessarily a truncated view of a more detailed study, it still clearly shows that many MNCs introduced new norms, practices, and organizations into a variety of Japanese sectors. These sectors experienced an influx of new, residual old, and hybrids as many of the older players adjusted.

Major regulatory shifts provided opportunities for new business models and organizational structures. Yet, in contrast to Hall and Soskice's VoC hypothesis, foreign MNCs, though benefitting most from the reforms, were not the primary drivers and the foreign MNCs that already had a presence in Japan did not push hard for change. In most cases, the influx followed regulatory shifts driven by domestic political dynamics that were specific to each sector.

In addition, in contrast to the VoC hypothesis about the movement of MNCs, foreign MNCs did not enter Japan to take advantage of the country's traditional "comparative institutional advantages." Instead, in most cases, it was the new regulatory structures that created a new set of competitive dynamics that were attractive to the MNCs. In several sectors, such as finance and pharmaceuticals, the foreign MNCs could introduce global products and services into the Japanese market in ways that they could not previously, thereby giving them competitive advantages in Japan. Their successes contributed to the syncretic model, as many Japanese competitors were forced to adjust and adapt to some degree, resulting in far greater diversity.

References

Amable, Bruno. *The Diversity of Modern Capitalism*. New York: Oxford University Press, 2003.

American Chamber of Commerce in Japan. "Kansai Sawayaka Bank (KS Bank): FDI to the Rescue," at http://www.accj.or.jp/doclib/fdi/1069040587.pdf, last accessed August 2010.

Anchordoguy, Marie. "Nippon Telegraph and Telephone Company (NTT) and the Building of a Telecommunications Industry in Japan." *Business History Review* 75, no. 3 (Autumn 2001): 507–41.

Aoki, Masahiko, Gregory Jackson, and Hideaki Miyajima, eds. *Corporate Governance in Japan: Institutional Change and Organizational Diversity*. Oxford: Oxford University Press, 2007.

Aoki, Masahiko, and Hugh Patrick, eds. *The Japanese Main Bank System: Its Relevance for Developing and Transforming Economies*. New York: Oxford University Press, 1994.

Berger, Suzanne, and Ronald Dore, eds. *National Diversity and Global Capitalism*. Ithaca, NY: Cornell University Press, 1996.

Boyer, Robert. "The Diversity of Institutions Governing the 'New Economy': Against Technological Determinism." Seminar on Institutional Complementarity. Paris, 2002.

———. "Coherence, Diversity, and the Evolution of Capitalisms: The Institutional Complementarity Hypothesis." *Evolutionary and Institutional Economics Review* 2, no. 1 (2005): 43-80.

"Brokerage Commissions Still Declining." *The Nikkei Weekly*, March 26, 2001.

Campbell, John Creighton, and Naoki Ikegami. *The Art of Balance in Health Policy: Maintaining Japan's Low-Cost, Egalitarian System*. New York: Cambridge University Press, 1998.

Campbell, John L. *Institutional Change and Globalization*. Princeton: Princeton University Press, 2004.

Clark, Tim, and Carl Kay. *Saying Yes to Japan: How Outsiders Are Reviving a Trillion Dollar Services Market*. New York: Vertical, 2005.

Conrad, Harald. "From Seniority to Performance Principle: The Evolution of Pay Practices in Japanese Firms since the 1990s." *Social Science Japan Journal* 13, no. 1 (2010): 115–35.

Crouch, Colin. *Capitalist Diversity and Change: Recombinant Governance and Institutional Entrepreneurs*. New York: Oxford University Press, 2005.

Crouch, Colin, Wolfgang Streeck, Robert Boyer, Bruno Amable, Peter A. Hall, and Gregory Jackson. "Dialogue on 'Institutional Complementarity and Political Economy.'" *Socio-Economic Review* 3, no. 2 (2005): 359–82.

Cusumano, Michael A. *The Japanese Automobile Industry: Technology and Management at Nissan and Toyota.* Cambridge: Council on East Asian Studies, Harvard University, 1985.

Duus, Peter. *Modern Japan*, 2nd ed. Boston: Houghton Mifflin, 1998.

"Foreign Funds Changing Regional Banks." *The Nikkei Weekly*, September 2, 2002.

"Foreign Innovations Lure Investors: Financial Institutions Tailor Higher Yielding Instruments to Japanese Individuals' Aversion to High Risk." *The Nikkei Weekly*, August 31, 1998.

"Gaishikei ga tainichi kōsei wo kakeru iyakuhin bijinesu gekihen no shōgeki" [The shock to pharmaceutical businesses caused by foreign firms on the offensive in Japan]. *Shukan Daiamondo* (2002): 52–54.

Hadjian, Ani Laura. "Nikko Salomon Logs a Stellar First Half in Japan, Which Leaves Rivals Frothing." *Investment Dealers' Digest* 66, no. 26 (2000): 3–4.

Hall, Peter A., and David Soskice, eds. *Varieties of Capitalism: The Institutional Foundations of Comparative Advantage.* New York: Oxford University Press, 2001.

Heller, Daniel Arturo. "An Inquiry into the Role of Interfirm Relationships in Recent Organizational Change Initiatives in Japanese Automobile Firms." *Shinshū Daigaku Keizaigaku Ronshū* [Shinshū University Economic Review], no. 49 (2003): 45–88.

———. "The Rebirth of Mazda under Ford's Shadow." In *The Second Automobile Revolution: Trajectories of the World Carmakers in the 21st Century*, edited by Michel Freyssenet, 129–40. Basingstoke: Palgrave Macmillan, 2009.

Jackson, Gregory. "The Origins of Nonliberal Corporate Governance in Germany and Japan." In *The Origins of Nonliberal Capitalism: Germany and Japan in Comparison,* edited by Kozo Yamamura and Wolfgang Streeck, 121–70. Ithaca, NY: Cornell University Press, 2001.

Jackson, Gregory, and Richard Deeg. "From Comparing Capitalisms to the Politics of Institutional Change." *Review of International Political Economy* 15, no. 4 (2008): 680–709.

"Kansai Sawayakai Bank Focused on Unsecured Loan Business." *The Nikkei Weekly*, April 15, 2002.

Kawahara, Akira. *The Origin of Competitive Strength: Fifty Years of the Auto Industry in Japan and the U.S.* New York: Springer, 1998.

Kishi, Nagami. *Gaishi kei seiyaku kigyō gekidō no jidai* [The era of upheaval, foreign pharmaceutical firms]. Tokyo: Nihon Noritsu Kyoukai Manejimento Senta, 1996.

Köhler, Holm-Detlev. "From the Marriage in Heaven to the Divorce on Earth: The DaimlerChrysler Trajectory since the Merger." In *The Second Automobile Revolution : Trajectories of the World Carmakers in the 21st Century*, edited by Michel Freyssenet, 309–31. Basingstoke: Palgrave Macmillan, 2009.

Kushida, Kenji E. "Japan's Telecommunications Regime Shift: Understanding Japan's Potential Resurgence." In *How Revolutionary Was the Digital Revolution? National Responses, Market Transitions, and Global Technology in the Digital Era*, edited by John Zysman and Abraham Newman, 125–47. Stanford: Stanford Business Books, 2006.

———. "Wireless Bound and Unbound: The Politics Shaping Cellular Markets in Japan and South Korea." *Journal of Information Technology and Politics* 5, no. 2 (2008): 231–54.

———. "Inside the Castle Gates: How Foreign Multinational Firms Navigate Japan's Policymaking Processes." Ph.D. diss., University of California, Berkeley, 2010.

———. "Leading without Followers: How Politics and Market Dynamics Trapped Innovations in Japan's Domestic 'Galapagos' Telecommunications Sector." *Journal of Industry, Competition and Trade* 11, no. 3 (2011): 279–307.

Laurence, Henry. *Money Rules: The New Politics of Finance in Britain and Japan*. Ithaca, NY: Cornell University Press, 2001.

Lincoln, James R., and Michael L. Gerlach. *Japan's Network Economy: Structure, Persistence, and Change*. New York: Cambridge University Press, 2004.

Liu, Shinhua. "Commission Deregulation and Performance of Securities Firms: Further Evidence from Japan." *Journal of Economics and Business* 60, no. 4 (2008): 355–68.

Milhaupt, Curtis J. "In the Shadow of Delaware? The Rise of Hostile Takeovers in Japan." *Columbia Law Review* 105 (2005): 2171–216.

Milhaupt, Curtis J., J. Mark Ramseyer, and Michael K. Young. *Japanese Law in Context: Readings in Society, the Economy, and Politics*. Cambridge: Asia Center, Harvard University, 2001.

Neimeth, Robert. "Japan's Pharmaceutical Industry Postwar Evolution." In *The Changing Economics of Medical Technology*, edited by Annetine C. Gelijns and Ethan Halm, 155–67. Washington, DC: National Academy Press, 1991.

"Nippon kōryaku Faizā hahiru: MR tsugitsugi hikinuki, uriagedaka mokuhyō kokunai toppu" [Pfizer rushes to capture Japan, hires away MRs, aims for top sales in the domestic market]. *Nikkei Sangyo Shimbun*, June 11, 2002, 13.

Noguchi, Makoto. *Yoku wakaru iyakuhin gyōkai* [Understanding the pharmaceutical industry]. Tokyo: Nihon Jitsugyo Shuppansha, 2003.

Noguchi, Yukio. "The 1940 System: Japan under the Wartime Economy." *American Economic Review* 88, no. 2 (1998): 404–7.

North, Douglass. *Institutions, Institutional Change and Economic Performance.* New York: Cambridge University Press, 1990.

Okimoto, Daniel I. *Between MITI and the Market: Japanese Industrial Policy for High Technology.* Stanford: Stanford University Press, 1989.

Paprzycki, Ralph, and Kyoji Fukao. *Foreign Direct Investment in Japan: Multinationals' Role in Growth and Globalization.* New York: Cambridge University Press, 2008.

Pauly, Louis W. *Regulatory Politics in Japan: The Case of Foreign Banking.* Ithaca, NY: China-Japan Program, Cornell University, 1987.

Pempel, T.J., and K. Tsunekawa. "Corporatism without Labor? The Japanese Anomaly." In *Trends toward Corporatist Intermediation*, edited by Philippe C. Schmitter and Gerhard Lehmbruch, 231–70. London: Sage, 1979.

Samuels, Richard J. *The Business of the Japanese State: Energy Markets in Comparative and Historical Perspective.* Ithaca, NY: Cornell University Press, 1987.

Satō, Makoto. "Realignments Sweep Trust-Bank Sector: Government Push to Speed Disposal of Bad Loans Adds to Impetus for Change." *The Nikkei Weekly*, January 25, 1999.

Schaede, Ulrike. *Choose and Focus: Japanese Business Strategies for the 21st Century.* Ithaca, NY: Cornell University Press, 2008.

"Seijikenkin, Kakusha goto ni, madoguchi ipponka wo shōkenkai minaoshi: Gaku wo kaiji no kaishamo" [Political donations reported on individual company basis: Securities industry association to revise consolidated donation window, considering reporting amounts]. *Nihon Keizai Shimbun*, March 20, 2004, 4.

Streeck, Wolfgang, and Kathleen Ann Thelen, eds. *Beyond Continuity: Institutional Change in Advanced Political Economies.* New York: Oxford University Press, 2005.

Suda, Yūko. *Tsūshin gurobaru ka no seijigaku: "Gaiatsu" to Nihon no denki tsūshin seisaku* [The politics of globalization in telecommunications: "External pressure" on Japanese policies]. Shohan ed. Tokyo: Yūshindō Kōbunsha, 2005.

Tanaka, Tatsuo, and Reiko Murakami. "Network Externalities in the Japanese Market of Routers." Competition Policy Research Center Discussion Paper, Fair Trade Commission of Japan no. 1-E (2003), at http://www.jftc.go.jp/en/cprc/discussionpapers/1-e_abstract.html, accessed April 25, 2013.

Tatewaki, Kazuo. *Gaikoku ginkō to Nihon: Zainichi gaigin hyaku-yonjūnen no kōbō.* [Foreign banks and Japan: 140 years of battles by foreign banks in Japan]. Tokyo: Sotensha Shuppan, 2004.

TDB. *TDB Report: Gyōkai dōkō 1998-I* [TDB report: Industry developments 1998-I]. Tokyo: Teikoku Databank, 1998.

———. *TDB Report: Gyōkai dōkō 1999-II* [TDB report: Industry developments 1999-II]. Tokyo: Teikoku Databank, 1999.

———. *TDB Report: Gyōkai dōkō 2000-II* [TDB report: Industry developments 2000-II]. Tokyo: Teikoku Databank, 2000.

———. *TDB Report: Gyōkai dōkō 2002-I* [TDB report: Industry developments 2002-I]. Tokyo: Teikoku Databank, 2002.

———. *TDB Report: Gyōkai dōkō 2003-I* [TDB report: Industry developments 2003-I]. Tokyo: Teikoku Databank, 2003.

———. *TDB Report: Gyōkai dōkō 2005-I* [TDB report: Industry developments 2005-I]. Tokyo: Teikoku Databank, 2005.

Tett, Gillian. *Saving the Sun: A Wall Street Gamble to Rescue Japan from Its Trillion-Dollar Meltdown.* New York: HarperBusiness, 2003.

Tokyo Stock Exchange (TSE). *TSE Factbook 2008.* Tokyo: Tokyo Stock Exchange, 2008, at http://www.tse.or.jp/english/market/data/factbook/index.html, accessed April 25, 2013.

Toya, Tetsurō. *The Political Economy of the Japanese Financial Big Bang: Institutional Change in Finance and Public Policymaking.* New York: Oxford University Press, 2006.

Tudor, Alison, and Petter Lattman. "Bankruptcy by Willcom Stings Carlyle." *Wall Street Journal,* February 19, 2010, 1, at http://online.wsj.com/article/SB20001424052748703315004575072830634735458.html, accessed April 25, 2013.

Tyson, Laura D'Andrea. *Who's Bashing Whom? Trade Conflicts in High-Technology Industries.* Washington, DC: Institute for International Economics, 1993.

Vogel, Steven K. *Japan Remodeled: How Government and Industry Are Reforming Japanese Capitalism.* Ithaca, NY: Cornell University Press, 2006.

White, Lawrence. "Asia: Is Japan Still a Tough Nut to Crack?" *Euromoney* 38, no. 453 (2007): 134–37.

Whitley, Richard. *Business Systems and Organizational Capabilities: The Institutional Structuring of Competitive Competences.* New York: Oxford University Press, 2007.

Yamamura, Kōzō, and Wolfgang Streeck. *The End of Diversity? Prospects for German and Japanese Capitalism.* Ithaca, NY: Cornell University Press, 2003.

Yamauchi, Mari. "Kinyū kikan ni okeru koyōseido no tayōsei" [Employment systems of financial institutions in Japan: Their varieties by capital, products, and individual strategies]. *Japan Journal of Human Resource Management* 12, no. 1 (2010):14–26.

———. "Tayōsei to shūren: Rīman shokku ikō no shōken gaisha ni okeru koyō seido no henka" [Convergence and divergence: Employment systems at Tokyo-based investment banks after the Lehman shock]. *Mita Business Review* 54, no. 2 (2011): 23–41.

Yoshikawa, Aki. "The Other Drug War: U.S.–Japan Trade in Pharmaceuticals." *California Management Review* 31, no. 2 (Winter 1989): 76–90.

Zysman, John, and Dan Breznitz. "The State in a Double Bind: Staying Wealthy in a Changing Global Economy." BRIE Working Paper 188 (2010), at http://brie.berkeley.edu/publications/wp188.pdf, accessed April 25, 2013.

Index

Page numbers in *italics* indicate figures and tables.

RECENT PUBLICATIONS OF THE
WALTER H. SHORENSTEIN ASIA-PACIFIC RESEARCH CENTER

BOOKS (distributed by the Brookings Institution Press)

Sang-Hun Choe, Gi-Wook Shin, and David Straub, eds. *Troubled Transition: North Korea's Politics, Economy and External Relations.* 2013.

Kenji E. Kushida and Phillip Y. Lipscy, eds. *Japan under the DPJ: The Politics of Transition and Governance.* 2013.

Joon-Woo Park, Donald Keyser, and Gi-Wook Shin, eds. *Asia's Middle Powers? The Identity and Regional Policy of South Korea and Vietnam.* 2013.

Jang-Jip Choi. *Democracy after Democratization: the Korean Experience.* 2012.

Byung-Kook Kim, Eun Mee Kim, and Jean C. Oi, eds. *Adapt, Fragment, Transform: Corporate Restructuring and System Reform in South Korea.* 2012.

John Everard. *Only Beautiful, Please: A British Diplomat in North Korea.* 2012.

Dong-won Lim. *Peacemaker: Twenty Years of Inter-Korean Relations and the North Korean Nuclear Issue.* 2012.

Byung Kwan Kim, Gi-Wook Shin, and David Straub, eds. Beyond North Korea: Future Challenges to South Korea's Security. 2011.

Jean C. Oi, ed. *Going Private in China: The Politics of Corporate Restructuring and System Reform.* 2011.

Karen Eggleston and Shripad Tuljapurkar, eds. *Aging Asia: The Economic and Social Implications of Rapid Demographic Change in China, Japan and South Korea.* 2010.

Rafiq Dossani, Daniel C. Sneider, and Vikram Sood, eds. *Does South Asia Exist? Prospects for Regional Integration.* 2010.

Jean C. Oi, Scott Rozelle, and Xueguang Zhou. *Growing Pains: Tensions and Opportunity in China's Transition.* 2010.

Karen Eggleston, ed. *Prescribing Cultures and Pharmaceutical Policy in the Asia-Pacific.* 2009.

Donald A. L. Macintyre, Daniel C. Sneider, and Gi-Wook Shin, eds. *First Drafts of Korea: The U.S. Media and Perceptions of the Last Cold War Frontier.* 2009.

Steven Reed, Kenneth Mori McElwain, and Kay Shimizu, eds. *Political Change in Japan: Electoral Behavior, Party Realignment, and the Koizumi Reforms.* 2009.

Donald K. Emmerson. *Hard Choices: Security, Democracy, and Regionalism in Southeast Asia*. 2008.

Henry S. Rowen, Marguerite Gong Hancock, and William F. Miller, eds. *Greater China's Quest for Innovation*. 2008.

Gi-Wook Shin and Daniel C. Sneider, eds. *Cross Currents: Regionalism and Nationalism in Northeast Asia*. 2007.

Philip W. Yun and Gi-Wook Shin, eds. *North Korea: 2005 and Beyond*. 2006.

STUDIES OF THE WALTER H. SHORENSTEIN
ASIA-PACIFIC RESEARCH CENTER (published with Stanford University Press)

Gene Park. Spending Without Taxation: FILP and the Politics of Public Finance in Japan. Stanford, CA: Stanford University Press, 2011.

Erik Martinez Kuhonta. The Institutional Imperative: The Politics of Equitable Development in Southeast Asia. Stanford, CA: Stanford University Press, 2011.

Yongshun Cai. *Collective Resistance in China: Why Popular Protests Succeed or Fail*. Stanford, CA: Stanford University Press, 2010.

Gi-Wook Shin. *One Alliance, Two Lenses: U.S.-Korea Relations in a New Era*. Stanford, CA: Stanford University Press, 2010.

Jean Oi and Nara Dillon, eds. *At the Crossroads of Empires: Middlemen, Social Networks, and State-building in Republican Shanghai*. Stanford, CA: Stanford University Press, 2007.

Henry S. Rowen, Marguerite Gong Hancock, and William F. Miller, eds. *Making IT: The Rise of Asia in High Tech*. Stanford, CA: Stanford University Press, 2006.

Gi-Wook Shin. *Ethnic Nationalism in Korea: Genealogy, Politics, and Legacy*. Stanford, CA: Stanford University Press, 2006.

Andrew Walder, Joseph Esherick, and Paul Pickowicz, eds. *The Chinese Cultural Revolution as History*. Stanford, CA: Stanford University Press, 2006.

Rafiq Dossani and Henry S. Rowen, eds. *Prospects for Peace in South Asia*. Stanford, CA: Stanford University Press, 2005.